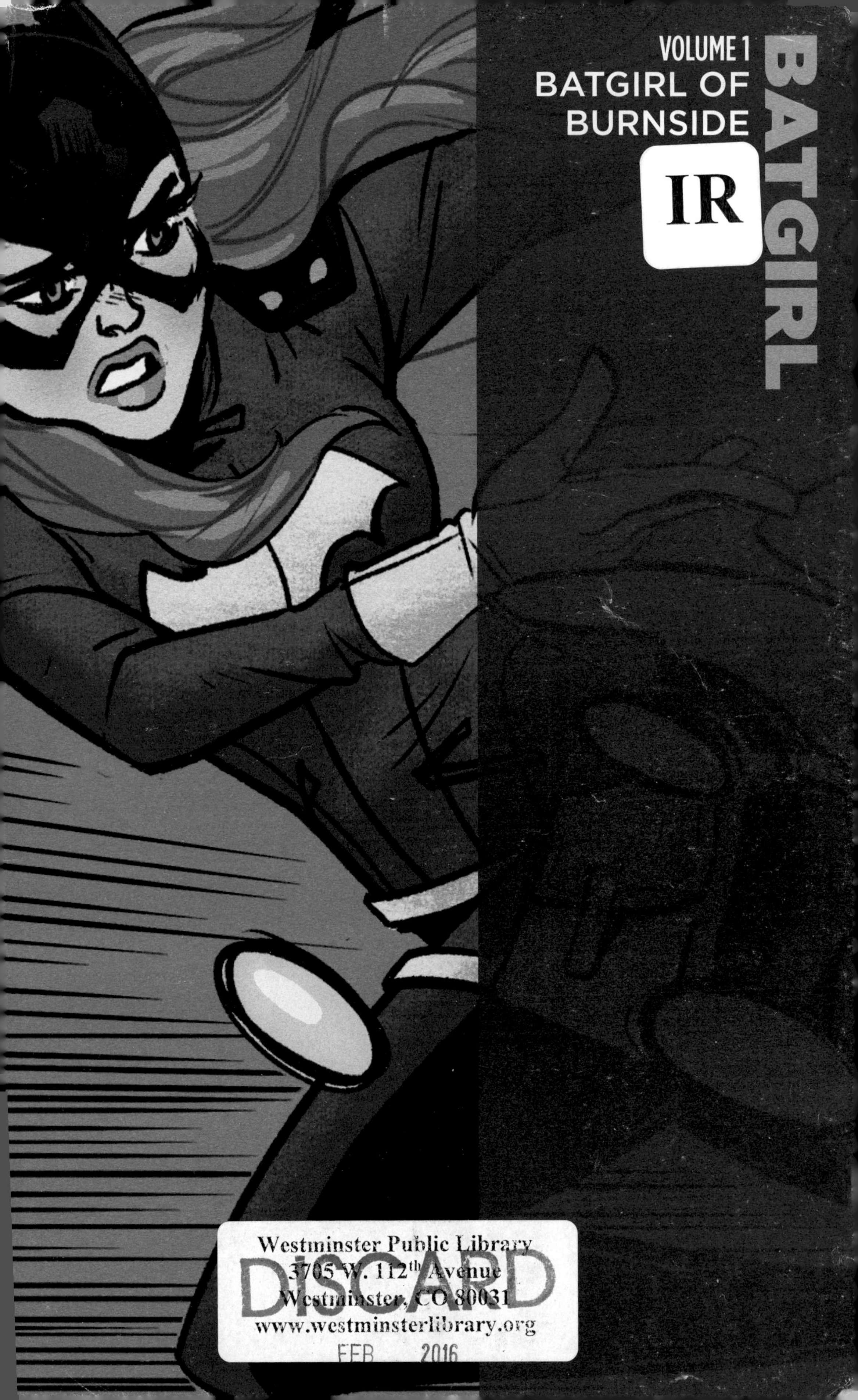
VOLUME 1
BATGIRL OF
BURNSIDE
BATGIRL

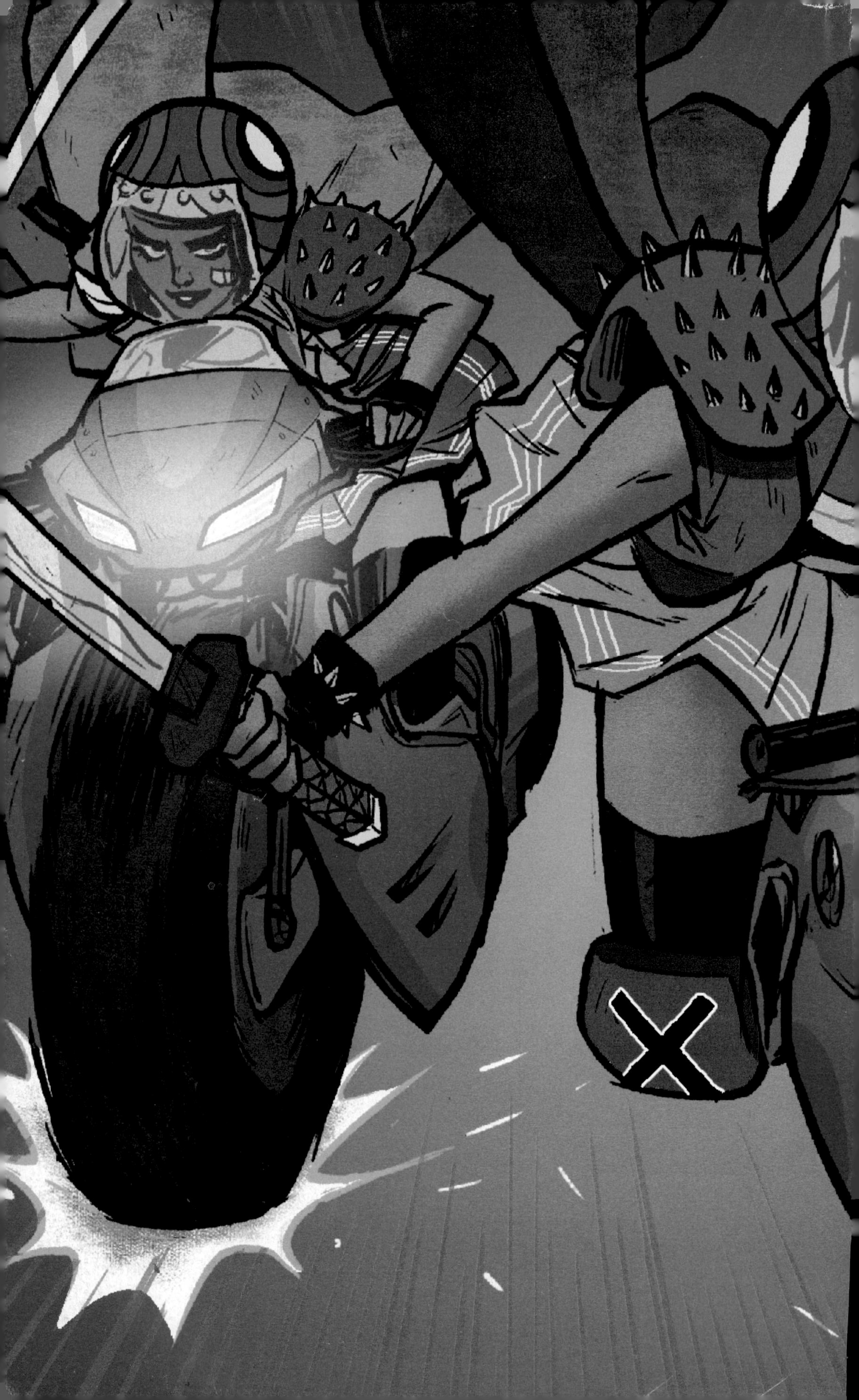

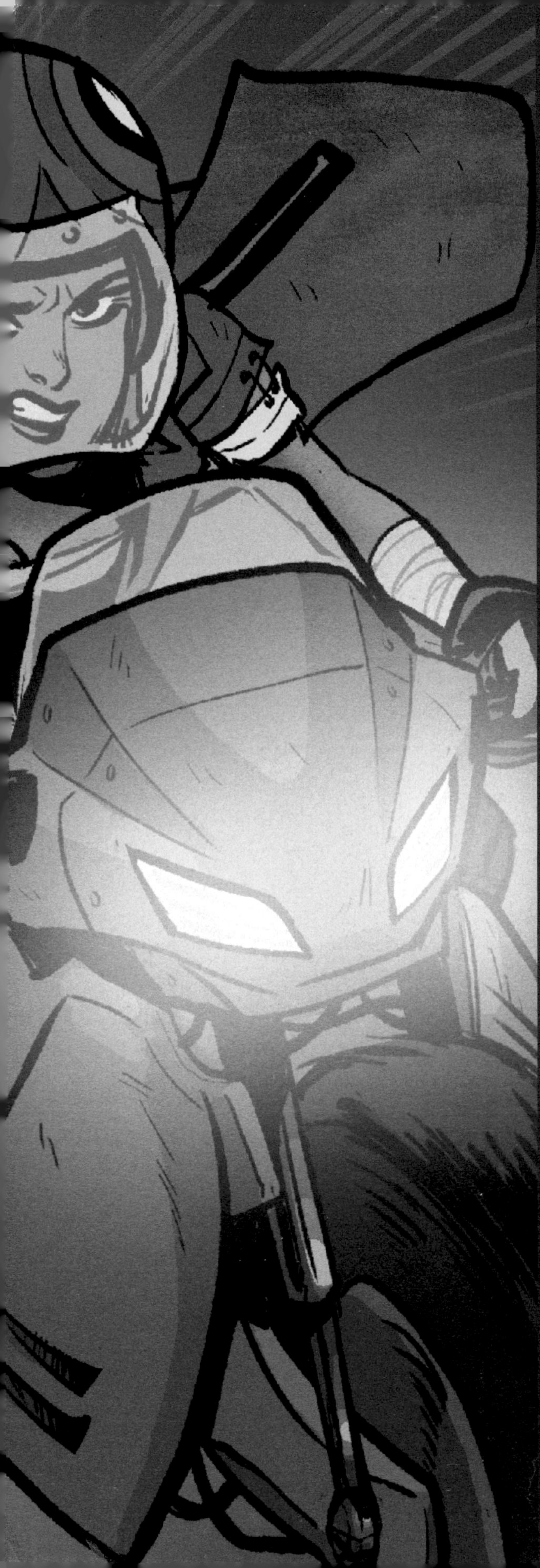

BATGIRL

VOLUME 1
BATGIRL OF BURNSIDE

WRITTEN BY
CAMERON STEWART
& BRENDEN FLETCHER

ART BY
BABS TARR

BREAKDOWN ART BY
CAMERON STEWART

SECRET ORIGIN ART BY
IRENE KOH

SECRET ORIGIN COLOR BY
HI-FI

COLOR BY
MARIS WICKS

LETTERS BY
JARED K. FLETCHER

ORIGINAL SERIES &
COLLECTION COVER ART BY
CAMERON STEWART

SECRET ORIGIN COVER BY
BRYAN HITCH

BATMAN CREATED BY
BOB KANE

CHRIS CONROY Editor – Original Series
DAVE WIELGOSZ Assistant Editor – Original Series
ROBIN WILDMAN Editor
ROBBIN BROSTERMAN Design Director – Books
DAMIAN RYLAND Publication Design

BOB HARRAS Senior VP – Editor-in-Chief, DC Comics

DIANE NELSON President
DAN DIDIO and JIM LEE Co-Publishers
GEOFF JOHNS Chief Creative Officer
AMIT DESAI Senior VP – Marketing & Franchise Management
AMY GENKINS Senior VP – Business & Legal Affairs
NAIRI GARDINER Senior VP – Finance
JEFF BOISON VP – Publishing Planning
MARK CHIARELLO VP – Art Direction & Design
JOHN CUNNINGHAM VP – Marketing
TERRI CUNNINGHAM VP – Editorial Administration
LARRY GANEM VP – Talent Relations & Services
ALISON GILL Senior VP – Manufacturing & Operations
HANK KANALZ Senior VP – Vertigo & Integrated Publishing
JAY KOGAN VP – Business & Legal Affairs, Publishing
JACK MAHAN VP – Business Affairs, Talent
NICK NAPOLITANO VP – Manufacturing Administration
SUE POHJA VP – Book Sales
FRED RUIZ VP – Manufacturing Operations
COURTNEY SIMMONS Senior VP – Publicity
BOB WAYNE Senior VP – Sales

BATGIRL VOLUME 1: BATGIRL OF BURNSIDE

DC Comics, 4000 Warner Blvd., Burbank, CA 91522
A Warner Bros. Entertainment Company.
Printed by RR Donnelley, Salem, VA, USA. 5/8/15. First Printing.
ISBN: 978-1-4012-5798-9

Library of Congress Cataloging-in-Publication Data

Stewart, Cameron, 1976- author.
Batgirl. Volume 1, The Batgirl of Burnside / Cameron Stewart, Brenden Fletcher, Babs Tarr.
pages cm. — (The New 52!)
ISBN 978-1-4012-5798-9
1. Graphic novels. I. Fletcher, Brenden, author. II. Tarr, Babs, illustrator. III. Title. IV. Title: Batgirl of Burnside.
PN6728.B358S74 2015
741.5'973—dc23
2015006319

SUSTAINABLE
FORESTRY
INITIATIVE

Certified Chain of Custody
20% Certified Forest Content,
80% Certified Sourcing
www.sfiprogram.org
SFI-01042
APPLIES TO TEXT STOCK ONLY

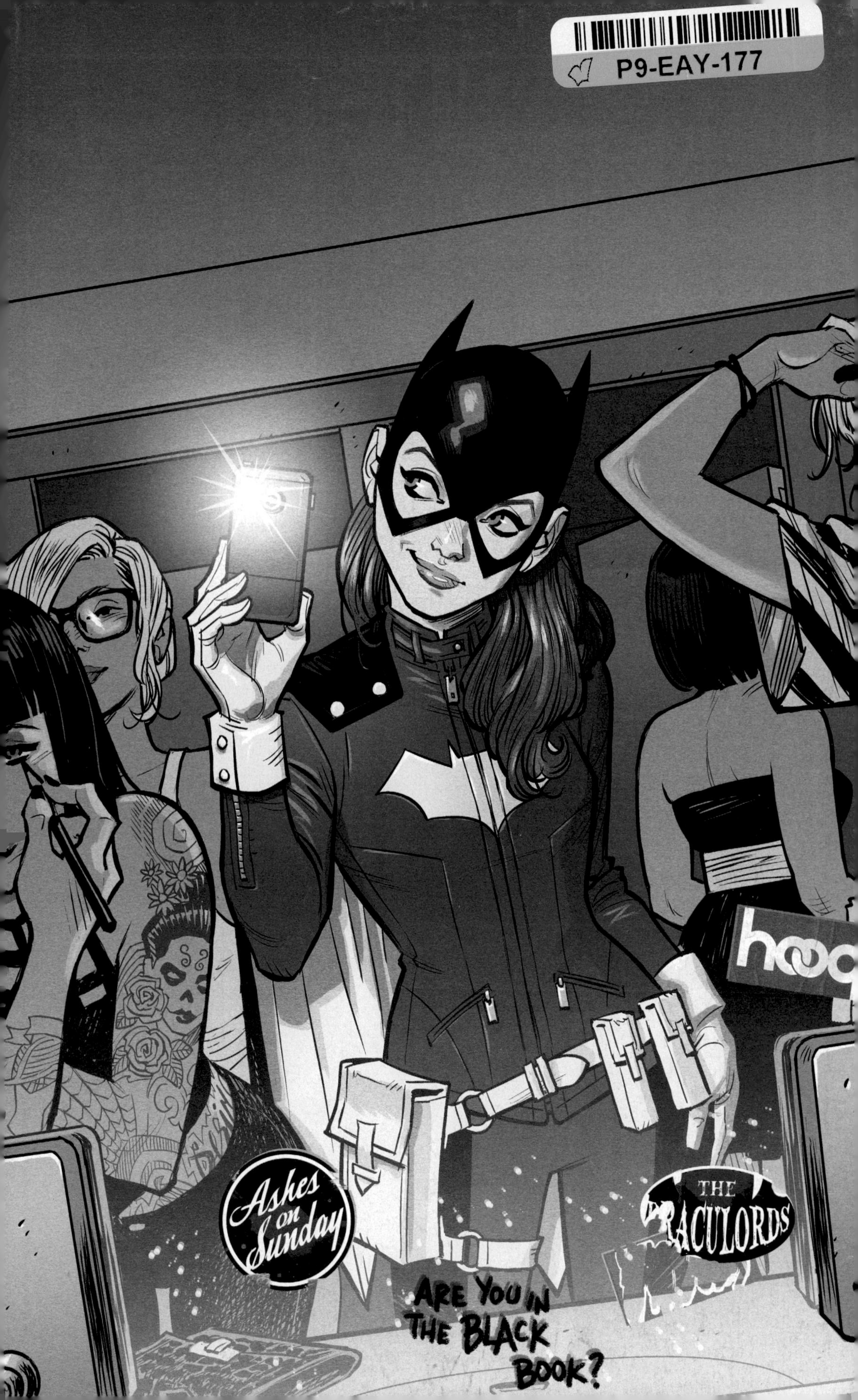
Ashes on Sunday
THE
RACULORDS
ARE YOU IN THE BLACK BOOK?

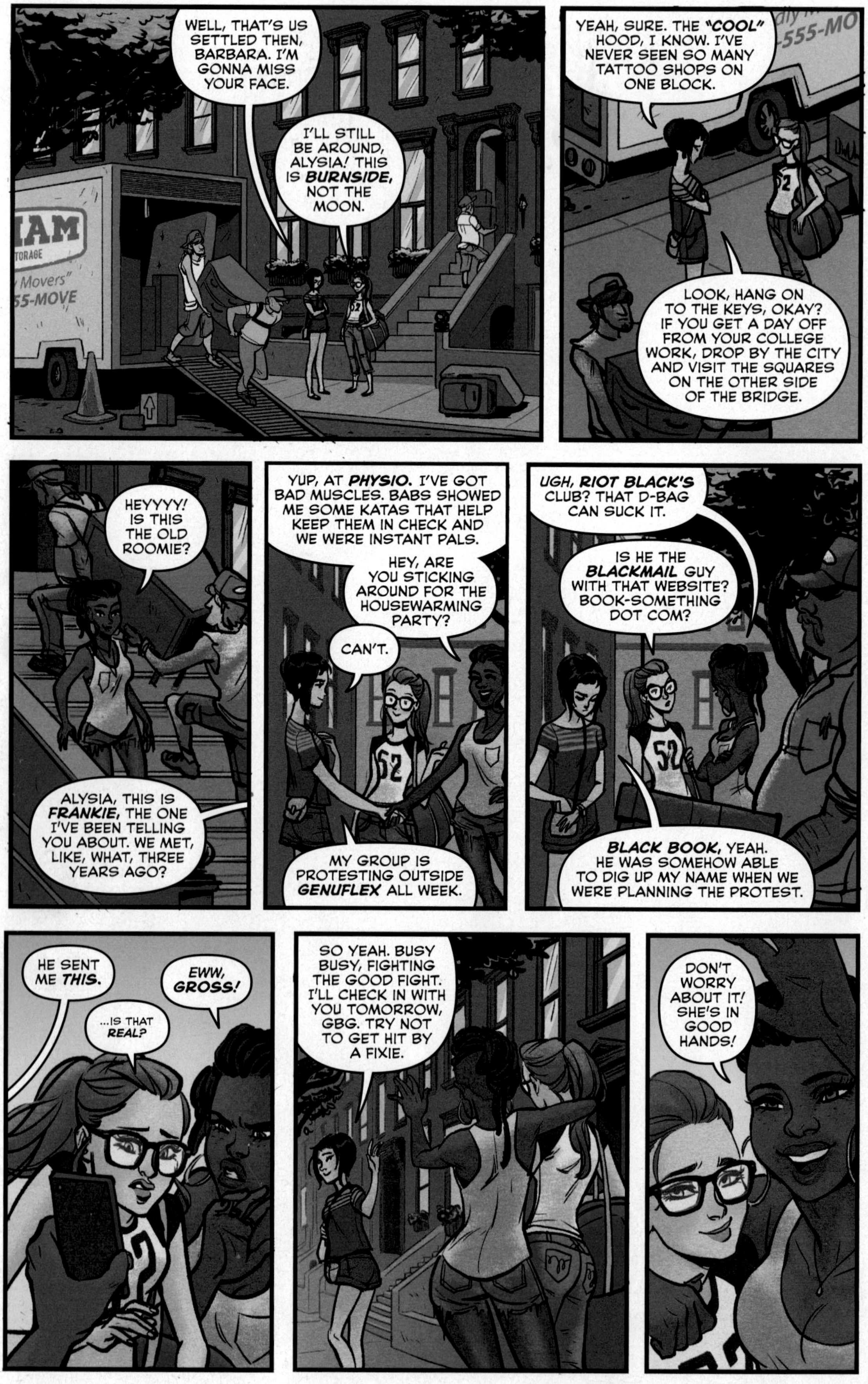
WELL, THAT'S US SETTLED THEN, BARBARA. I'M GONNA MISS YOUR FACE.
I'LL STILL BE AROUND, ALYSIA! THIS IS BURNSIDE, NOT THE MOON.
YEAH, SURE. THE "COOL" HOOD, I KNOW. I'VE NEVER SEEN SO MANY TATTOO SHOPS ON ONE BLOCK.
LOOK, HANG ON TO THE KEYS, OKAY? IF YOU GET A DAY OFF FROM YOUR COLLEGE WORK, DROP BY THE CITY AND VISIT THE SQUARES ON THE OTHER SIDE OF THE BRIDGE.
HEYYYY! IS THIS THE OLD ROOMIE?
ALYSIA, THIS IS FRANKIE, THE ONE I'VE BEEN TELLING YOU ABOUT. WE MET, LIKE, WHAT, THREE YEARS AGO?
YUP, AT PHYSIO. I'VE GOT BAD MUSCLES. BABS SHOWED ME SOME KATAS THAT HELP KEEP THEM IN CHECK AND WE WERE INSTANT PALS.
HEY, ARE YOU STICKING AROUND FOR THE HOUSEWARMING PARTY?
CAN'T.
MY GROUP IS PROTESTING OUTSIDE GENUFLEX ALL WEEK.
UGH, RIOT BLACK'S CLUB? THAT D-BAG CAN SUCK IT.
IS HE THE BLACKMAIL GUY WITH THAT WEBSITE? BOOK-SOMETHING DOT COM?
BLACK BOOK, YEAH. HE WAS SOMEHOW ABLE TO DIG UP MY NAME WHEN WE WERE PLANNING THE PROTEST.
HE SENT ME THIS.
...IS THAT REAL?
EWW, GROSS!
SO YEAH. BUSY BUSY, FIGHTING THE GOOD FIGHT. I'LL CHECK IN WITH YOU TOMORROW, GBG. TRY NOT TO GET HIT BY A FIXIE.
DON'T WORRY ABOUT IT! SHE'S IN GOOD HANDS!

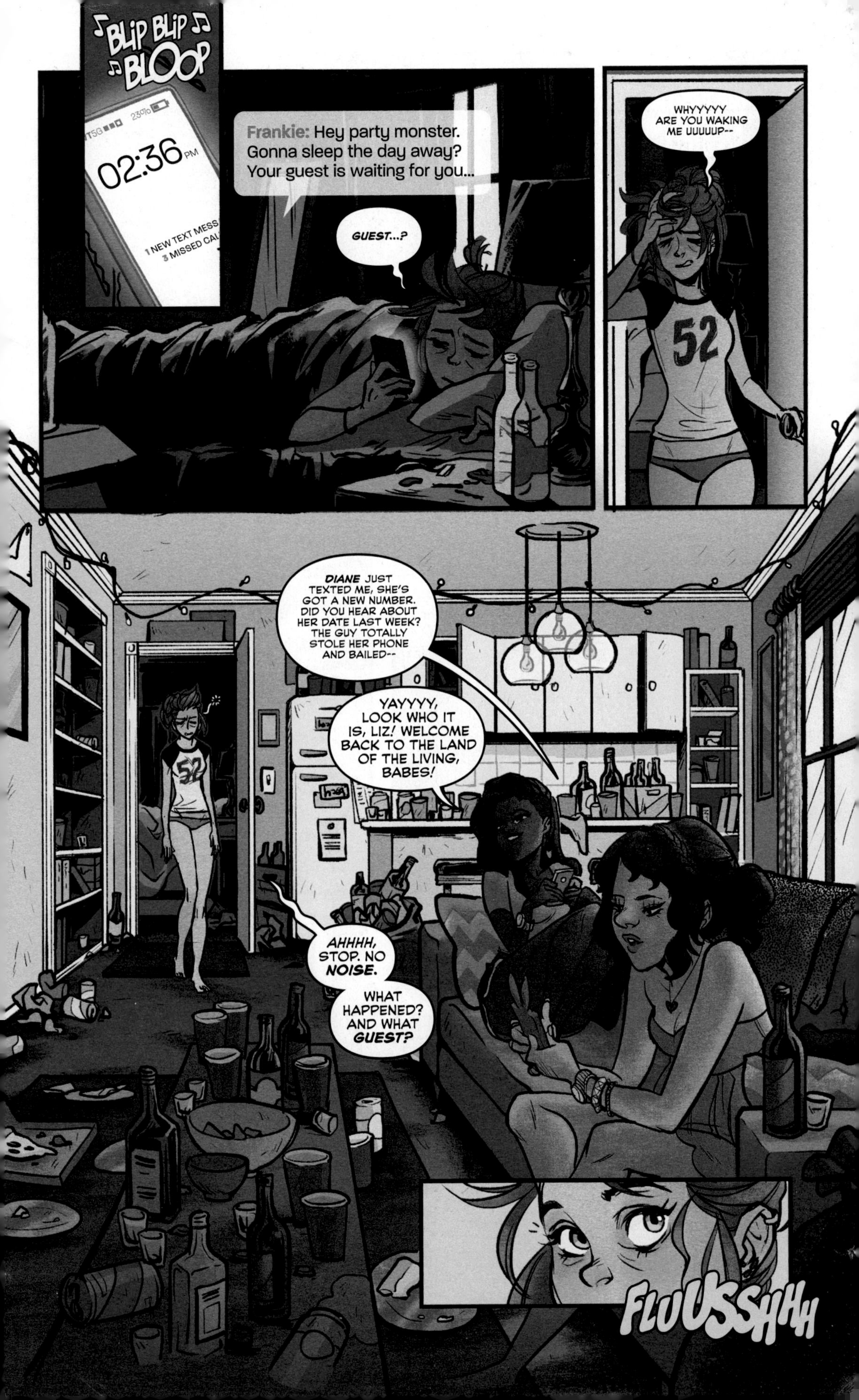

BLIP BLIP BLOOP
02:36 PM
23%
1 NEW TEXT MESS
3 MISSED CAL
Frankie: Hey party monster. Gonna sleep the day away? Your guest is waiting for you...
GUEST...?
WHYYYYY ARE YOU WAKING ME UUUUUP--
52
DIANE JUST TEXTED ME, SHE'S GOT A NEW NUMBER. DID YOU HEAR ABOUT HER DATE LAST WEEK? THE GUY TOTALLY STOLE HER PHONE AND BAILED--
YAYYYY, LOOK WHO IT IS, LIZ! WELCOME BACK TO THE LAND OF THE LIVING, BABES!
AHHHH, STOP. NO NOISE.
WHAT HAPPENED? AND WHAT GUEST?
FLUUSSHHH

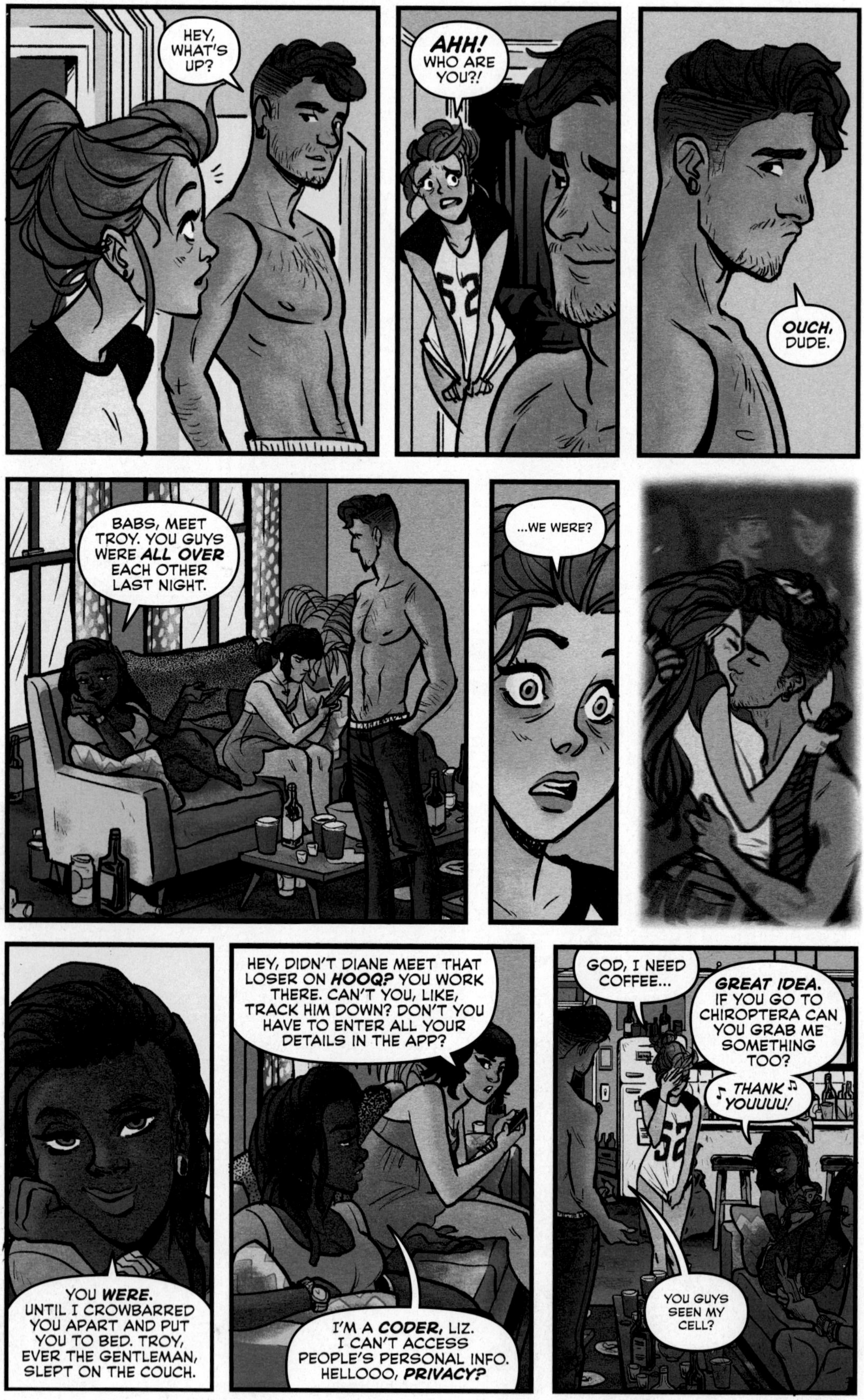
HEY, WHAT'S UP?
AHH! WHO ARE YOU?!
OUCH, DUDE.
BABS, MEET TROY. YOU GUYS WERE ALL OVER EACH OTHER LAST NIGHT.
...WE WERE?
YOU WERE. UNTIL I CROWBARRED YOU APART AND PUT YOU TO BED. TROY, EVER THE GENTLEMAN, SLEPT ON THE COUCH.
HEY, DIDN'T DIANE MEET THAT LOSER ON HOOQ? YOU WORK THERE. CAN'T YOU, LIKE, TRACK HIM DOWN? DON'T YOU HAVE TO ENTER ALL YOUR DETAILS IN THE APP?
I'M A CODER, LIZ. I CAN'T ACCESS PEOPLE'S PERSONAL INFO. HELLOOO, PRIVACY?
GOD, I NEED COFFEE...
GREAT IDEA. IF YOU GO TO CHIROPTERA CAN YOU GRAB ME SOMETHING TOO?
♪ THANK YOUUUU! ♫
YOU GUYS SEEN MY CELL?

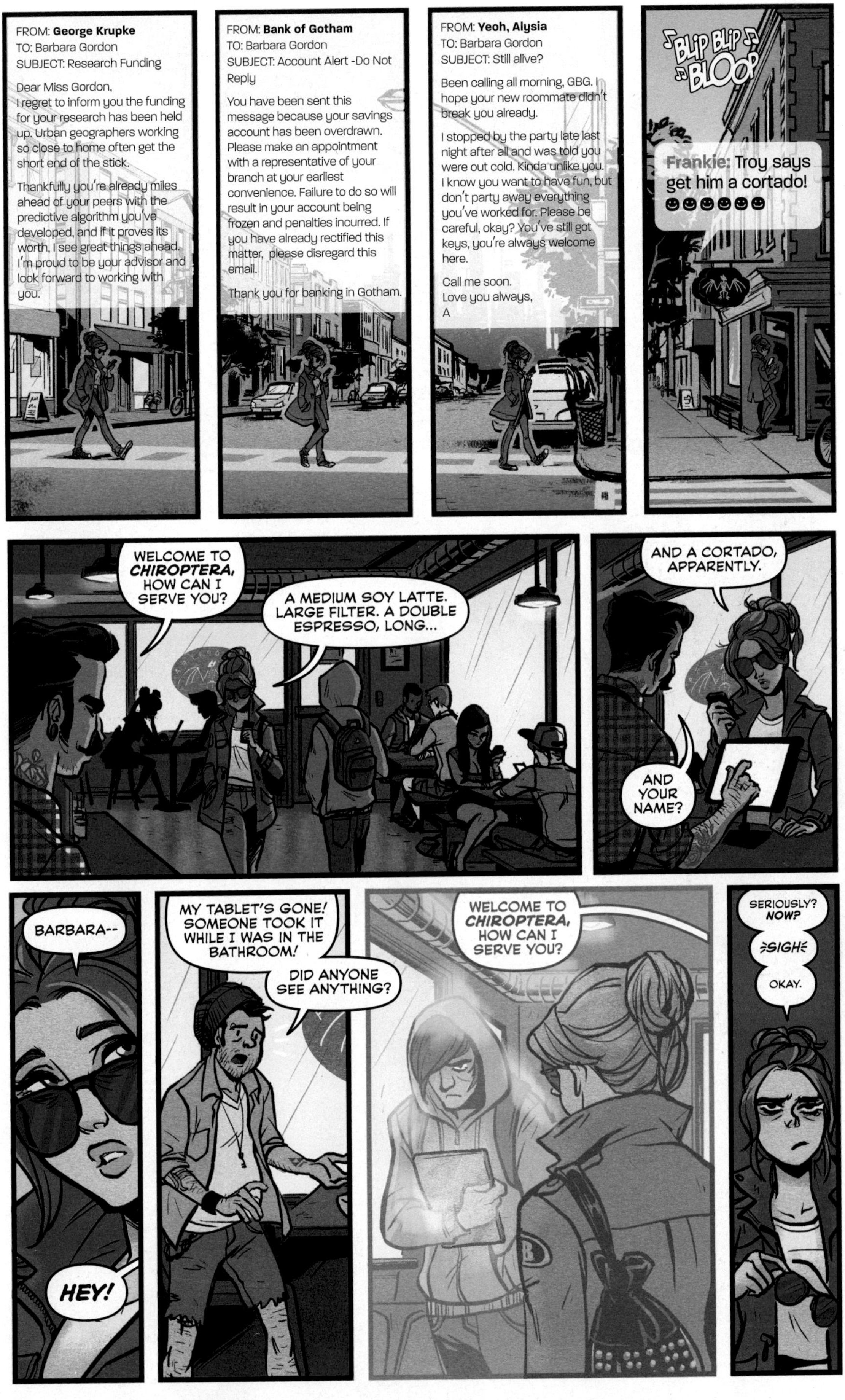
FROM: George Krupke
TO: Barbara Gordon
SUBJECT: Research Funding
Dear Miss Gordon,
I regret to inform you the funding for your research has been held up. Urban geographers working so close to home often get the short end of the stick.
Thankfully you're already miles ahead of your peers with the predictive algorithm you've developed, and if it proves its worth, I see great things ahead. I'm proud to be your advisor and look forward to working with you.
FROM: Bank of Gotham
TO: Barbara Gordon
SUBJECT: Account Alert -Do Not Reply
You have been sent this message because your savings account has been overdrawn. Please make an appointment with a representative of your branch at your earliest convenience. Failure to do so will result in your account being frozen and penalties incurred. If you have already rectified this matter, please disregard this email.
Thank you for banking in Gotham.
FROM: Yeoh, Alysia
TO: Barbara Gordon
SUBJECT: Still alive?
Been calling all morning, GBG. I hope your new roommate didn't break you already.
I stopped by the party late last night after all and was told you were out cold. Kinda unlike you. I know you want to have fun, but don't party away everything you've worked for. Please be careful, okay? You've still got keys, you're always welcome here.
Call me soon.
Love you always,
A
BLIP BLIP BLOOP
Frankie: Troy says get him a cortado!
WELCOME TO CHIROPTERA, HOW CAN I SERVE YOU?
A MEDIUM SOY LATTE. LARGE FILTER. A DOUBLE ESPRESSO, LONG...
AND A CORTADO, APPARENTLY.
AND YOUR NAME?
BARBARA--
HEY!
MY TABLET'S GONE! SOMEONE TOOK IT WHILE I WAS IN THE BATHROOM!
DID ANYONE SEE ANYTHING?
WELCOME TO CHIROPTERA, HOW CAN I SERVE YOU?
SERIOUSLY? NOW?
SIGH
OKAY.

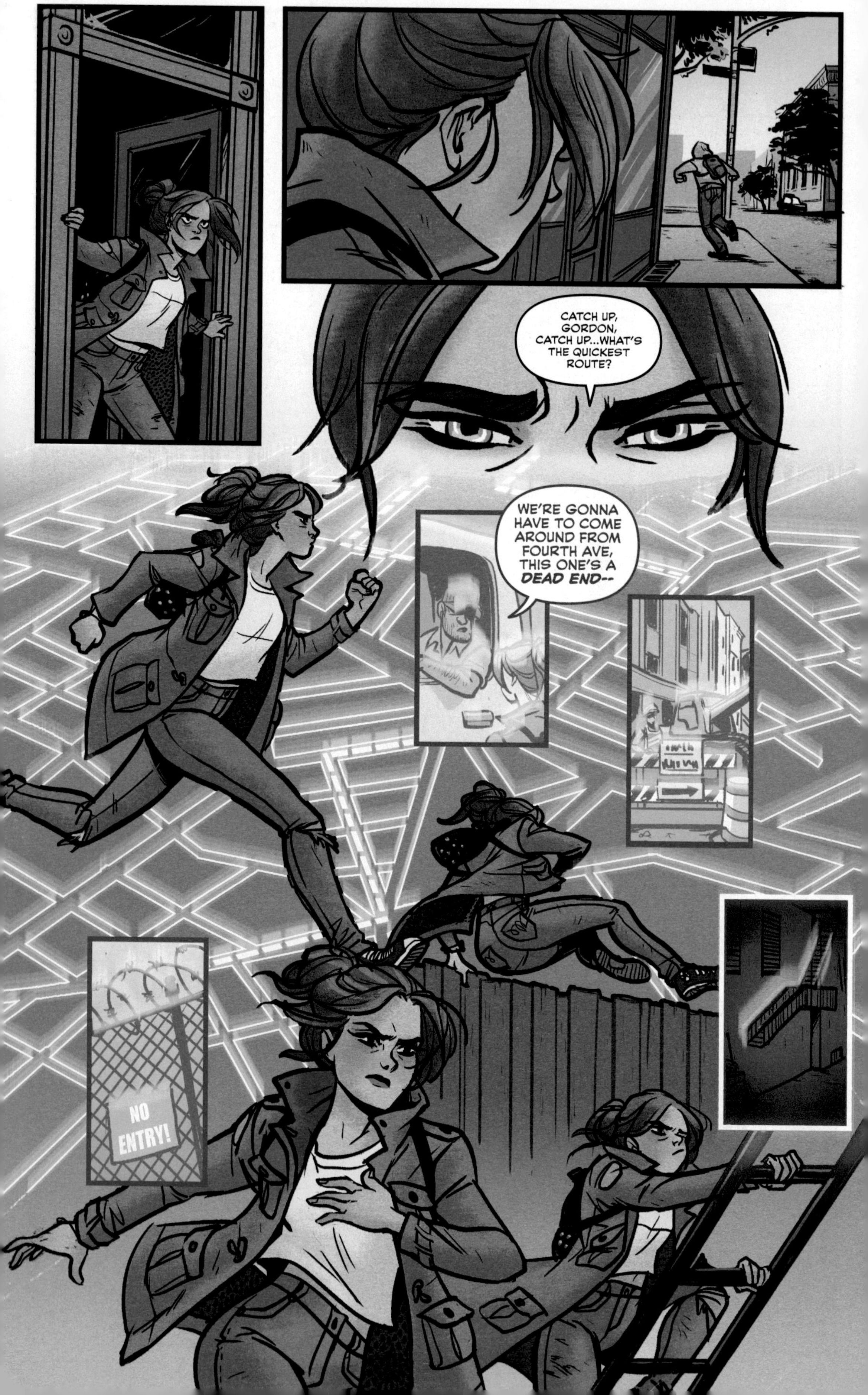
CATCH UP, GORDON, CATCH UP...WHAT'S THE QUICKEST ROUTE?
WE'RE GONNA HAVE TO COME AROUND FROM FOURTH AVE, THIS ONE'S A *DEAD END--*
NO ENTRY!

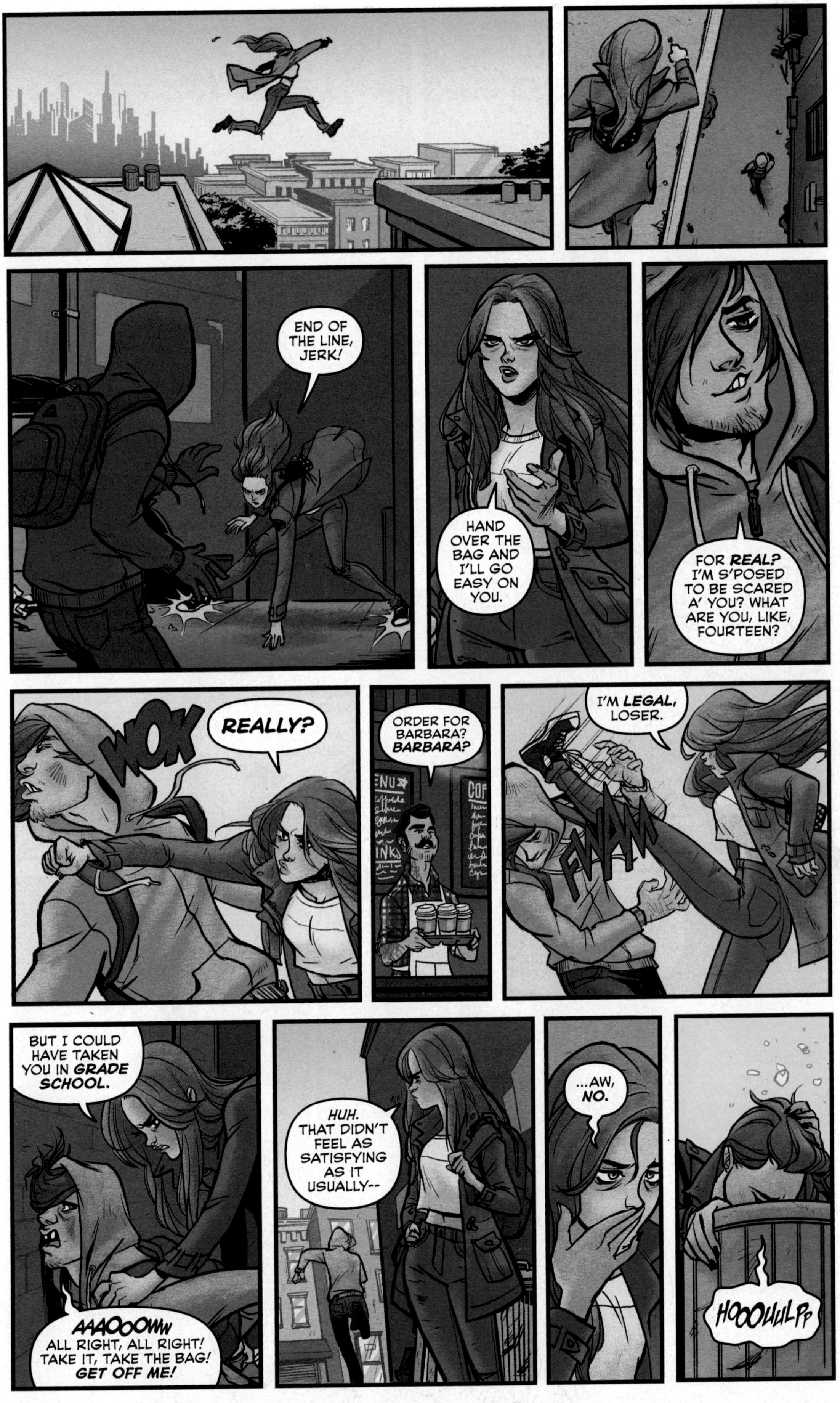
END OF THE LINE, JERK!
HAND OVER THE BAG AND I'LL GO EASY ON YOU.
FOR **REAL?** I'M S'POSED TO BE SCARED A' YOU? WHAT ARE YOU, LIKE, FOURTEEN?
WOK
REALLY?
ORDER FOR BARBARA? ***BARBARA?***
I'M ***LEGAL,*** LOSER.
FWAM
BUT I COULD HAVE TAKEN YOU IN ***GRADE SCHOOL.***
AAAOOOWW
ALL RIGHT, ALL RIGHT! TAKE IT, TAKE THE BAG! ***GET OFF ME!***
HUH. THAT DIDN'T FEEL AS SATISFYING AS IT USUALLY--
...AW, ***NO.***
HOOOUULPP

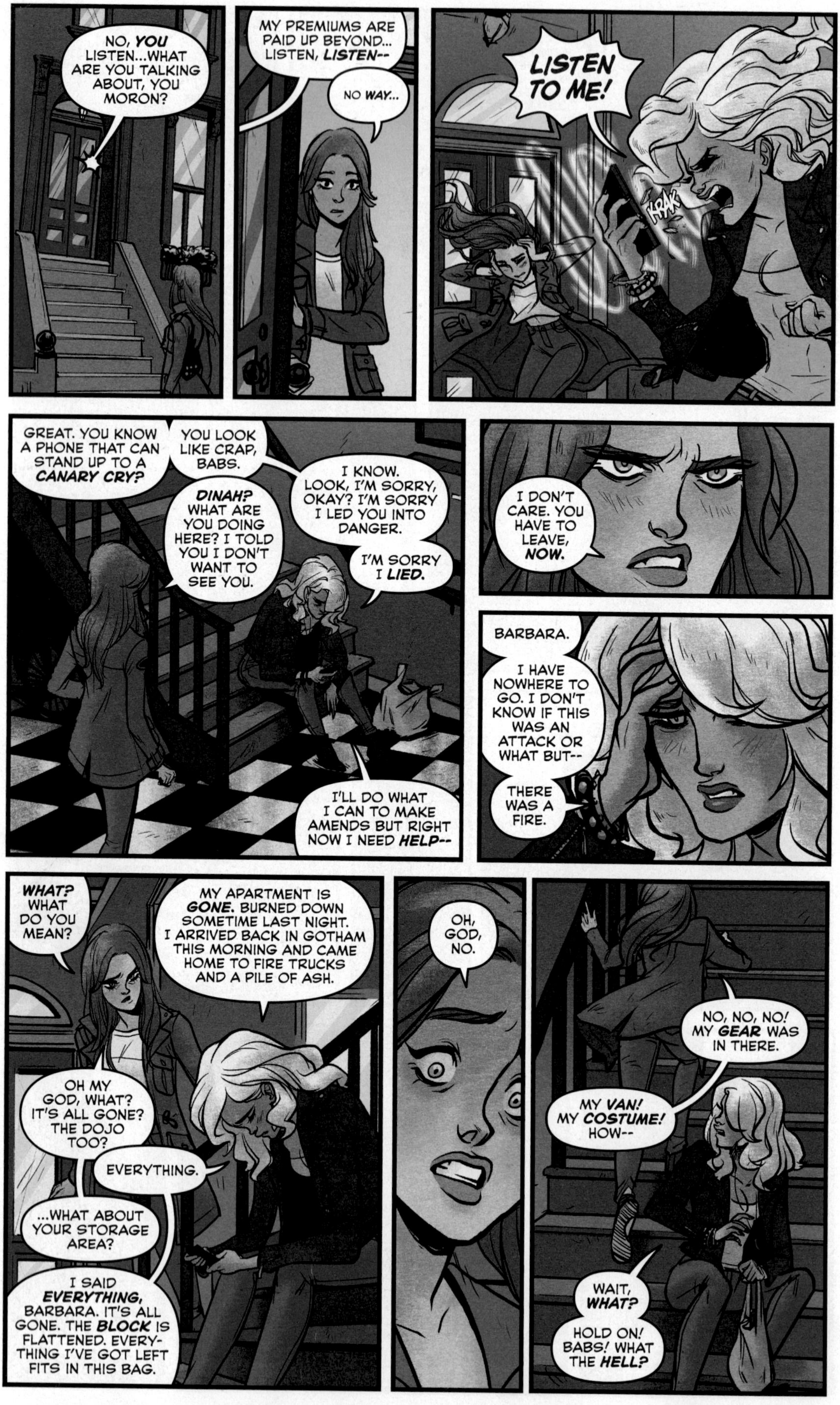
NO, YOU LISTEN...WHAT ARE YOU TALKING ABOUT, YOU MORON?
MY PREMIUMS ARE PAID UP BEYOND... LISTEN, LISTEN--
NO WAY...
LISTEN TO ME!
KRAK
GREAT. YOU KNOW A PHONE THAT CAN STAND UP TO A CANARY CRY?
YOU LOOK LIKE CRAP, BABS.
DINAH? WHAT ARE YOU DOING HERE? I TOLD YOU I DON'T WANT TO SEE YOU.
I KNOW. LOOK, I'M SORRY, OKAY? I'M SORRY I LED YOU INTO DANGER.
I'M SORRY I LIED.
I'LL DO WHAT I CAN TO MAKE AMENDS BUT RIGHT NOW I NEED HELP--
I DON'T CARE. YOU HAVE TO LEAVE, NOW.
BARBARA.
I HAVE NOWHERE TO GO. I DON'T KNOW IF THIS WAS AN ATTACK OR WHAT BUT--
THERE WAS A FIRE.
WHAT? WHAT DO YOU MEAN?
MY APARTMENT IS GONE. BURNED DOWN SOMETIME LAST NIGHT. I ARRIVED BACK IN GOTHAM THIS MORNING AND CAME HOME TO FIRE TRUCKS AND A PILE OF ASH.
OH MY GOD, WHAT? IT'S ALL GONE? THE DOJO TOO?
EVERYTHING.
...WHAT ABOUT YOUR STORAGE AREA?
I SAID EVERYTHING, BARBARA. IT'S ALL GONE. THE BLOCK IS FLATTENED. EVERY-THING I'VE GOT LEFT FITS IN THIS BAG.
OH, GOD, NO.
NO, NO, NO! MY GEAR WAS IN THERE.
MY VAN! MY COSTUME! HOW--
WAIT, WHAT?
HOLD ON! BABS! WHAT THE HELL?

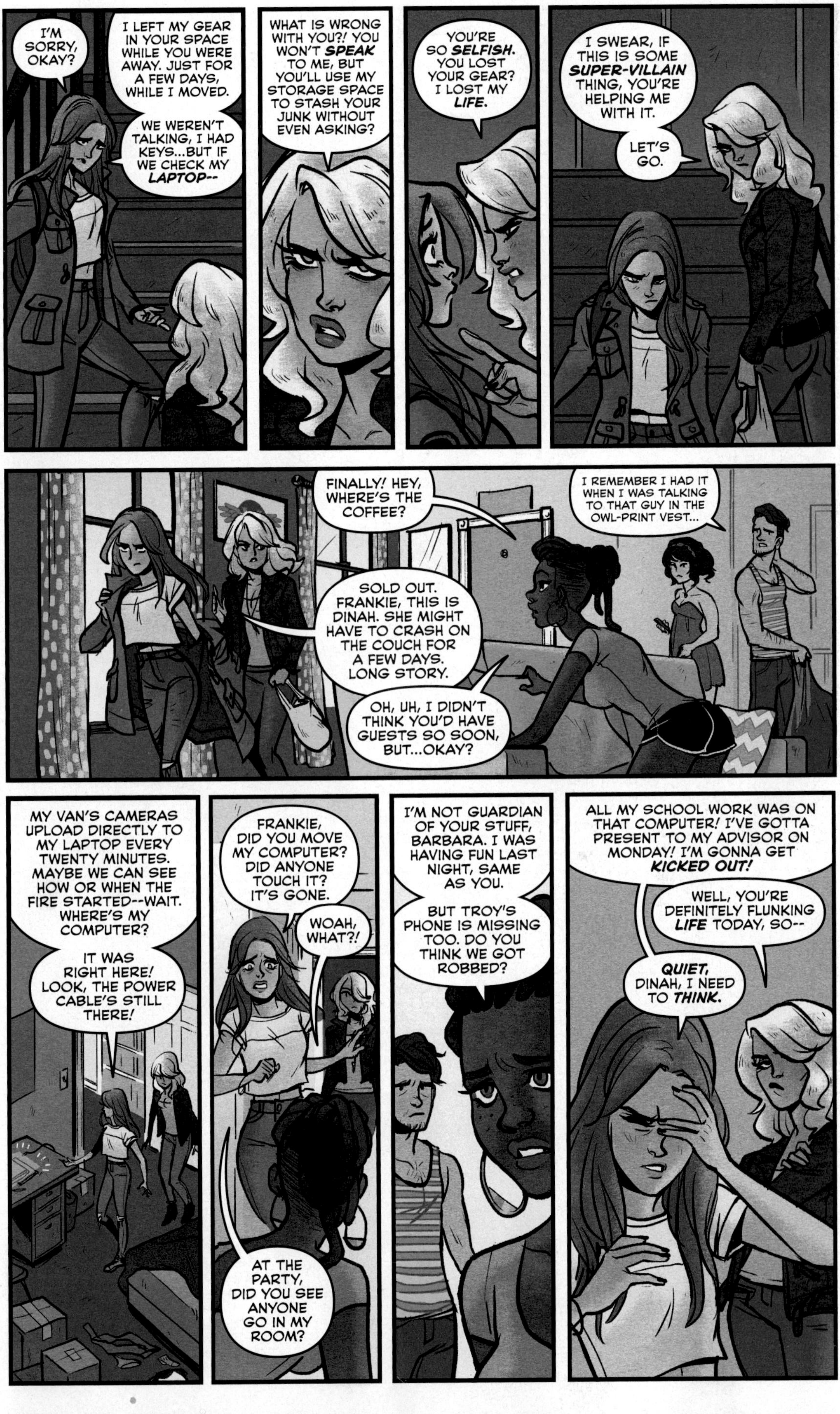
I'M SORRY, OKAY?
I LEFT MY GEAR IN YOUR SPACE WHILE YOU WERE AWAY. JUST FOR A FEW DAYS, WHILE I MOVED.
WE WEREN'T TALKING, I HAD KEYS...BUT IF WE CHECK MY LAPTOP--
WHAT IS WRONG WITH YOU?! YOU WON'T SPEAK TO ME, BUT YOU'LL USE MY STORAGE SPACE TO STASH YOUR JUNK WITHOUT EVEN ASKING?
YOU'RE SO SELFISH. YOU LOST YOUR GEAR? I LOST MY LIFE.
I SWEAR, IF THIS IS SOME SUPER-VILLAIN THING, YOU'RE HELPING ME WITH IT.
LET'S GO.
FINALLY! HEY, WHERE'S THE COFFEE?
I REMEMBER I HAD IT WHEN I WAS TALKING TO THAT GUY IN THE OWL-PRINT VEST...
SOLD OUT. FRANKIE, THIS IS DINAH. SHE MIGHT HAVE TO CRASH ON THE COUCH FOR A FEW DAYS. LONG STORY.
OH, UH, I DIDN'T THINK YOU'D HAVE GUESTS SO SOON, BUT...OKAY?
MY VAN'S CAMERAS UPLOAD DIRECTLY TO MY LAPTOP EVERY TWENTY MINUTES. MAYBE WE CAN SEE HOW OR WHEN THE FIRE STARTED--WAIT. WHERE'S MY COMPUTER?
IT WAS RIGHT HERE! LOOK, THE POWER CABLE'S STILL THERE!
FRANKIE, DID YOU MOVE MY COMPUTER? DID ANYONE TOUCH IT? IT'S GONE.
WOAH, WHAT?!
AT THE PARTY, DID YOU SEE ANYONE GO IN MY ROOM?
I'M NOT GUARDIAN OF YOUR STUFF, BARBARA. I WAS HAVING FUN LAST NIGHT, SAME AS YOU.
BUT TROY'S PHONE IS MISSING TOO. DO YOU THINK WE GOT ROBBED?
ALL MY SCHOOL WORK WAS ON THAT COMPUTER! I'VE GOTTA PRESENT TO MY ADVISOR ON MONDAY! I'M GONNA GET KICKED OUT!
WELL, YOU'RE DEFINITELY FLUNKING LIFE TODAY, SO--
QUIET, DINAH, I NEED TO THINK.

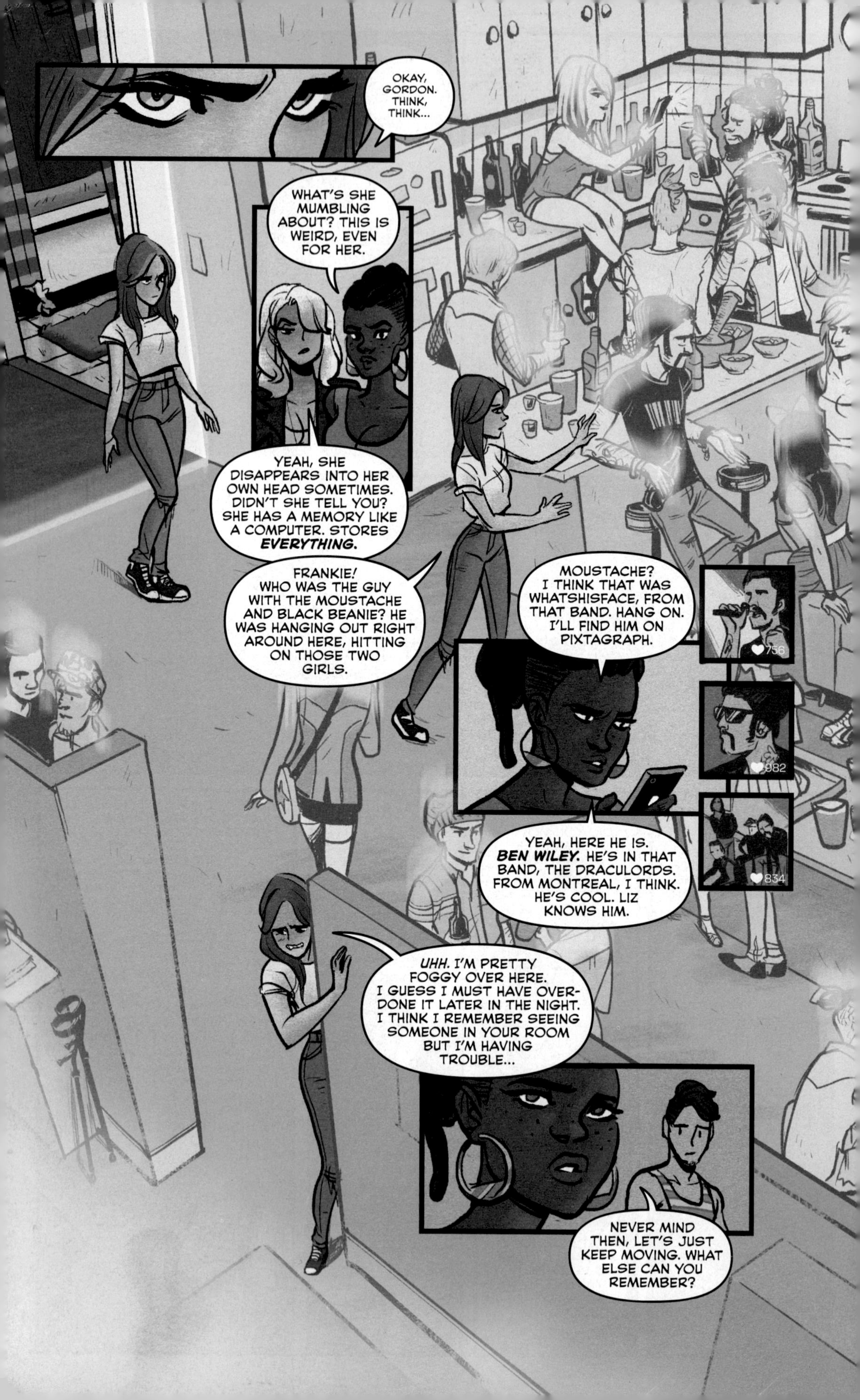
OKAY, GORDON. THINK, THINK...
WHAT'S SHE MUMBLING ABOUT? THIS IS WEIRD, EVEN FOR HER.
YEAH, SHE DISAPPEARS INTO HER OWN HEAD SOMETIMES. DIDN'T SHE TELL YOU? SHE HAS A MEMORY LIKE A COMPUTER. STORES *EVERYTHING.*
FRANKIE! WHO WAS THE GUY WITH THE MOUSTACHE AND BLACK BEANIE? HE WAS HANGING OUT RIGHT AROUND HERE, HITTING ON THOSE TWO GIRLS.
MOUSTACHE? I THINK THAT WAS WHATSHISFACE, FROM THAT BAND. HANG ON. I'LL FIND HIM ON PIXTAGRAPH.
756
982
834
YEAH, HERE HE IS. ***BEN WILEY.*** HE'S IN THAT BAND, THE DRACULORDS. FROM MONTREAL, I THINK. HE'S COOL. LIZ KNOWS HIM.
UHH. I'M PRETTY FOGGY OVER HERE. I GUESS I MUST HAVE OVER-DONE IT LATER IN THE NIGHT. I THINK I REMEMBER SEEING SOMEONE IN YOUR ROOM BUT I'M HAVING TROUBLE...
NEVER MIND THEN, LET'S JUST KEEP MOVING. WHAT ELSE CAN YOU REMEMBER?

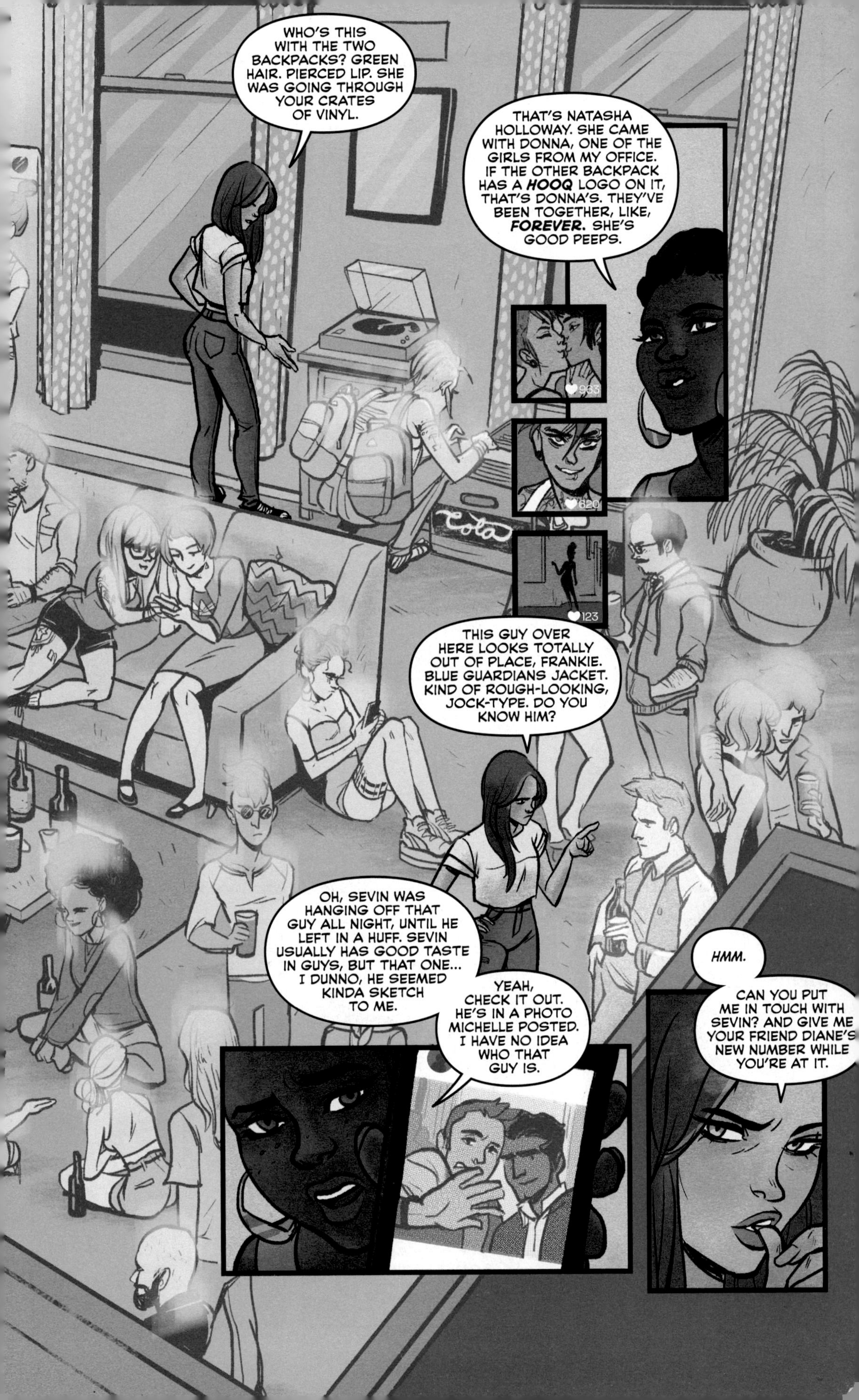
WHO'S THIS WITH THE TWO BACKPACKS? GREEN HAIR. PIERCED LIP. SHE WAS GOING THROUGH YOUR CRATES OF VINYL.
THAT'S NATASHA HOLLOWAY. SHE CAME WITH DONNA, ONE OF THE GIRLS FROM MY OFFICE. IF THE OTHER BACKPACK HAS A **HOOQ** LOGO ON IT, THAT'S DONNA'S. THEY'VE BEEN TOGETHER, LIKE, ***FOREVER.*** SHE'S GOOD PEEPS.
963
620
123
COLA
THIS GUY OVER HERE LOOKS TOTALLY OUT OF PLACE, FRANKIE. BLUE GUARDIANS JACKET. KIND OF ROUGH-LOOKING, JOCK-TYPE. DO YOU KNOW HIM?
OH, SEVIN WAS HANGING OFF THAT GUY ALL NIGHT, UNTIL HE LEFT IN A HUFF. SEVIN USUALLY HAS GOOD TASTE IN GUYS, BUT THAT ONE... I DUNNO, HE SEEMED KINDA SKETCH TO ME.
YEAH, CHECK IT OUT. HE'S IN A PHOTO MICHELLE POSTED. I HAVE NO IDEA WHO THAT GUY IS.
HMM.
CAN YOU PUT ME IN TOUCH WITH SEVIN? AND GIVE ME YOUR FRIEND DIANE'S NEW NUMBER WHILE YOU'RE AT IT.

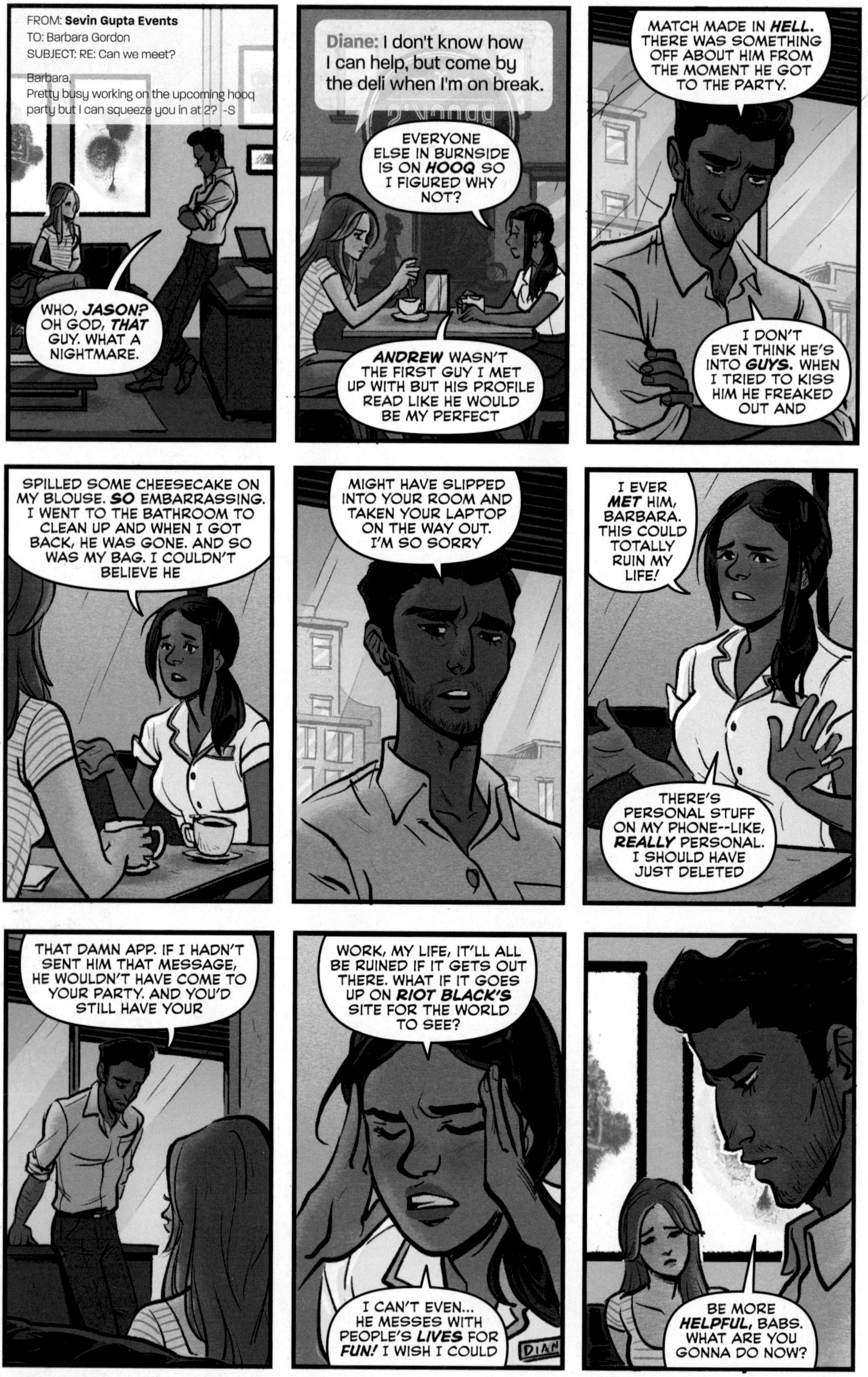
FROM: Sevin Gupta Events
TO: Barbara Gordon
SUBJECT: RE: Can we meet?
Barbara,
Pretty busy working on the upcoming hooq party but I can squeeze you in at 2? -S
WHO, JASON? OH GOD, THAT GUY. WHAT A NIGHTMARE.
Diane: I don't know how I can help, but come by the deli when I'm on break.
EVERYONE ELSE IN BURNSIDE IS ON HOOQ SO I FIGURED WHY NOT?
ANDREW WASN'T THE FIRST GUY I MET UP WITH BUT HIS PROFILE READ LIKE HE WOULD BE MY PERFECT
MATCH MADE IN HELL. THERE WAS SOMETHING OFF ABOUT HIM FROM THE MOMENT HE GOT TO THE PARTY.
I DON'T EVEN THINK HE'S INTO GUYS. WHEN I TRIED TO KISS HIM HE FREAKED OUT AND
SPILLED SOME CHEESECAKE ON MY BLOUSE. SO EMBARRASSING. I WENT TO THE BATHROOM TO CLEAN UP AND WHEN I GOT BACK, HE WAS GONE. AND SO WAS MY BAG. I COULDN'T BELIEVE HE
MIGHT HAVE SLIPPED INTO YOUR ROOM AND TAKEN YOUR LAPTOP ON THE WAY OUT. I'M SO SORRY
I EVER MET HIM, BARBARA. THIS COULD TOTALLY RUIN MY LIFE!
THERE'S PERSONAL STUFF ON MY PHONE--LIKE, REALLY PERSONAL. I SHOULD HAVE JUST DELETED
THAT DAMN APP. IF I HADN'T SENT HIM THAT MESSAGE, HE WOULDN'T HAVE COME TO YOUR PARTY. AND YOU'D STILL HAVE YOUR
WORK, MY LIFE, IT'LL ALL BE RUINED IF IT GETS OUT THERE. WHAT IF IT GOES UP ON RIOT BLACK'S SITE FOR THE WORLD TO SEE?
I CAN'T EVEN... HE MESSES WITH PEOPLE'S LIVES FOR FUN! I WISH I COULD
BE MORE HELPFUL, BABS. WHAT ARE YOU GONNA DO NOW?

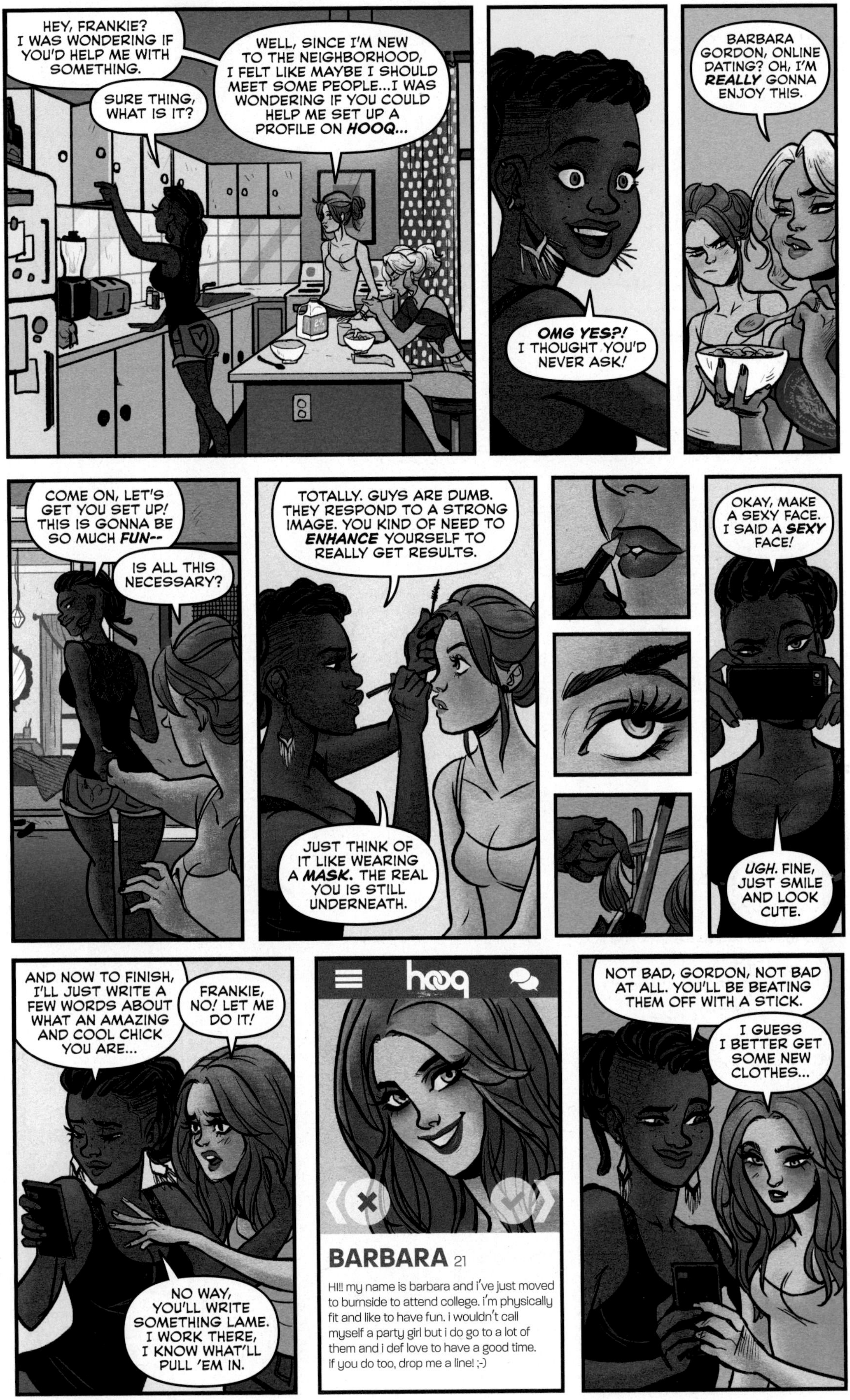
HEY, FRANKIE? I WAS WONDERING IF YOU'D HELP ME WITH SOMETHING.
SURE THING, WHAT IS IT?
WELL, SINCE I'M NEW TO THE NEIGHBORHOOD, I FELT LIKE MAYBE I SHOULD MEET SOME PEOPLE...I WAS WONDERING IF YOU COULD HELP ME SET UP A PROFILE ON HOOQ...
OMG YES?! I THOUGHT YOU'D NEVER ASK!
BARBARA GORDON, ONLINE DATING? OH, I'M REALLY GONNA ENJOY THIS.
COME ON, LET'S GET YOU SET UP! THIS IS GONNA BE SO MUCH FUN--
IS ALL THIS NECESSARY?
TOTALLY. GUYS ARE DUMB. THEY RESPOND TO A STRONG IMAGE. YOU KIND OF NEED TO ENHANCE YOURSELF TO REALLY GET RESULTS.
JUST THINK OF IT LIKE WEARING A MASK. THE REAL YOU IS STILL UNDERNEATH.
OKAY, MAKE A SEXY FACE. I SAID A SEXY FACE!
UGH. FINE, JUST SMILE AND LOOK CUTE.
AND NOW TO FINISH, I'LL JUST WRITE A FEW WORDS ABOUT WHAT AN AMAZING AND COOL CHICK YOU ARE...
FRANKIE, NO! LET ME DO IT!
NO WAY, YOU'LL WRITE SOMETHING LAME. I WORK THERE, I KNOW WHAT'LL PULL 'EM IN.
hooq
BARBARA 21
HI!! my name is barbara and i've just moved to burnside to attend college. i'm physically fit and like to have fun. i wouldn't call myself a party girl but i do go to a lot of them and i def love to have a good time. if you do too, drop me a line! ;-)
NOT BAD, GORDON, NOT BAD AT ALL. YOU'LL BE BEATING THEM OFF WITH A STICK.
I GUESS I BETTER GET SOME NEW CLOTHES...

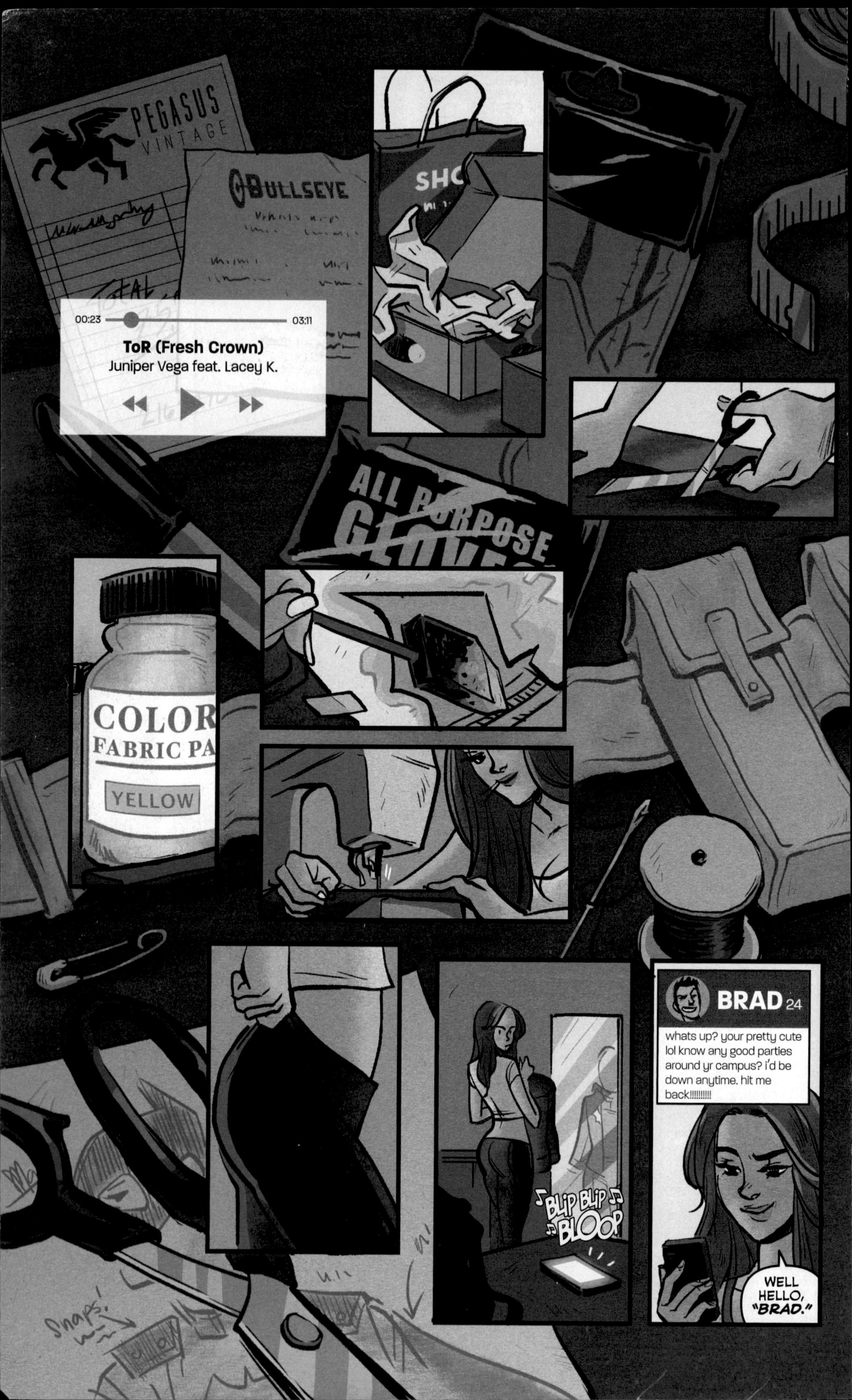
PEGASUS VINTAGE
BULLSEYE
00:23
03:11
ToR (Fresh Crown)
Juniper Vega feat. Lacey K.
ALL PURPOSE GLOVES
COLOR FABRIC PA
YELLOW
BLIP BLIP BLOOP
BRAD 24
whats up? your pretty cute lol know any good parties around yr campus? i'd be down anytime. hit me back!!!!!!!!!!
WELL HELLO, "BRAD."
Snaps!

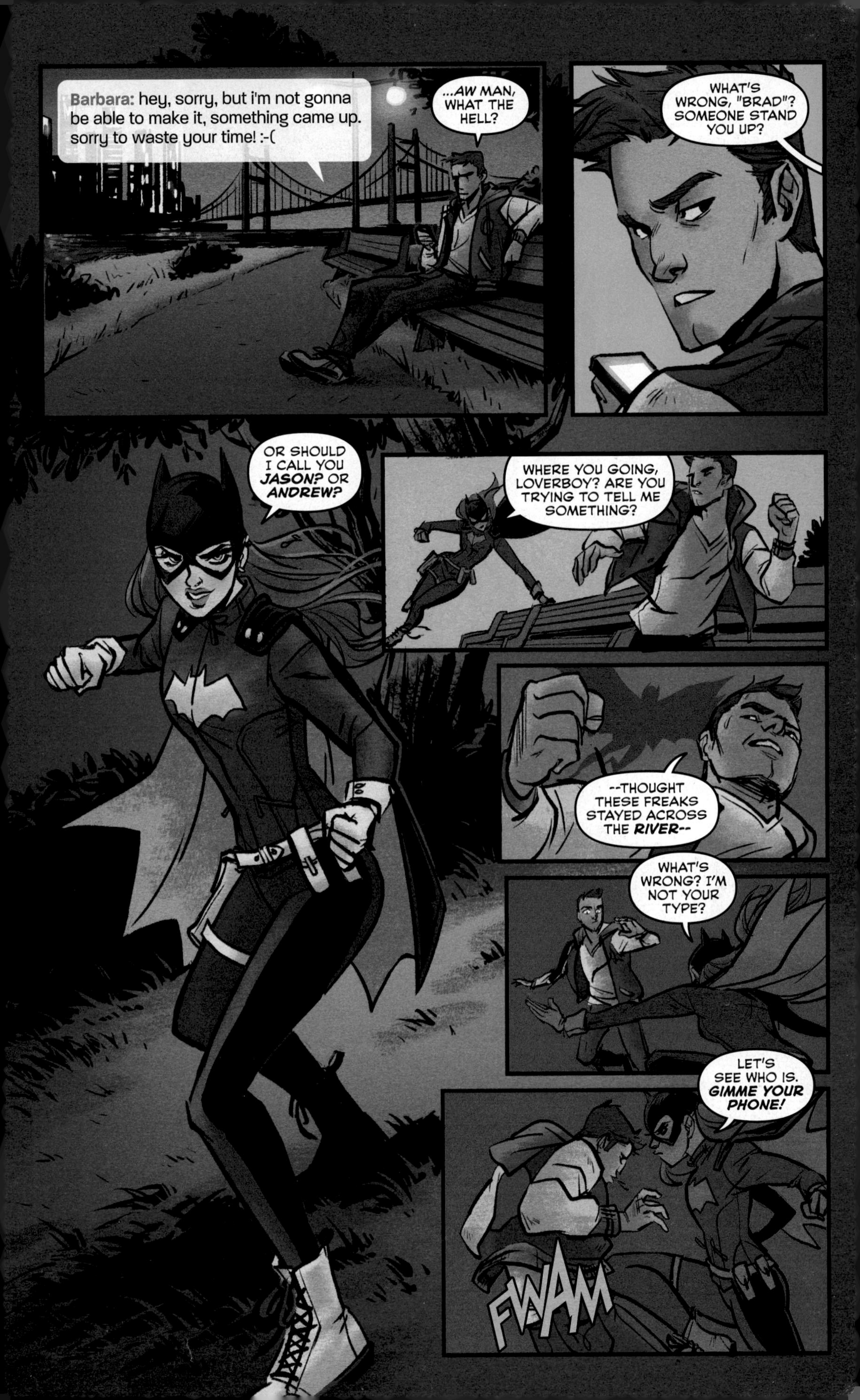
Barbara: hey, sorry, but i'm not gonna be able to make it, something came up. sorry to waste your time! :-(
...AW MAN, WHAT THE HELL?
WHAT'S WRONG, "BRAD"? SOMEONE STAND YOU UP?
OR SHOULD I CALL YOU JASON? OR ANDREW?
WHERE YOU GOING, LOVERBOY? ARE YOU TRYING TO TELL ME SOMETHING?
--THOUGHT THESE FREAKS STAYED ACROSS THE RIVER--
WHAT'S WRONG? I'M NOT YOUR TYPE?
LET'S SEE WHO IS. GIMME YOUR PHONE!
FWAM

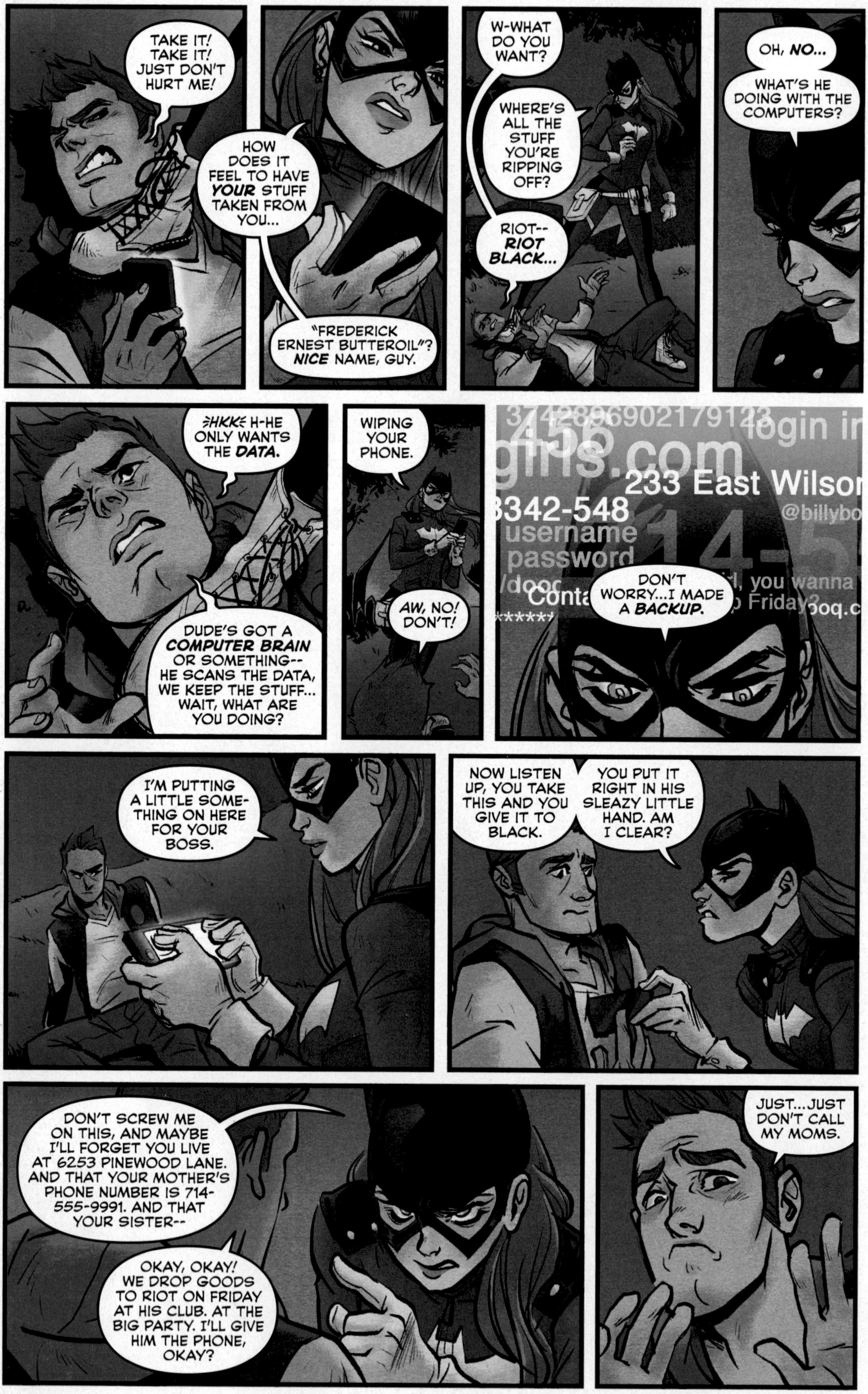
TAKE IT! TAKE IT! JUST DON'T HURT ME!
HOW DOES IT FEEL TO HAVE YOUR STUFF TAKEN FROM YOU...
"FREDERICK ERNEST BUTTEROIL"? NICE NAME, GUY.
W-WHAT DO YOU WANT?
WHERE'S ALL THE STUFF YOU'RE RIPPING OFF?
RIOT-- RIOT BLACK...
OH, NO...
WHAT'S HE DOING WITH THE COMPUTERS?
HKK H-HE ONLY WANTS THE DATA.
DUDE'S GOT A COMPUTER BRAIN OR SOMETHING-- HE SCANS THE DATA, WE KEEP THE STUFF... WAIT, WHAT ARE YOU DOING?
WIPING YOUR PHONE.
AW, NO! DON'T!
233 East Wilson
username
password
DON'T WORRY...I MADE A BACKUP.
I'M PUTTING A LITTLE SOMETHING ON HERE FOR YOUR BOSS.
NOW LISTEN UP, YOU TAKE THIS AND YOU GIVE IT TO BLACK.
YOU PUT IT RIGHT IN HIS SLEAZY LITTLE HAND. AM I CLEAR?
DON'T SCREW ME ON THIS, AND MAYBE I'LL FORGET YOU LIVE AT 6253 PINEWOOD LANE. AND THAT YOUR MOTHER'S PHONE NUMBER IS 714-555-9991. AND THAT YOUR SISTER--
OKAY, OKAY! WE DROP GOODS TO RIOT ON FRIDAY AT HIS CLUB. AT THE BIG PARTY. I'LL GIVE HIM THE PHONE, OKAY?
JUST...JUST DON'T CALL MY MOMS.

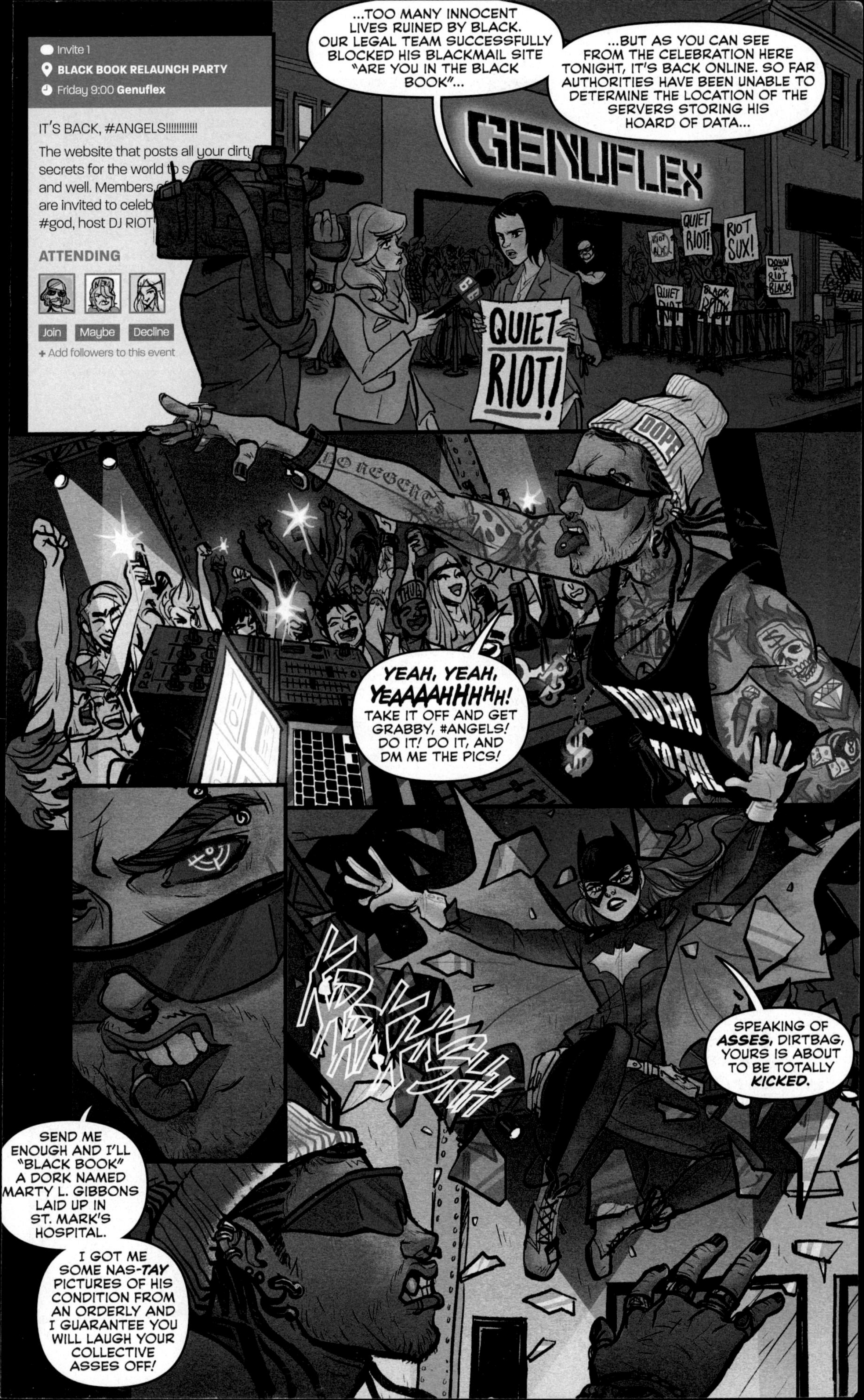

Invite 1
BLACK BOOK RELAUNCH PARTY
Friday 9:00 Genuflex
IT'S BACK, #ANGELS!!!!!!!!!!!
The website that posts all your dirty secrets for the world t
and well. Members
are invited to celeb
#god, host DJ RIOT
ATTENDING
Join
Maybe
Decline
+ Add followers to this event
...TOO MANY INNOCENT LIVES RUINED BY BLACK. OUR LEGAL TEAM SUCCESSFULLY BLOCKED HIS BLACKMAIL SITE "ARE YOU IN THE BLACK BOOK"...
...BUT AS YOU CAN SEE FROM THE CELEBRATION HERE TONIGHT, IT'S BACK ONLINE. SO FAR AUTHORITIES HAVE BEEN UNABLE TO DETERMINE THE LOCATION OF THE SERVERS STORING HIS HOARD OF DATA...
GENUFLEX
QUIET RIOT!
RIOT SUX!
QUIET RIOT!
DOWN WITH RIOT BLACK
DOPE
NO REGERTS
TOO EPIC TO FAIL
YEAH, YEAH, YEAAAAAHHHHH! TAKE IT OFF AND GET GRABBY, #ANGELS! DO IT! DO IT, AND DM ME THE PICS!
SEND ME ENOUGH AND I'LL "BLACK BOOK" A DORK NAMED MARTY L. GIBBONS LAID UP IN ST. MARK'S HOSPITAL.
I GOT ME SOME NAS-TAY PICTURES OF HIS CONDITION FROM AN ORDERLY AND I GUARANTEE YOU WILL LAUGH YOUR COLLECTIVE ASSES OFF!
SPEAKING OF ASSES, DIRTBAG, YOURS IS ABOUT TO BE TOTALLY KICKED.

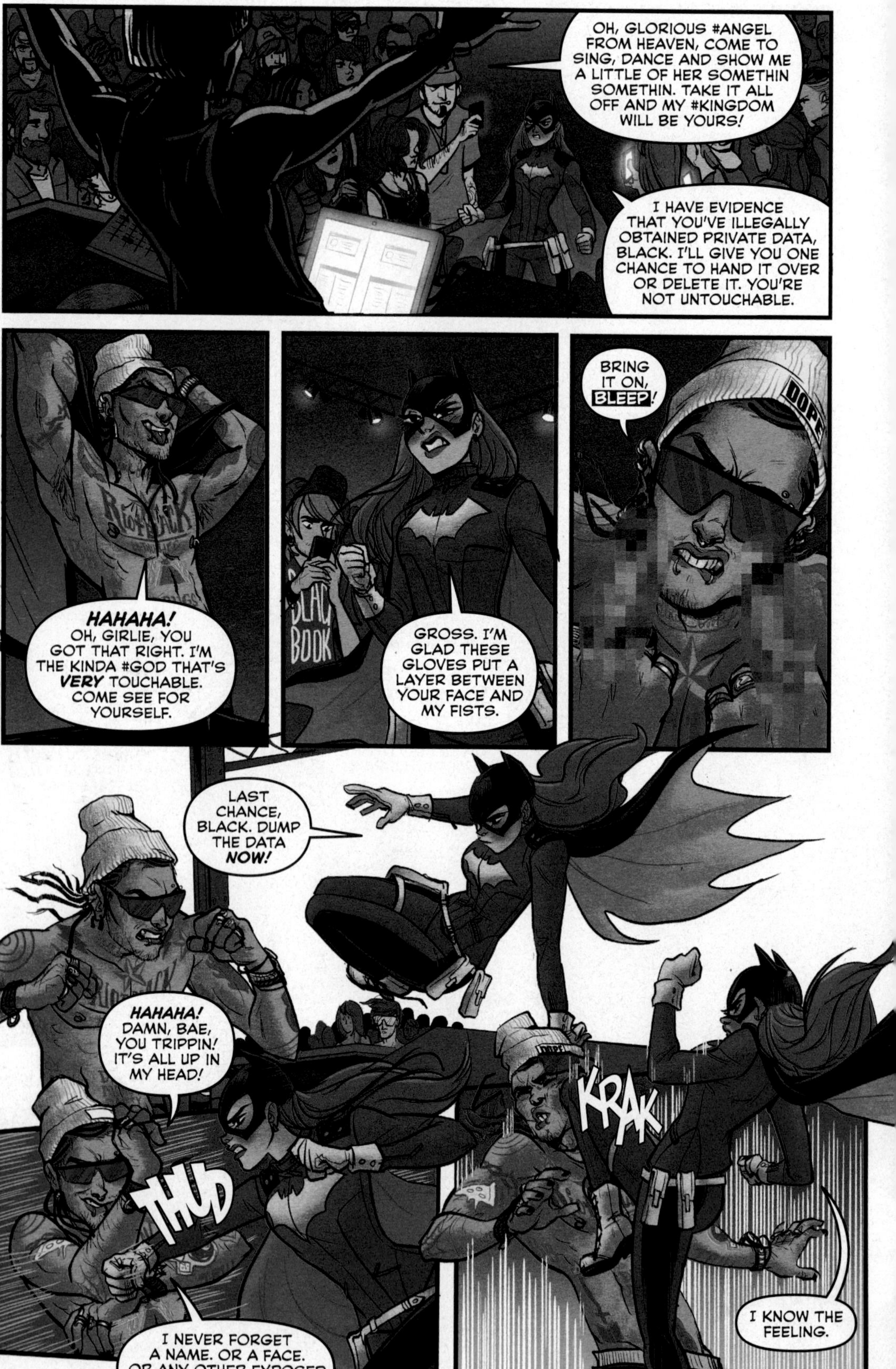
OH, GLORIOUS #ANGEL FROM HEAVEN, COME TO SING, DANCE AND SHOW ME A LITTLE OF HER SOMETHIN SOMETHIN. TAKE IT ALL OFF AND MY #KINGDOM WILL BE YOURS!
I HAVE EVIDENCE THAT YOU'VE ILLEGALLY OBTAINED PRIVATE DATA, BLACK. I'LL GIVE YOU ONE CHANCE TO HAND IT OVER OR DELETE IT. YOU'RE NOT UNTOUCHABLE.
HAHAHA! OH, GIRLIE, YOU GOT THAT RIGHT. I'M THE KINDA #GOD THAT'S ***VERY*** TOUCHABLE. COME SEE FOR YOURSELF.
GROSS. I'M GLAD THESE GLOVES PUT A LAYER BETWEEN YOUR FACE AND MY FISTS.
BRING IT ON, BLEEP!
DOPE
LAST CHANCE, BLACK. DUMP THE DATA ***NOW!***
HAHAHA! DAMN, BAE, YOU TRIPPIN! IT'S ALL UP IN MY HEAD!
THUD
I NEVER FORGET A NAME. OR A FACE. OR ANY OTHER EXPOSED BODY PART, FOR THAT MATTER!
KRAK
I KNOW THE FEELING.

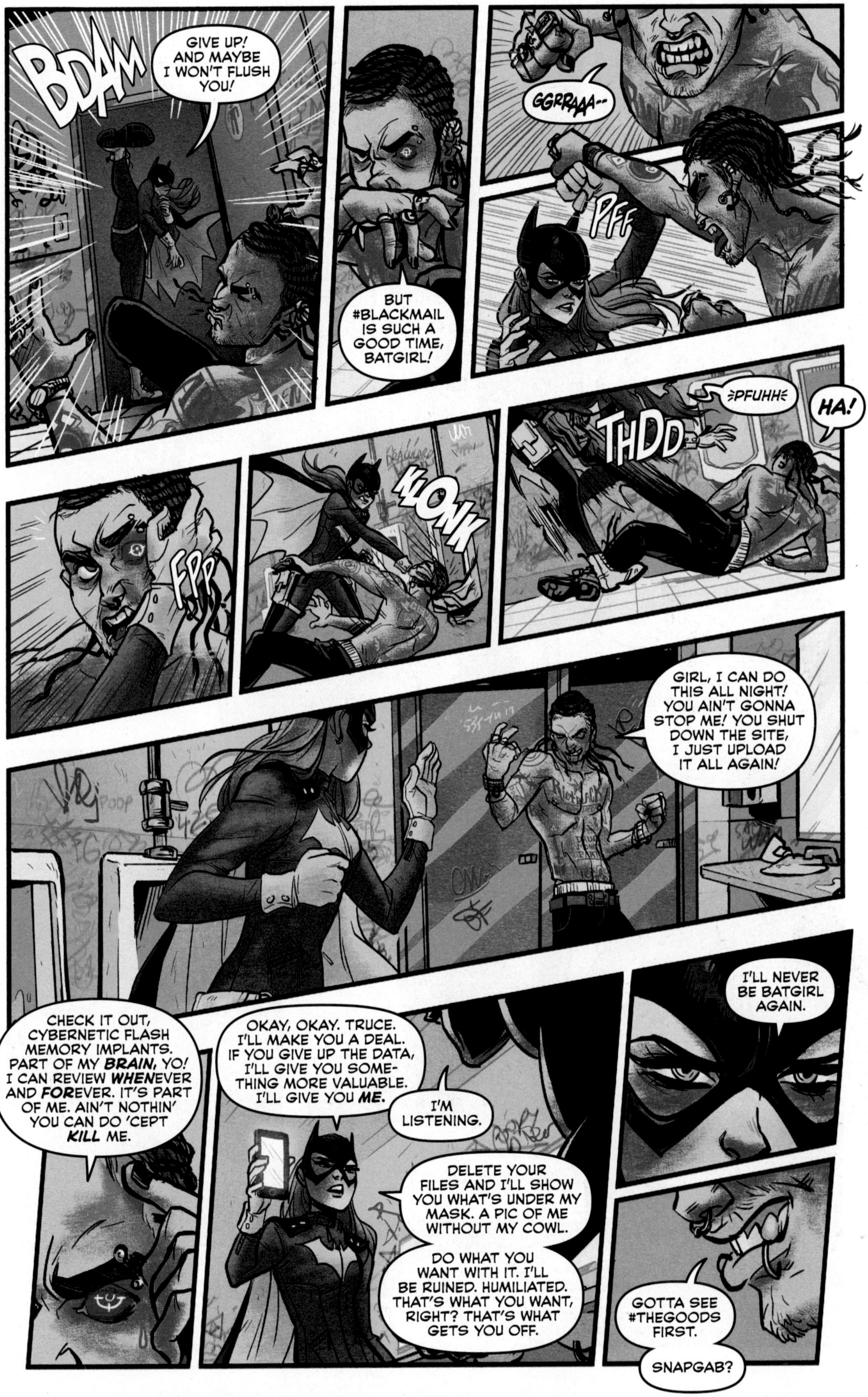
BDAM
GIVE UP! AND MAYBE I WON'T FLUSH YOU!
BUT #BLACKMAIL IS SUCH A GOOD TIME, BATGIRL!
GGRRAAA--
PFF
FPP
KLONK
THDD
PFUHH
HA!
GIRL, I CAN DO THIS ALL NIGHT! YOU AIN'T GONNA STOP ME! YOU SHUT DOWN THE SITE, I JUST UPLOAD IT ALL AGAIN!
CHECK IT OUT, CYBERNETIC FLASH MEMORY IMPLANTS. PART OF MY BRAIN, YO! I CAN REVIEW WHENEVER AND FOREVER. IT'S PART OF ME. AIN'T NOTHIN' YOU CAN DO 'CEPT KILL ME.
OKAY, OKAY. TRUCE. I'LL MAKE YOU A DEAL. IF YOU GIVE UP THE DATA, I'LL GIVE YOU SOMETHING MORE VALUABLE. I'LL GIVE YOU ME.
I'M LISTENING.
DELETE YOUR FILES AND I'LL SHOW YOU WHAT'S UNDER MY MASK. A PIC OF ME WITHOUT MY COWL.
DO WHAT YOU WANT WITH IT. I'LL BE RUINED. HUMILIATED. THAT'S WHAT YOU WANT, RIGHT? THAT'S WHAT GETS YOU OFF.
I'LL NEVER BE BATGIRL AGAIN.
GOTTA SEE #THEGOODS FIRST.
SNAPGAB?

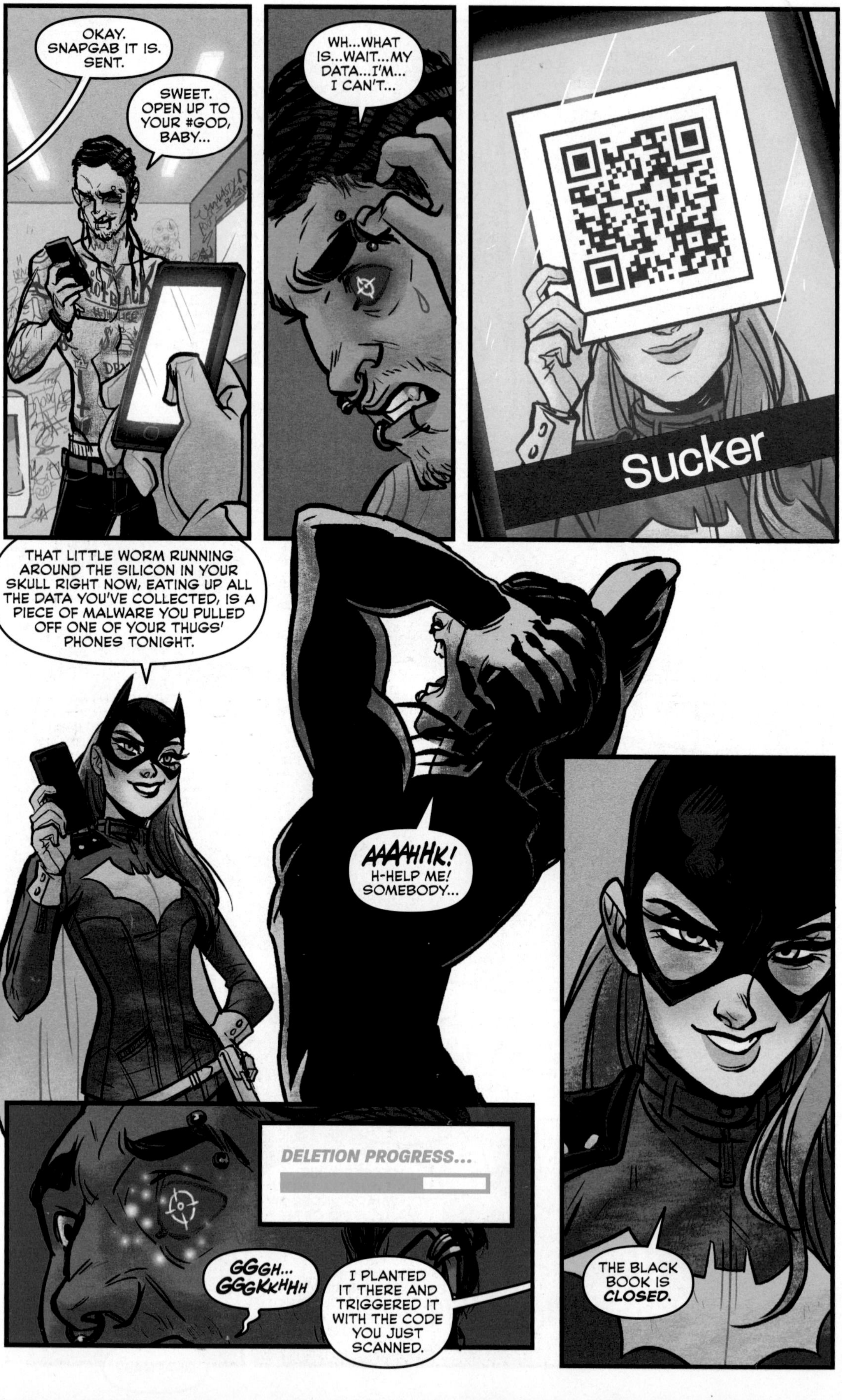
OKAY. SNAPGAB IT IS. SENT.
SWEET. OPEN UP TO YOUR #GOD, BABY...
WH...WHAT IS...WAIT...MY DATA...I'M... I CAN'T...
Sucker
THAT LITTLE WORM RUNNING AROUND THE SILICON IN YOUR SKULL RIGHT NOW, EATING UP ALL THE DATA YOU'VE COLLECTED, IS A PIECE OF MALWARE YOU PULLED OFF ONE OF YOUR THUGS' PHONES TONIGHT.
AAAAHHK! H-HELP ME! SOMEBODY...
DELETION PROGRESS...
GGGH... GGGKKHHH
I PLANTED IT THERE AND TRIGGERED IT WITH THE CODE YOU JUST SCANNED.
THE BLACK BOOK IS CLOSED.

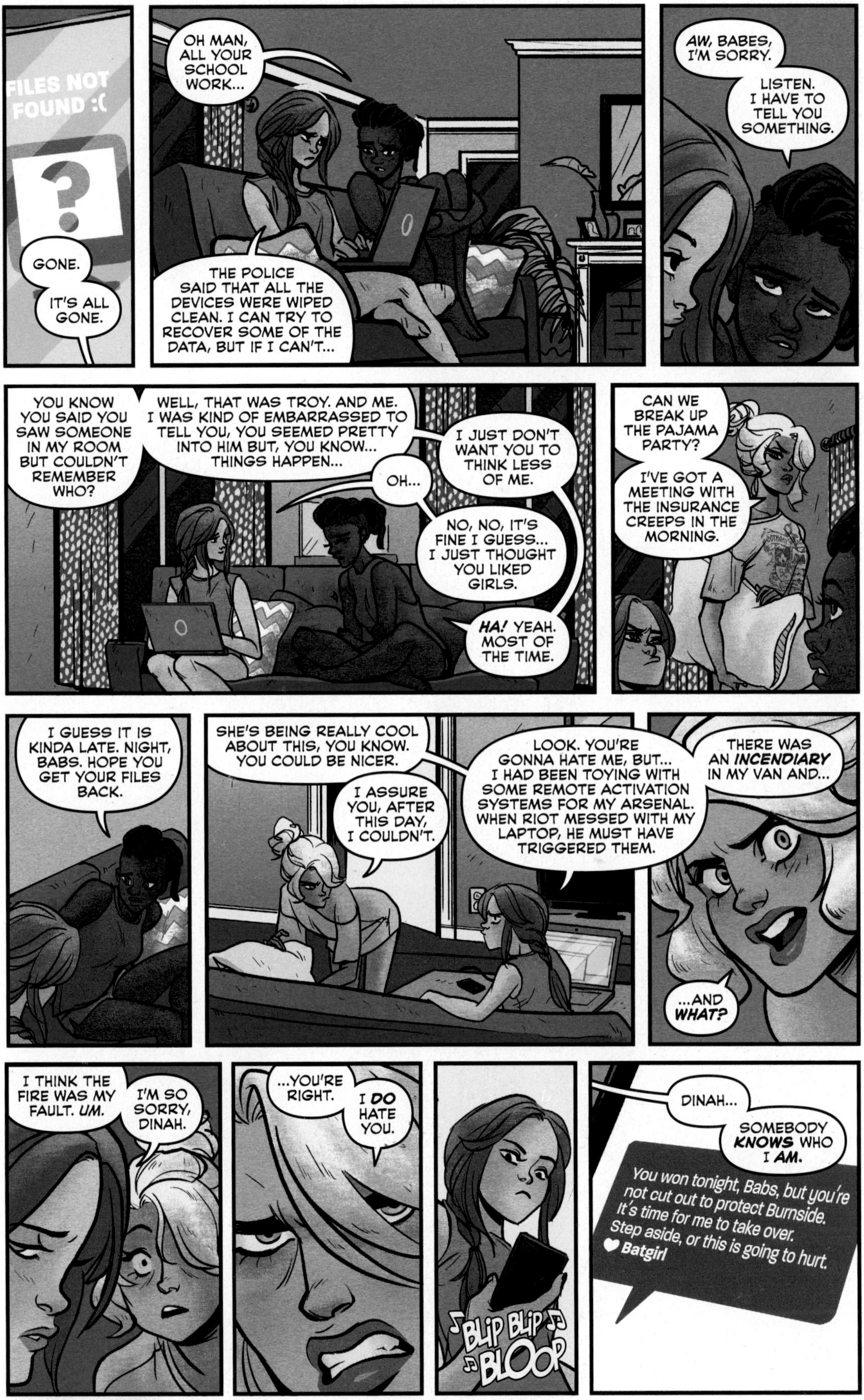
FILES NOT FOUND :(
GONE.
IT'S ALL GONE.
OH MAN, ALL YOUR SCHOOL WORK...
THE POLICE SAID THAT ALL THE DEVICES WERE WIPED CLEAN. I CAN TRY TO RECOVER SOME OF THE DATA, BUT IF I CAN'T...
AW, BABES, I'M SORRY.
LISTEN. I HAVE TO TELL YOU SOMETHING.
YOU KNOW YOU SAID YOU SAW SOMEONE IN MY ROOM BUT COULDN'T REMEMBER WHO?
WELL, THAT WAS TROY. AND ME. I WAS KIND OF EMBARRASSED TO TELL YOU, YOU SEEMED PRETTY INTO HIM BUT, YOU KNOW... THINGS HAPPEN...
I JUST DON'T WANT YOU TO THINK LESS OF ME.
OH...
NO, NO, IT'S FINE I GUESS... I JUST THOUGHT YOU LIKED GIRLS.
HA! YEAH. MOST OF THE TIME.
CAN WE BREAK UP THE PAJAMA PARTY?
I'VE GOT A MEETING WITH THE INSURANCE CREEPS IN THE MORNING.
I GUESS IT IS KINDA LATE. NIGHT, BABS. HOPE YOU GET YOUR FILES BACK.
SHE'S BEING REALLY COOL ABOUT THIS, YOU KNOW. YOU COULD BE NICER.
I ASSURE YOU, AFTER THIS DAY, I COULDN'T.
LOOK. YOU'RE GONNA HATE ME, BUT... I HAD BEEN TOYING WITH SOME REMOTE ACTIVATION SYSTEMS FOR MY ARSENAL. WHEN RIOT MESSED WITH MY LAPTOP, HE MUST HAVE TRIGGERED THEM.
THERE WAS AN INCENDIARY IN MY VAN AND...
...AND WHAT?
I THINK THE FIRE WAS MY FAULT. UM.
I'M SO SORRY, DINAH.
...YOU'RE RIGHT.
I DO HATE YOU.
BLIP BLIP BLOOP
DINAH...
SOMEBODY KNOWS WHO I AM.
You won tonight, Babs, but you're not cut out to protect Burnside. It's time for me to take over. Step aside, or this is going to hurt.
Batgirl

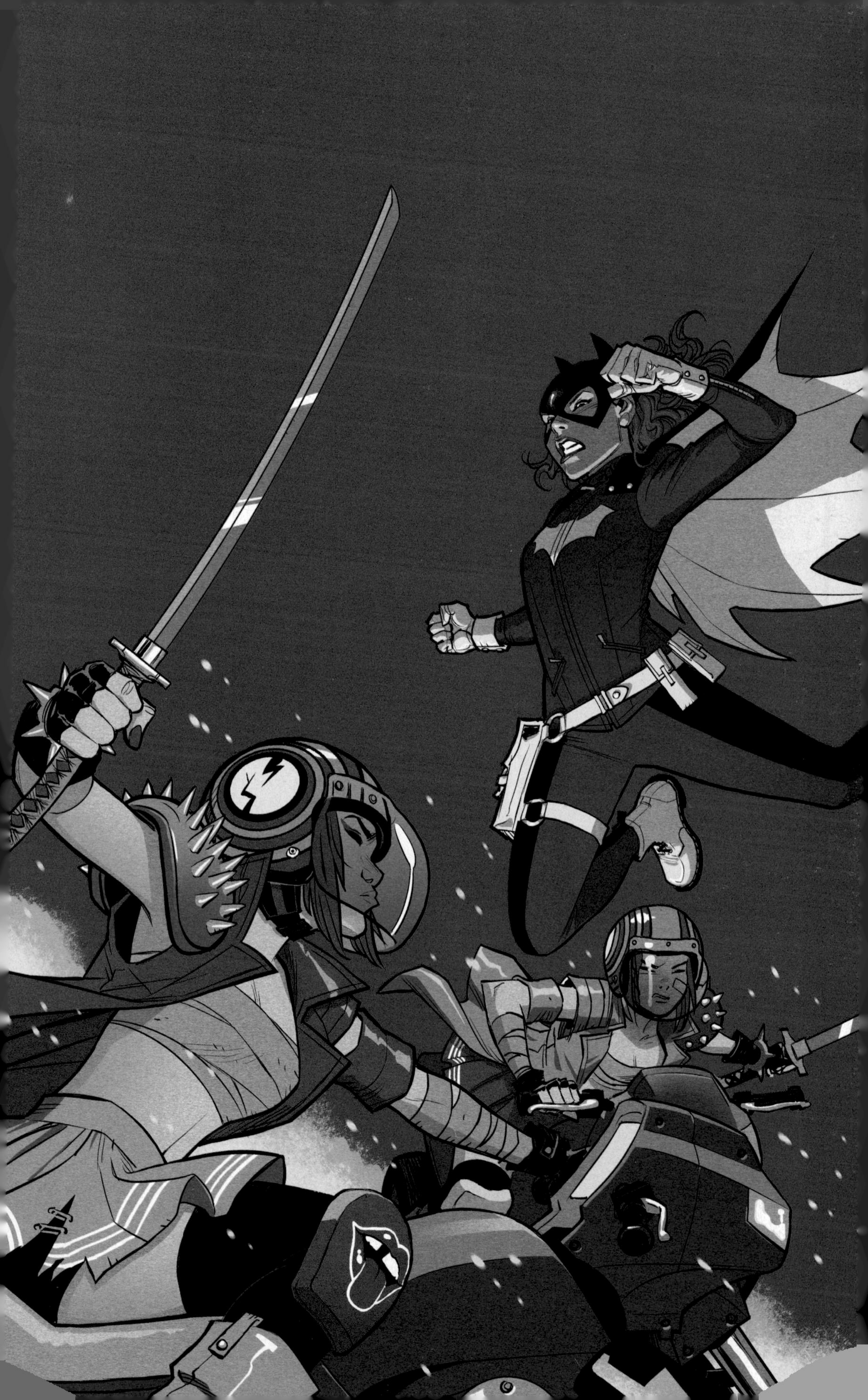

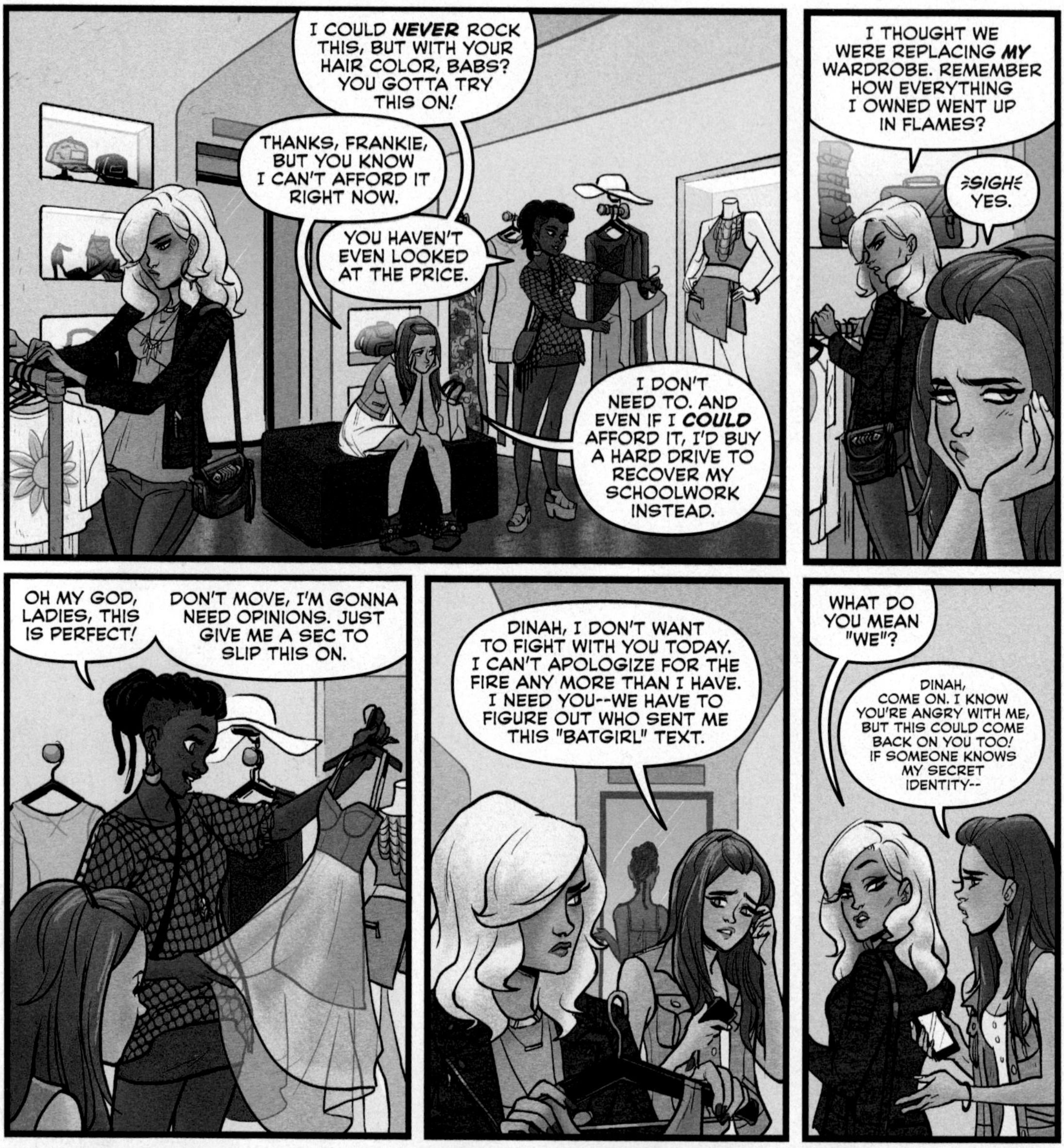
I COULD NEVER ROCK THIS, BUT WITH YOUR HAIR COLOR, BABS? YOU GOTTA TRY THIS ON!
THANKS, FRANKIE, BUT YOU KNOW I CAN'T AFFORD IT RIGHT NOW.
YOU HAVEN'T EVEN LOOKED AT THE PRICE.
I DON'T NEED TO. AND EVEN IF I COULD AFFORD IT, I'D BUY A HARD DRIVE TO RECOVER MY SCHOOLWORK INSTEAD.
I THOUGHT WE WERE REPLACING MY WARDROBE. REMEMBER HOW EVERYTHING I OWNED WENT UP IN FLAMES?
SIGH YES.
OH MY GOD, LADIES, THIS IS PERFECT!
DON'T MOVE, I'M GONNA NEED OPINIONS. JUST GIVE ME A SEC TO SLIP THIS ON.
DINAH, I DON'T WANT TO FIGHT WITH YOU TODAY. I CAN'T APOLOGIZE FOR THE FIRE ANY MORE THAN I HAVE. I NEED YOU--WE HAVE TO FIGURE OUT WHO SENT ME THIS "BATGIRL" TEXT.
WHAT DO YOU MEAN "WE"?
DINAH, COME ON. I KNOW YOU'RE ANGRY WITH ME, BUT THIS COULD COME BACK ON YOU TOO! IF SOMEONE KNOWS MY SECRET IDENTITY--
--THEN YOU HAVEN'T DONE A VERY GOOD JOB OF PROTECTING IT. IF YOU HAD, THEN YOU WOULDN'T BE GETTING CREEPY TEXTS FROM SOMEONE CALLING THEMSELVES "BATGIRL"--
BATGIRL?! SHE'S SO COOL, HEY?
YOU SAW THE PHOTOS FROM HER TAKEDOWN OF RIOT BLACK THE OTHER NIGHT, RIGHT?
UH, YEAH, WOW...
SHE'S SO BADASS. LOOK AT THAT OUTFIT!
Instagraph
J2Starsss
1052 Likes
WHO DO YOU THINK SHE IS?

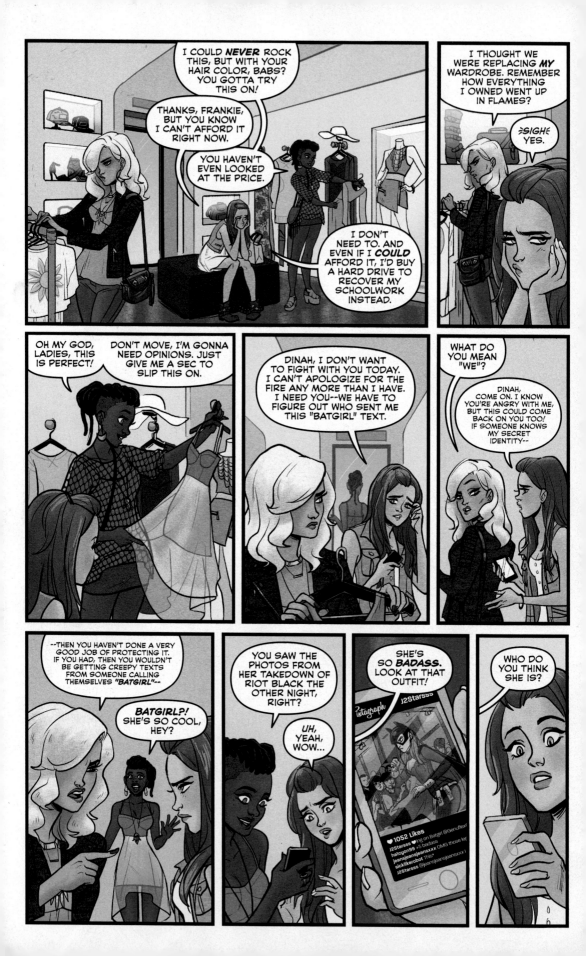

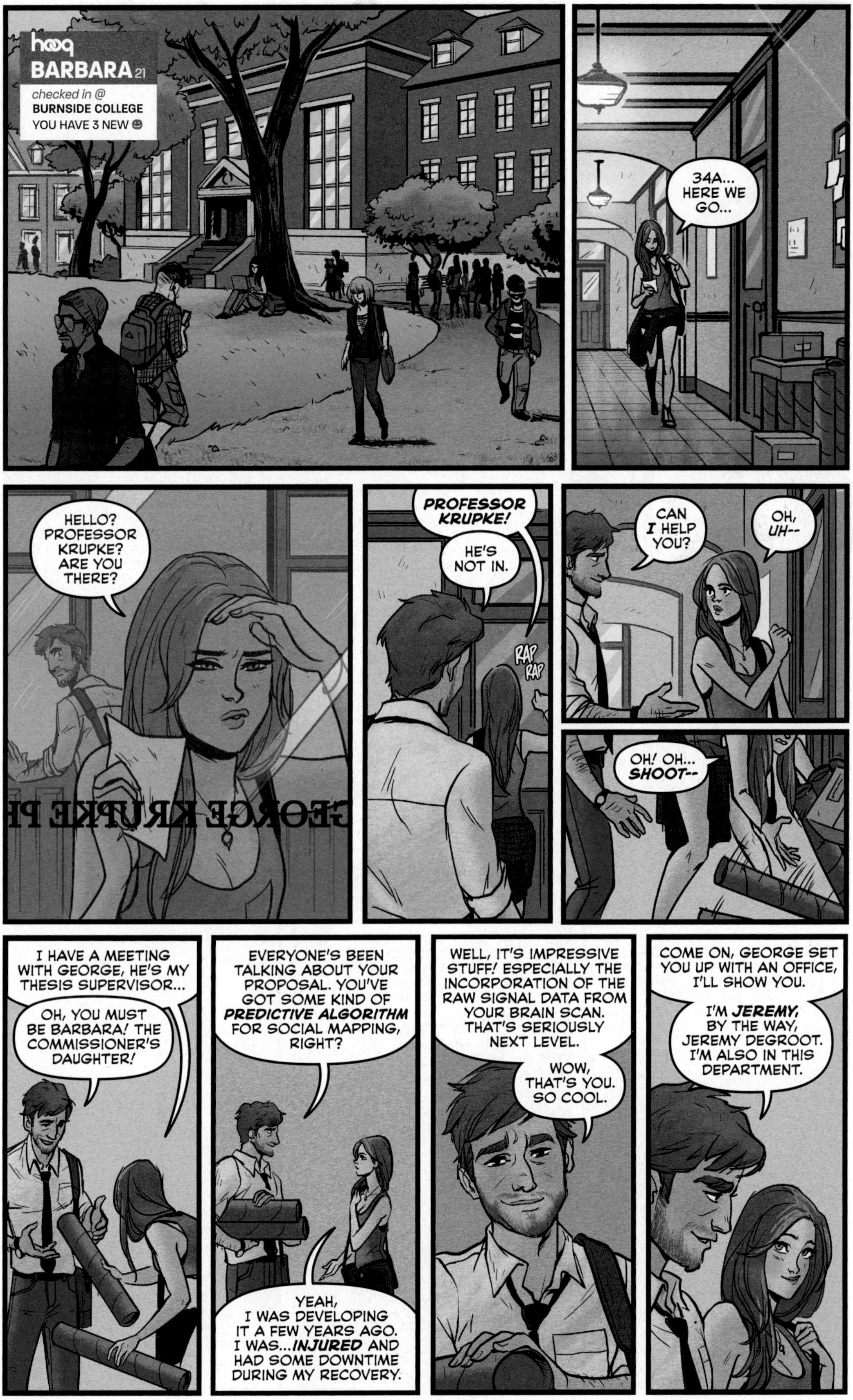
hooq
BARBARA 21
checked in @
BURNSIDE COLLEGE
YOU HAVE 3 NEW
34A... HERE WE GO...
HELLO? PROFESSOR KRUPKE? ARE YOU THERE?
GEORGE KRUPKE PH
PROFESSOR KRUPKE!
HE'S NOT IN.
RAP RAP
CAN I HELP YOU?
OH, UH--
OH! OH... SHOOT--
I HAVE A MEETING WITH GEORGE, HE'S MY THESIS SUPERVISOR...
OH, YOU MUST BE BARBARA! THE COMMISSIONER'S DAUGHTER!
EVERYONE'S BEEN TALKING ABOUT YOUR PROPOSAL. YOU'VE GOT SOME KIND OF PREDICTIVE ALGORITHM FOR SOCIAL MAPPING, RIGHT?
YEAH, I WAS DEVELOPING IT A FEW YEARS AGO. I WAS...INJURED AND HAD SOME DOWNTIME DURING MY RECOVERY.
WELL, IT'S IMPRESSIVE STUFF! ESPECIALLY THE INCORPORATION OF THE RAW SIGNAL DATA FROM YOUR BRAIN SCAN. THAT'S SERIOUSLY NEXT LEVEL.
WOW, THAT'S YOU. SO COOL.
COME ON, GEORGE SET YOU UP WITH AN OFFICE, I'LL SHOW YOU.
I'M JEREMY, BY THE WAY, JEREMY DEGROOT. I'M ALSO IN THIS DEPARTMENT.

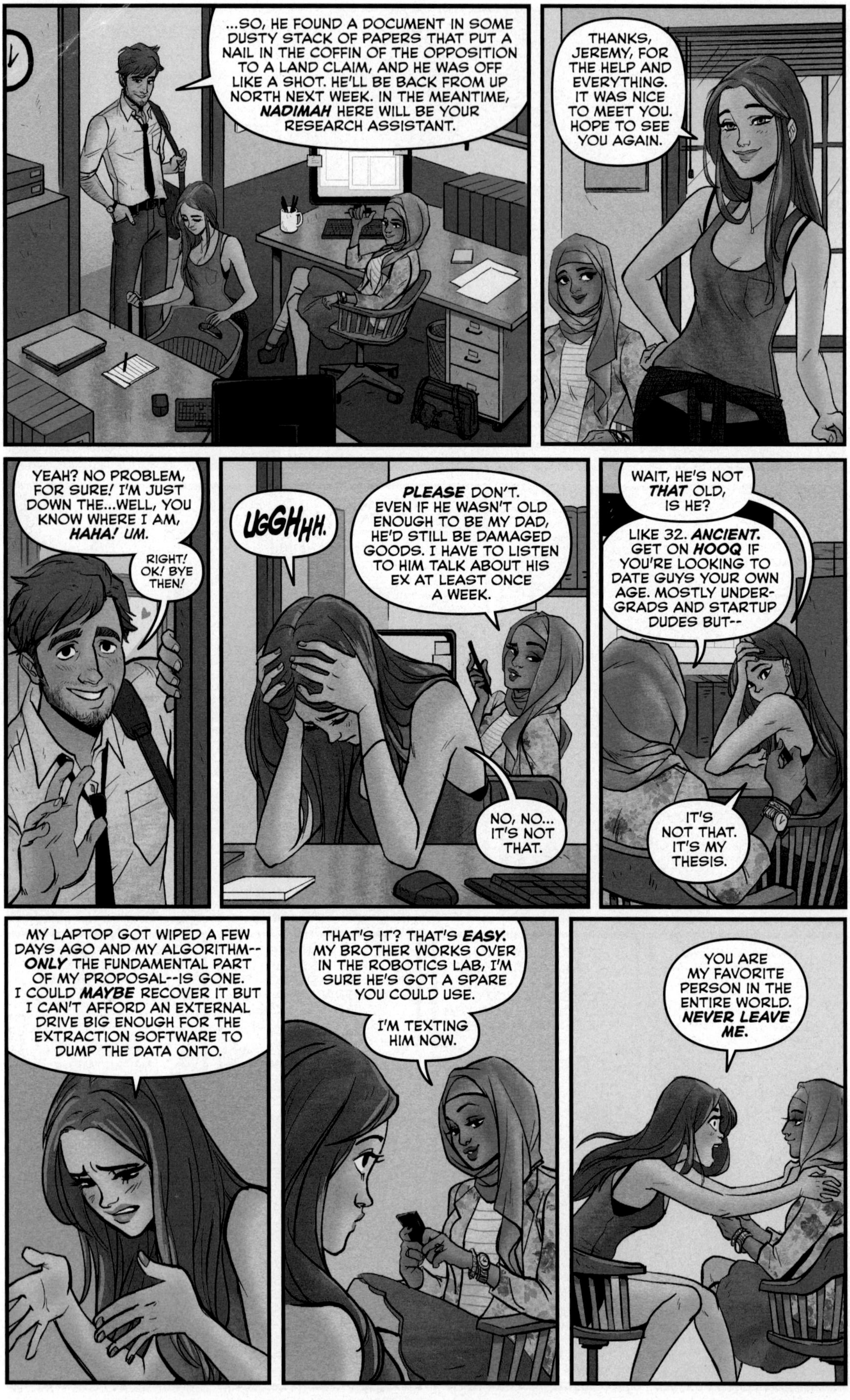
...SO, HE FOUND A DOCUMENT IN SOME DUSTY STACK OF PAPERS THAT PUT A NAIL IN THE COFFIN OF THE OPPOSITION TO A LAND CLAIM, AND HE WAS OFF LIKE A SHOT. HE'LL BE BACK FROM UP NORTH NEXT WEEK. IN THE MEANTIME, NADIMAH HERE WILL BE YOUR RESEARCH ASSISTANT.
THANKS, JEREMY, FOR THE HELP AND EVERYTHING. IT WAS NICE TO MEET YOU. HOPE TO SEE YOU AGAIN.
YEAH? NO PROBLEM, FOR SURE! I'M JUST DOWN THE...WELL, YOU KNOW WHERE I AM, HAHA! UM.
RIGHT! OK! BYE THEN!
UGGHHH.
PLEASE DON'T. EVEN IF HE WASN'T OLD ENOUGH TO BE MY DAD, HE'D STILL BE DAMAGED GOODS. I HAVE TO LISTEN TO HIM TALK ABOUT HIS EX AT LEAST ONCE A WEEK.
NO, NO... IT'S NOT THAT.
WAIT, HE'S NOT THAT OLD, IS HE?
LIKE 32. ANCIENT. GET ON HOOQ IF YOU'RE LOOKING TO DATE GUYS YOUR OWN AGE. MOSTLY UNDERGRADS AND STARTUP DUDES BUT--
IT'S NOT THAT. IT'S MY THESIS.
MY LAPTOP GOT WIPED A FEW DAYS AGO AND MY ALGORITHM--ONLY THE FUNDAMENTAL PART OF MY PROPOSAL--IS GONE. I COULD MAYBE RECOVER IT BUT I CAN'T AFFORD AN EXTERNAL DRIVE BIG ENOUGH FOR THE EXTRACTION SOFTWARE TO DUMP THE DATA ONTO.
THAT'S IT? THAT'S EASY. MY BROTHER WORKS OVER IN THE ROBOTICS LAB, I'M SURE HE'S GOT A SPARE YOU COULD USE.
I'M TEXTING HIM NOW.
YOU ARE MY FAVORITE PERSON IN THE ENTIRE WORLD. NEVER LEAVE ME.

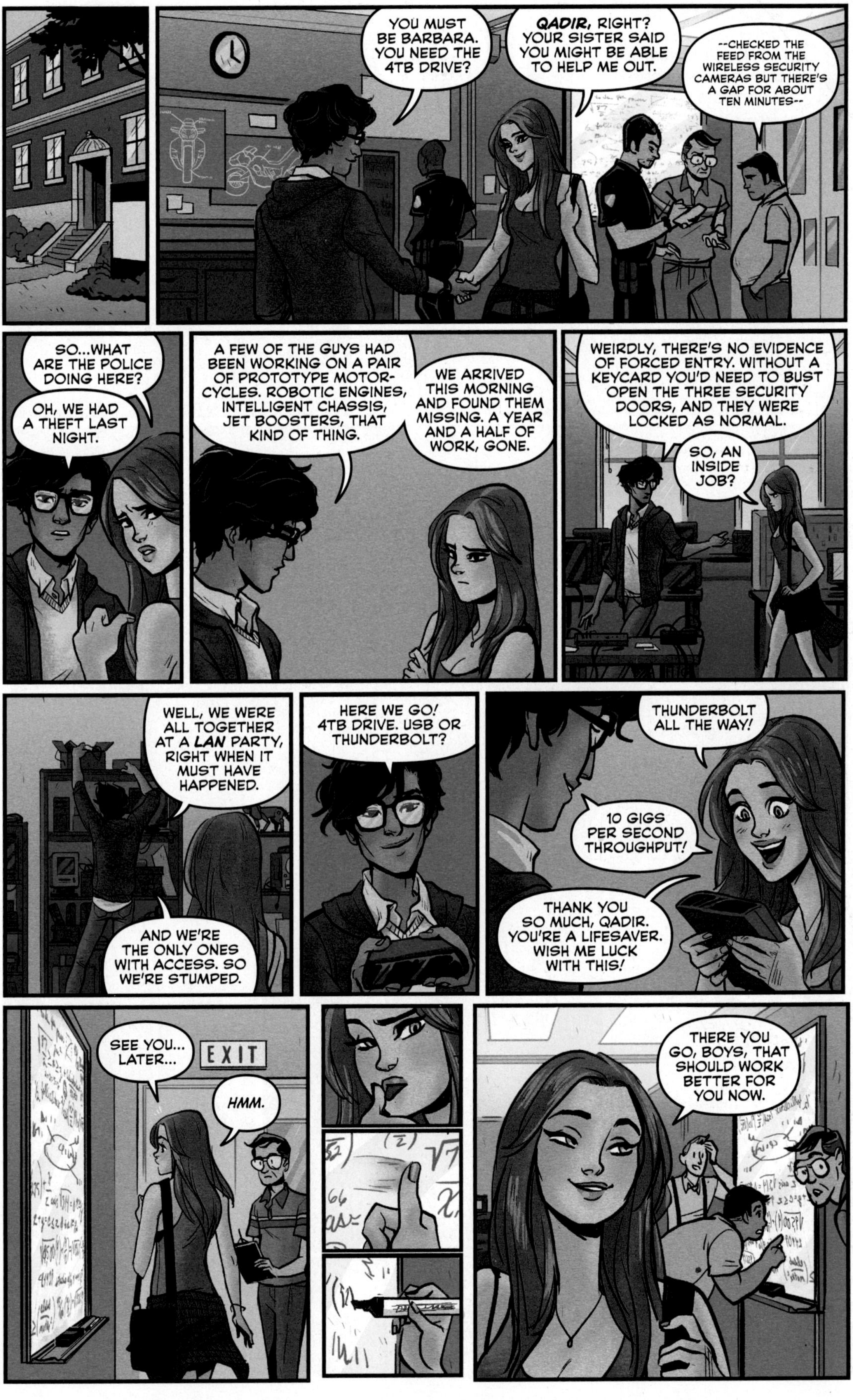

YOU MUST BE BARBARA. YOU NEED THE 4TB DRIVE?
QADIR, RIGHT? YOUR SISTER SAID YOU MIGHT BE ABLE TO HELP ME OUT.
--CHECKED THE FEED FROM THE WIRELESS SECURITY CAMERAS BUT THERE'S A GAP FOR ABOUT TEN MINUTES--
SO...WHAT ARE THE POLICE DOING HERE?
OH, WE HAD A THEFT LAST NIGHT.
A FEW OF THE GUYS HAD BEEN WORKING ON A PAIR OF PROTOTYPE MOTOR-CYCLES. ROBOTIC ENGINES, INTELLIGENT CHASSIS, JET BOOSTERS, THAT KIND OF THING.
WE ARRIVED THIS MORNING AND FOUND THEM MISSING. A YEAR AND A HALF OF WORK, GONE.
WEIRDLY, THERE'S NO EVIDENCE OF FORCED ENTRY. WITHOUT A KEYCARD YOU'D NEED TO BUST OPEN THE THREE SECURITY DOORS, AND THEY WERE LOCKED AS NORMAL.
SO, AN INSIDE JOB?
WELL, WE WERE ALL TOGETHER AT A LAN PARTY, RIGHT WHEN IT MUST HAVE HAPPENED.
AND WE'RE THE ONLY ONES WITH ACCESS. SO WE'RE STUMPED.
HERE WE GO! 4TB DRIVE. USB OR THUNDERBOLT?
THUNDERBOLT ALL THE WAY!
10 GIGS PER SECOND THROUGHPUT!
THANK YOU SO MUCH, QADIR. YOU'RE A LIFESAVER. WISH ME LUCK WITH THIS!
SEE YOU... LATER...
EXIT
HMM.
THERE YOU GO, BOYS, THAT SHOULD WORK BETTER FOR YOU NOW.

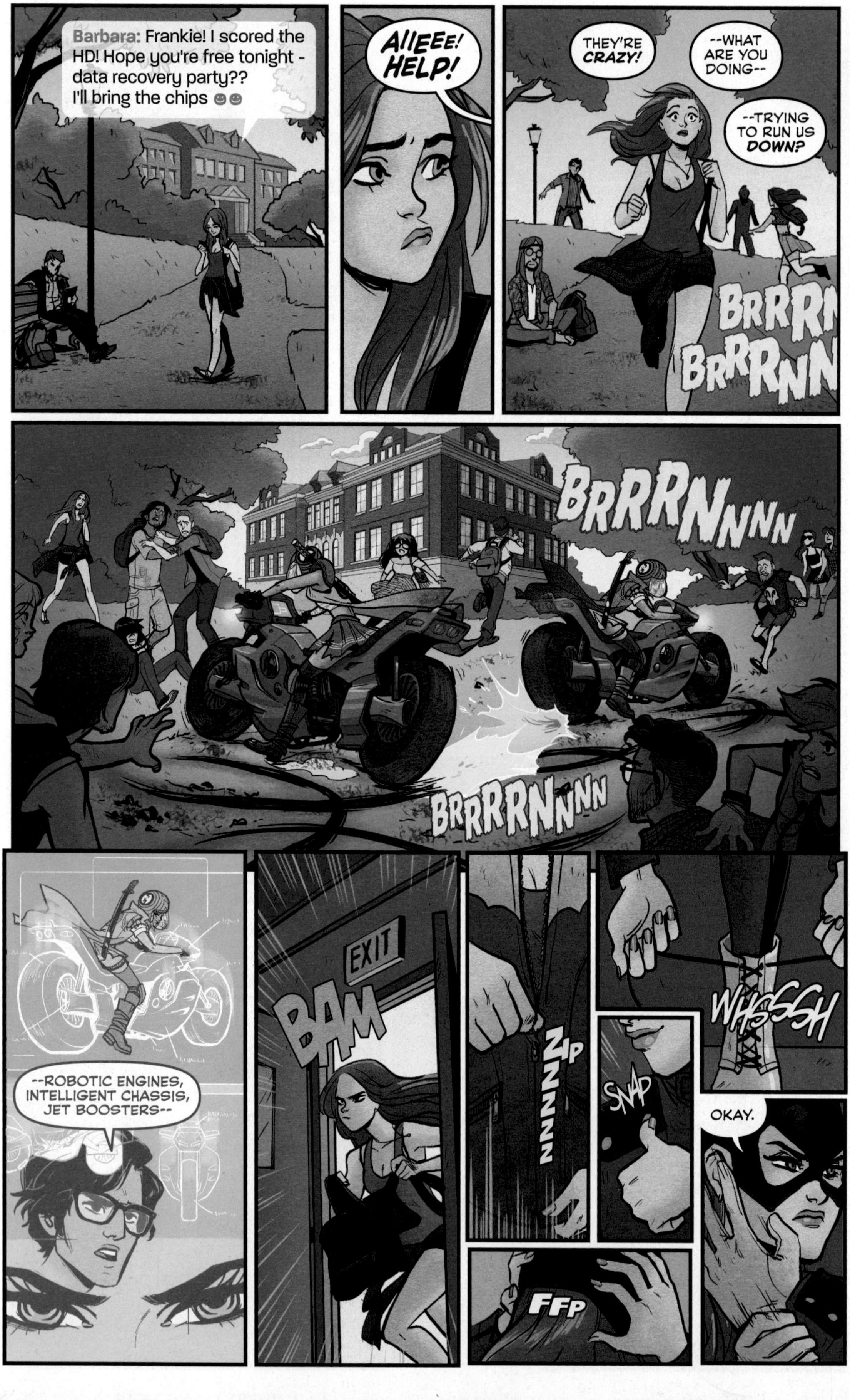
Barbara: Frankie! I scored the HD! Hope you're free tonight - data recovery party?? I'll bring the chips ☻☻
AIIEEE! HELP!
THEY'RE CRAZY!
--WHAT ARE YOU DOING--
--TRYING TO RUN US DOWN?
BRRRN
BRRRNN
BRRRNnnn
BRRRRNNNN
--ROBOTIC ENGINES, INTELLIGENT CHASSIS, JET BOOSTERS--
EXIT
BAM
ZIP
ZZZZZZ
WHSSSH
SNAP
FFP
OKAY.

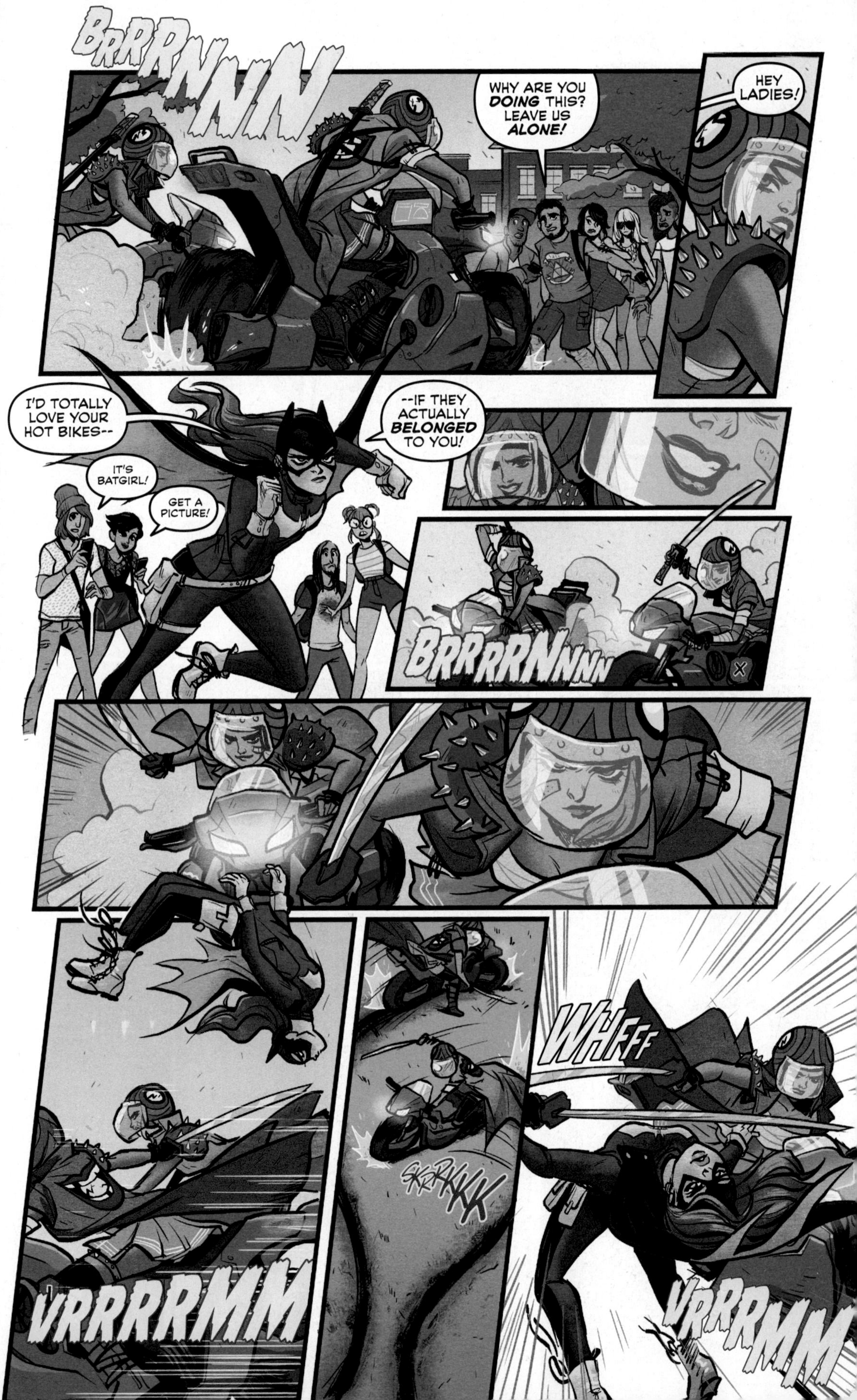

BRRRNNNN
WHY ARE YOU DOING THIS? LEAVE US ALONE!
HEY LADIES!
I'D TOTALLY LOVE YOUR HOT BIKES--
--IF THEY ACTUALLY BELONGED TO YOU!
IT'S BATGIRL!
GET A PICTURE!
BRRRRRNnnn
WHFFF
SKRRKKK
VRRRRRMM
VRRRMM

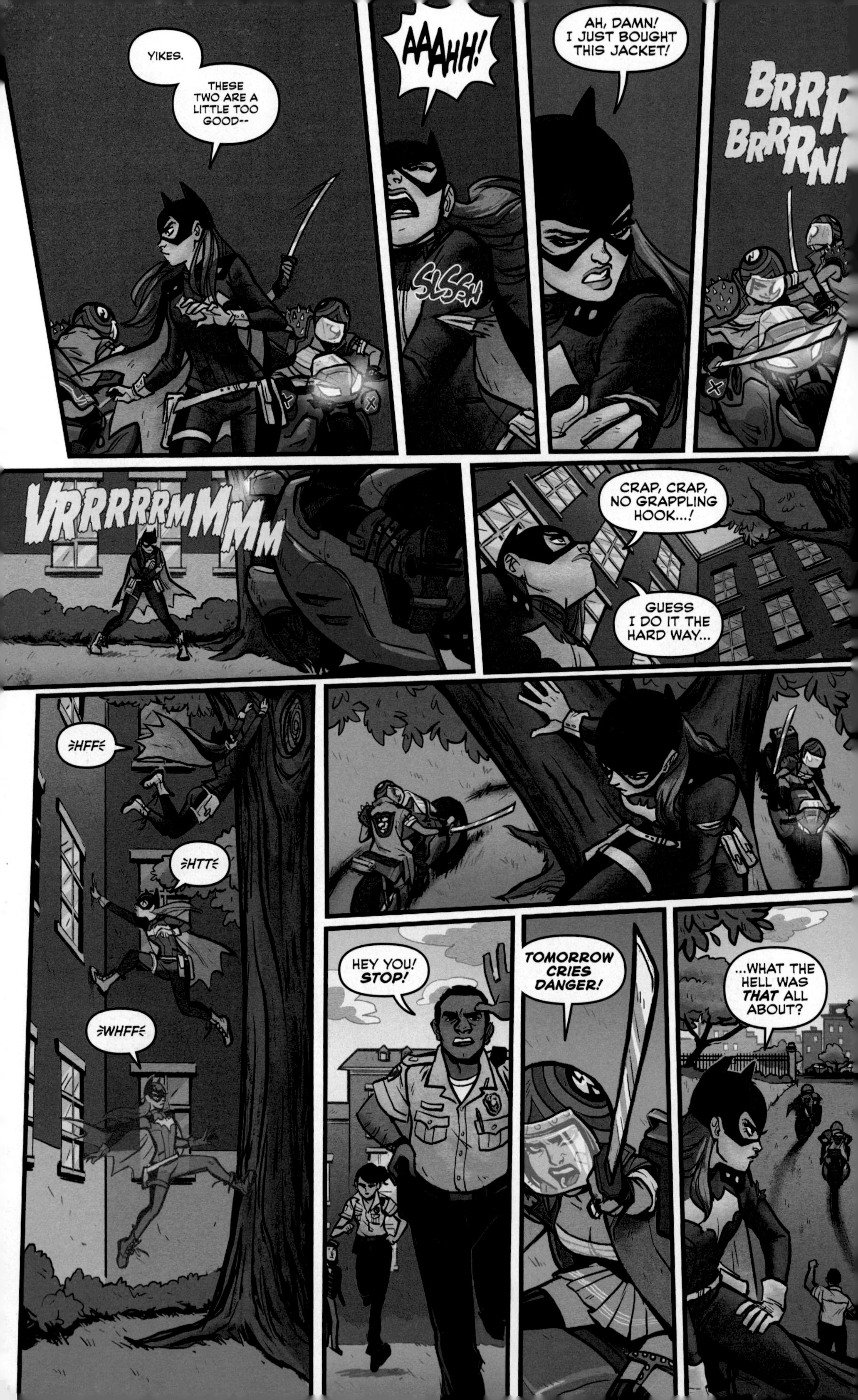

YIKES.
THESE TWO ARE A LITTLE TOO GOOD--
AAAHH!
SLSSH
AH, DAMN! I JUST BOUGHT THIS JACKET!
BRRR BRRRRNI
VRRRRRMMMMM
CRAP, CRAP, NO GRAPPLING HOOK...!
GUESS I DO IT THE HARD WAY...
HFF
HTT
WHFF
HEY YOU! STOP!
TOMORROW CRIES DANGER!
...WHAT THE HELL WAS THAT ALL ABOUT?

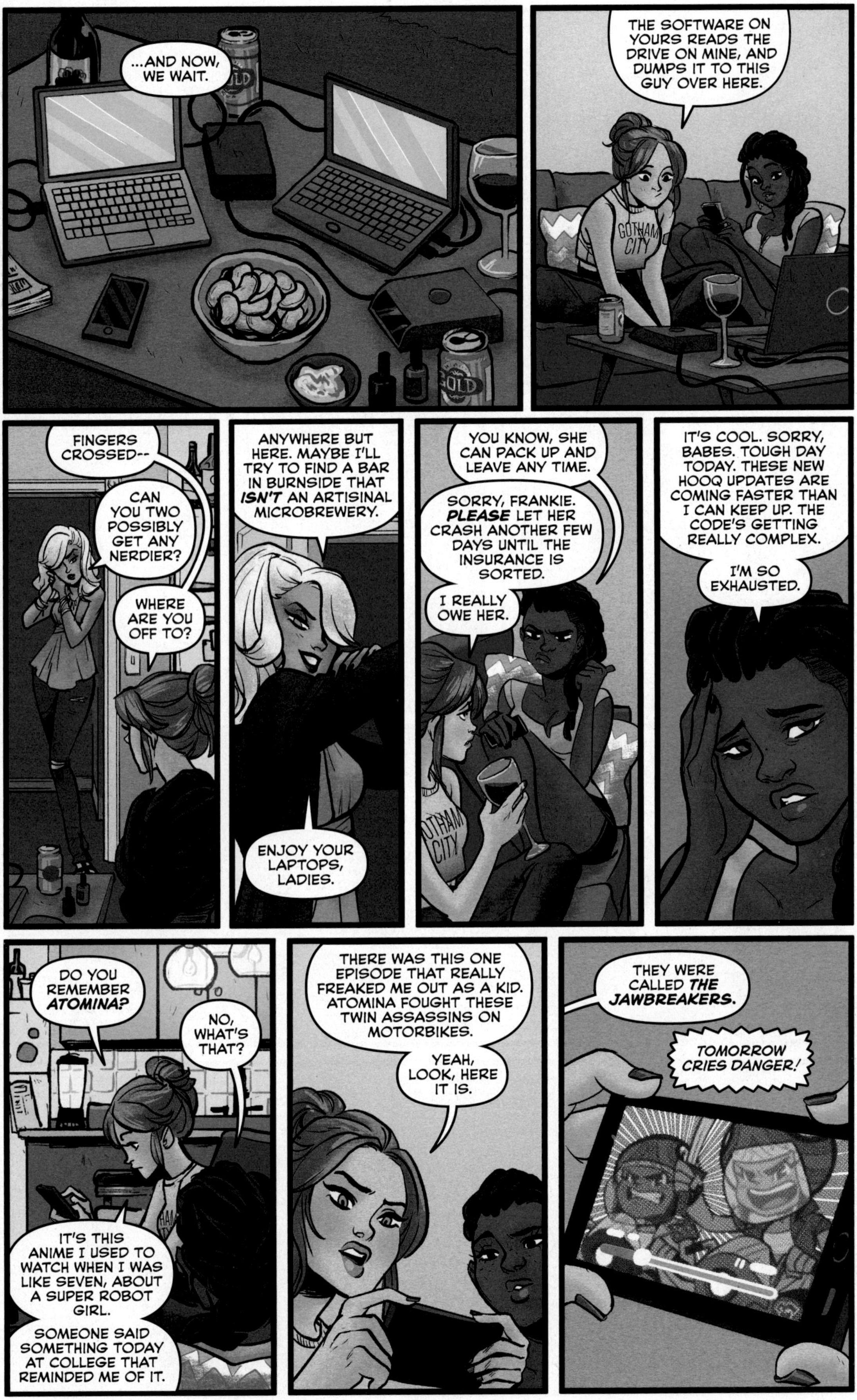

...AND NOW, WE WAIT.
THE SOFTWARE ON YOURS READS THE DRIVE ON MINE, AND DUMPS IT TO THIS GUY OVER HERE.
GOTHAM CITY
FINGERS CROSSED--
CAN YOU TWO POSSIBLY GET ANY NERDIER?
WHERE ARE YOU OFF TO?
ANYWHERE BUT HERE. MAYBE I'LL TRY TO FIND A BAR IN BURNSIDE THAT *ISN'T* AN ARTISINAL MICROBREWERY.
ENJOY YOUR LAPTOPS, LADIES.
YOU KNOW, SHE CAN PACK UP AND LEAVE ANY TIME.
SORRY, FRANKIE. *PLEASE* LET HER CRASH ANOTHER FEW DAYS UNTIL THE INSURANCE IS SORTED.
I REALLY OWE HER.
IT'S COOL. SORRY, BABES. TOUGH DAY TODAY. THESE NEW HOOQ UPDATES ARE COMING FASTER THAN I CAN KEEP UP. THE CODE'S GETTING REALLY COMPLEX.
I'M SO EXHAUSTED.
DO YOU REMEMBER *ATOMINA?*
NO, WHAT'S THAT?
IT'S THIS ANIME I USED TO WATCH WHEN I WAS LIKE SEVEN, ABOUT A SUPER ROBOT GIRL.
SOMEONE SAID SOMETHING TODAY AT COLLEGE THAT REMINDED ME OF IT.
THERE WAS THIS ONE EPISODE THAT REALLY FREAKED ME OUT AS A KID. ATOMINA FOUGHT THESE TWIN ASSASSINS ON MOTORBIKES.
YEAH, LOOK, HERE IT IS.
THEY WERE CALLED *THE JAWBREAKERS.*
TOMORROW CRIES DANGER!

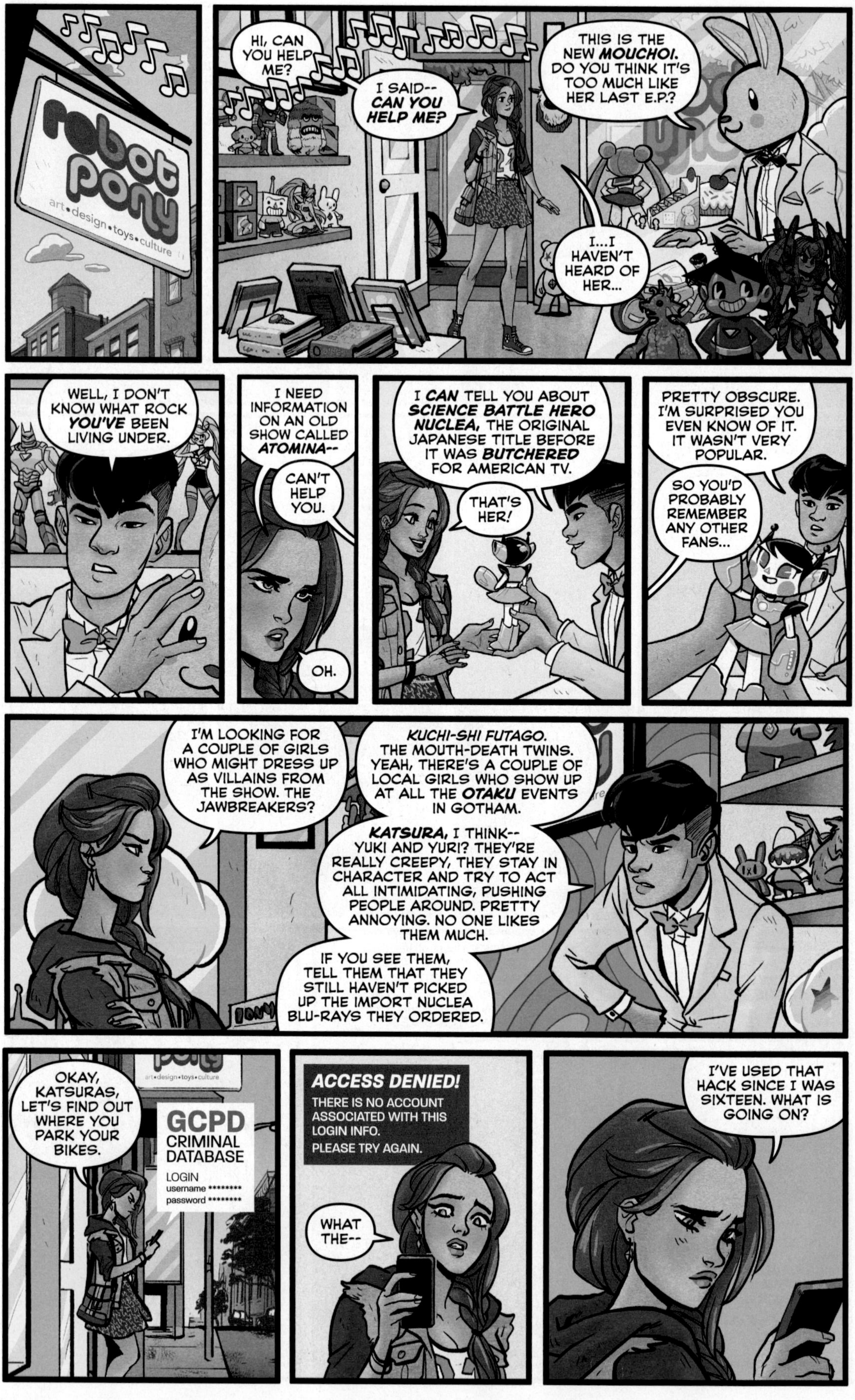
robot pony
art•design•toys•culture
HI, CAN YOU HELP ME?
I SAID-- CAN YOU HELP ME?
THIS IS THE NEW MOUCHOI. DO YOU THINK IT'S TOO MUCH LIKE HER LAST E.P.?
I...I HAVEN'T HEARD OF HER...
WELL, I DON'T KNOW WHAT ROCK YOU'VE BEEN LIVING UNDER.
I NEED INFORMATION ON AN OLD SHOW CALLED ATOMINA--
CAN'T HELP YOU.
OH.
I CAN TELL YOU ABOUT SCIENCE BATTLE HERO NUCLEA, THE ORIGINAL JAPANESE TITLE BEFORE IT WAS BUTCHERED FOR AMERICAN TV.
THAT'S HER!
PRETTY OBSCURE. I'M SURPRISED YOU EVEN KNOW OF IT. IT WASN'T VERY POPULAR.
SO YOU'D PROBABLY REMEMBER ANY OTHER FANS...
I'M LOOKING FOR A COUPLE OF GIRLS WHO MIGHT DRESS UP AS VILLAINS FROM THE SHOW. THE JAWBREAKERS?
KUCHI-SHI FUTAGO. THE MOUTH-DEATH TWINS. YEAH, THERE'S A COUPLE OF LOCAL GIRLS WHO SHOW UP AT ALL THE OTAKU EVENTS IN GOTHAM.
KATSURA, I THINK-- YUKI AND YURI? THEY'RE REALLY CREEPY, THEY STAY IN CHARACTER AND TRY TO ACT ALL INTIMIDATING, PUSHING PEOPLE AROUND. PRETTY ANNOYING. NO ONE LIKES THEM MUCH.
IF YOU SEE THEM, TELL THEM THAT THEY STILL HAVEN'T PICKED UP THE IMPORT NUCLEA BLU-RAYS THEY ORDERED.
art•design•toys•culture
OKAY, KATSURAS, LET'S FIND OUT WHERE YOU PARK YOUR BIKES.
GCPD CRIMINAL DATABASE
LOGIN
username ********
password ********
ACCESS DENIED!
THERE IS NO ACCOUNT ASSOCIATED WITH THIS LOGIN INFO.
PLEASE TRY AGAIN.
WHAT THE--
I'VE USED THAT HACK SINCE I WAS SIXTEEN. WHAT IS GOING ON?

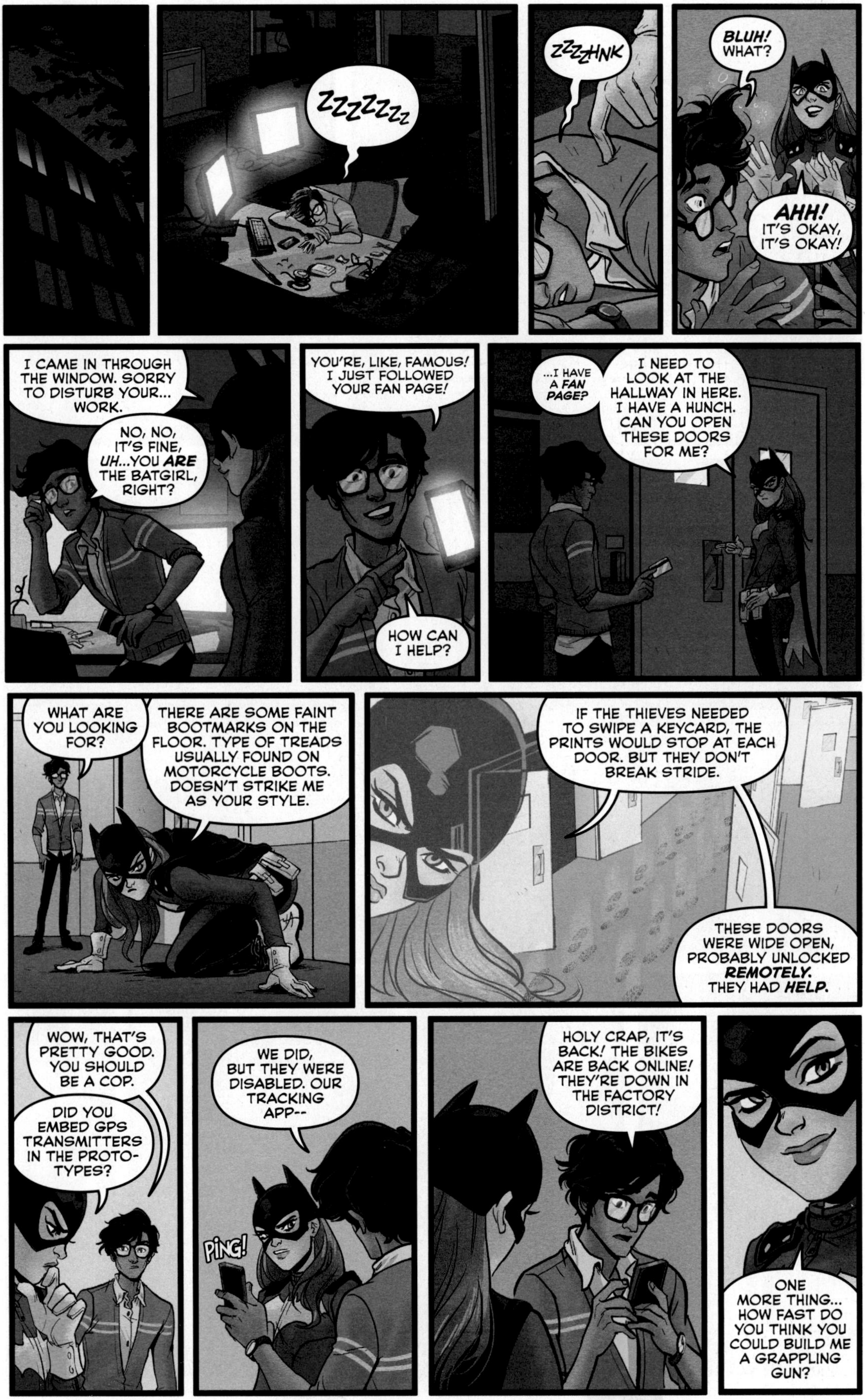

ZZZZZZZz
ZZZZHNK
BLUH! WHAT?
AHH! IT'S OKAY, IT'S OKAY!
I CAME IN THROUGH THE WINDOW. SORRY TO DISTURB YOUR... WORK.
NO, NO, IT'S FINE, UH...YOU ARE THE BATGIRL, RIGHT?
YOU'RE, LIKE, FAMOUS! I JUST FOLLOWED YOUR FAN PAGE!
HOW CAN I HELP?
...I HAVE A FAN PAGE?
I NEED TO LOOK AT THE HALLWAY IN HERE. I HAVE A HUNCH. CAN YOU OPEN THESE DOORS FOR ME?
WHAT ARE YOU LOOKING FOR?
THERE ARE SOME FAINT BOOTMARKS ON THE FLOOR. TYPE OF TREADS USUALLY FOUND ON MOTORCYCLE BOOTS. DOESN'T STRIKE ME AS YOUR STYLE.
IF THE THIEVES NEEDED TO SWIPE A KEYCARD, THE PRINTS WOULD STOP AT EACH DOOR. BUT THEY DON'T BREAK STRIDE.
THESE DOORS WERE WIDE OPEN, PROBABLY UNLOCKED REMOTELY. THEY HAD HELP.
WOW, THAT'S PRETTY GOOD. YOU SHOULD BE A COP.
DID YOU EMBED GPS TRANSMITTERS IN THE PROTO-TYPES?
WE DID, BUT THEY WERE DISABLED. OUR TRACKING APP--
PING!
HOLY CRAP, IT'S BACK! THE BIKES ARE BACK ONLINE! THEY'RE DOWN IN THE FACTORY DISTRICT!
ONE MORE THING... HOW FAST DO YOU THINK YOU COULD BUILD ME A GRAPPLING GUN?

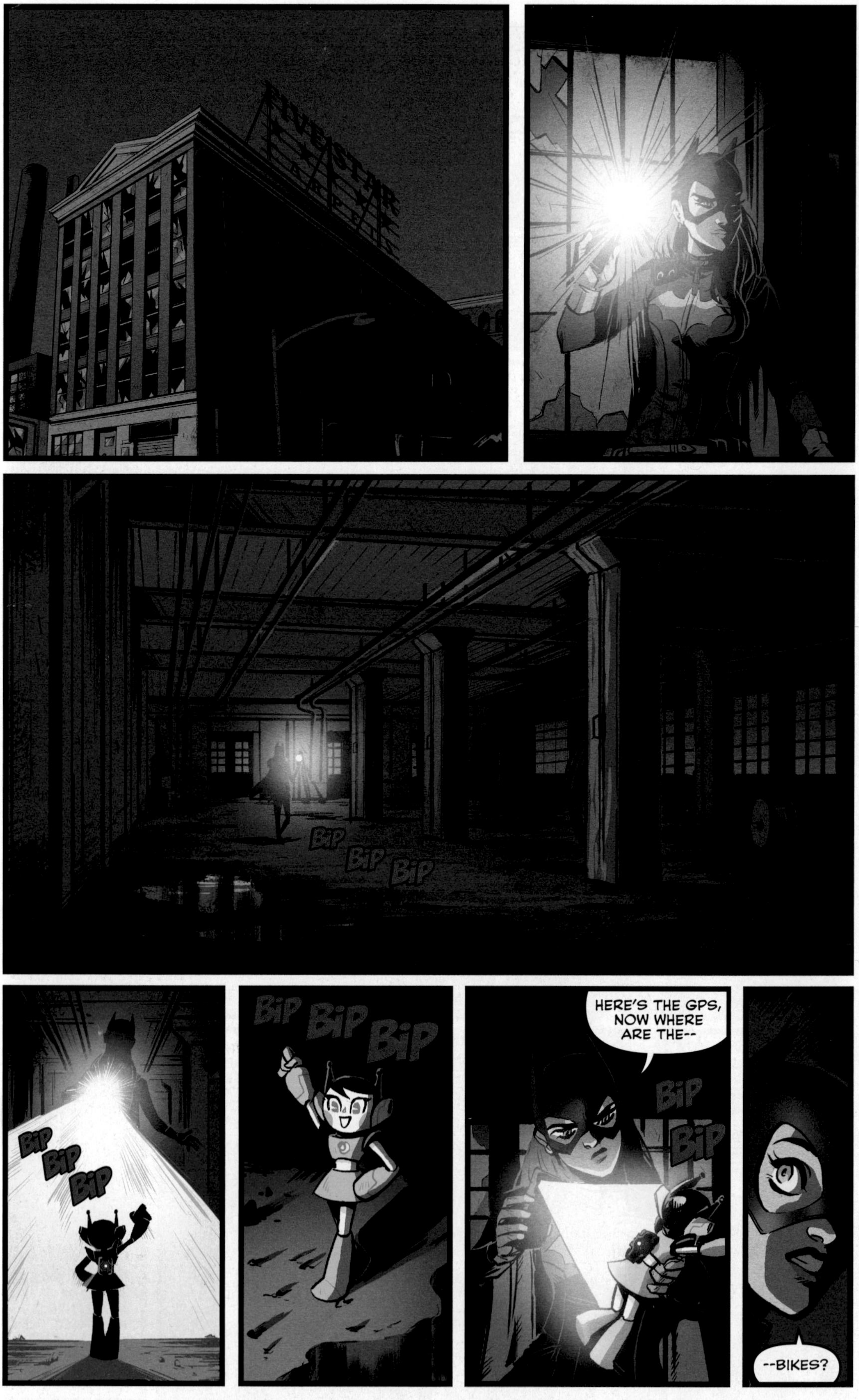
BIP
BIP
BIP
BIP
BIP
BIP
BIP
BIP
BIP
HERE'S THE GPS, NOW WHERE ARE THE--
BIP
BIP
--BIKES?

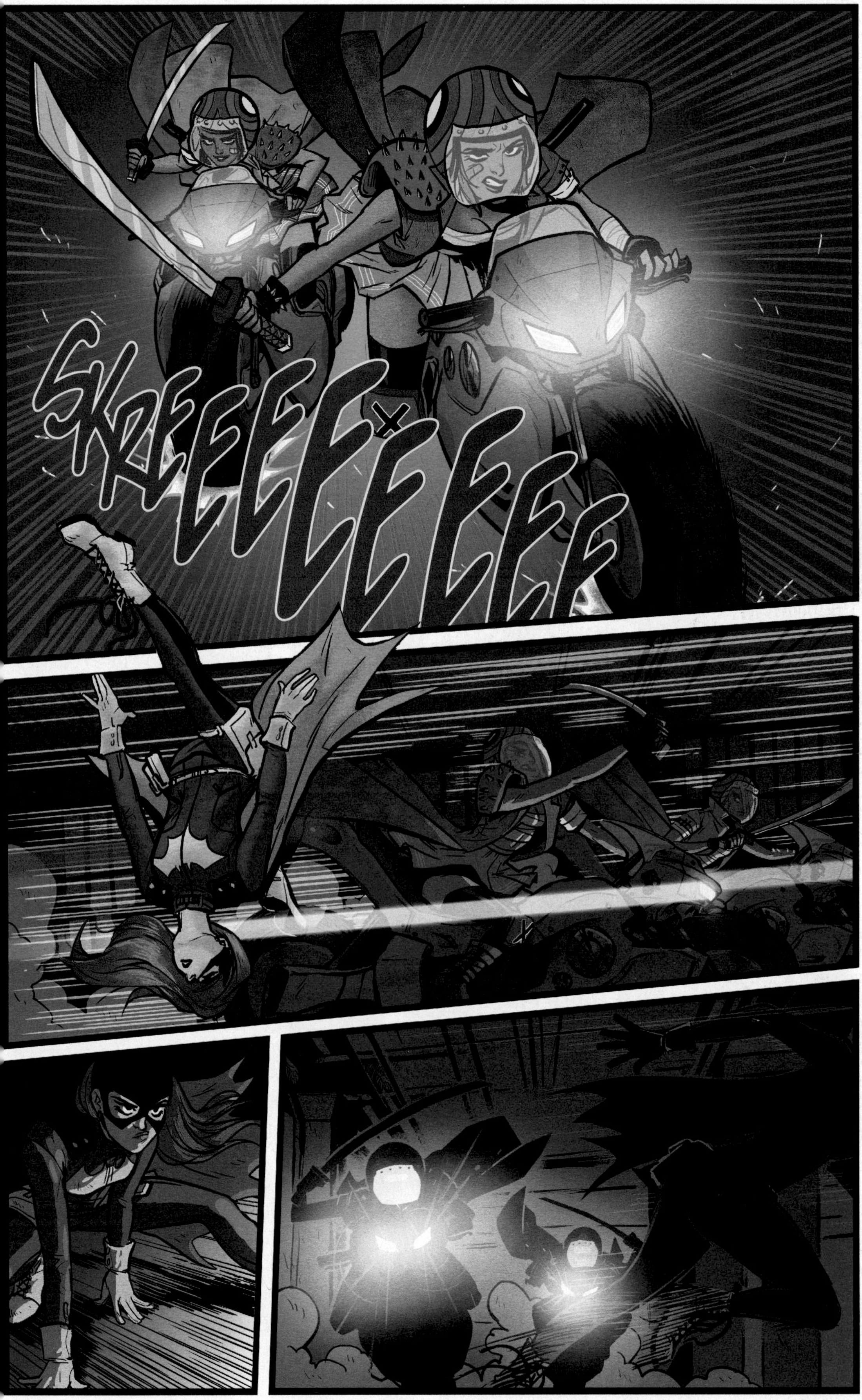
SKREEEEEEEEER

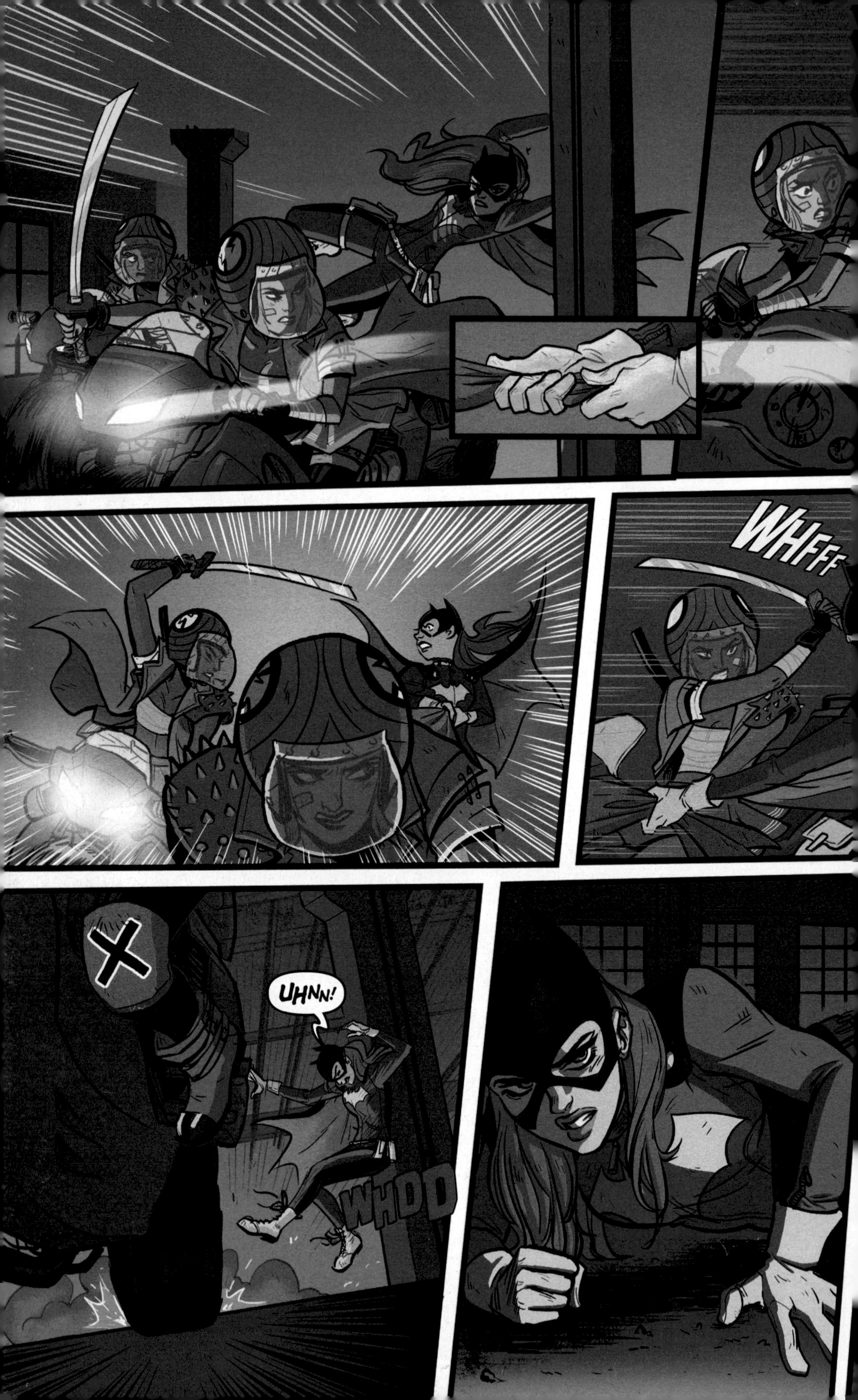
WHFFF
UHNN!
WHOD

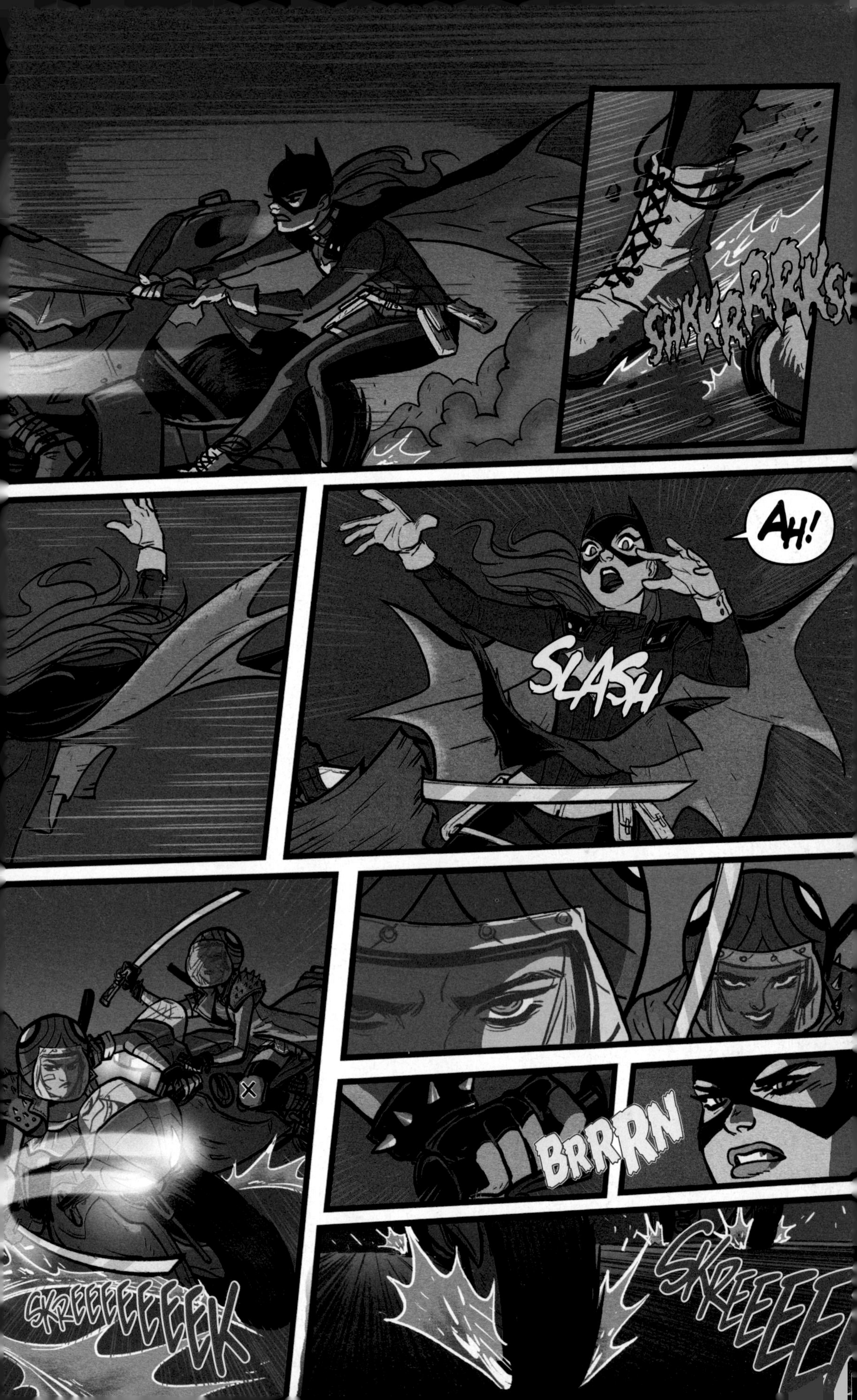
SHKRRRKS
AH!
SLASH
BRRRN
SKREEEEEEEEK
SKREEEEE

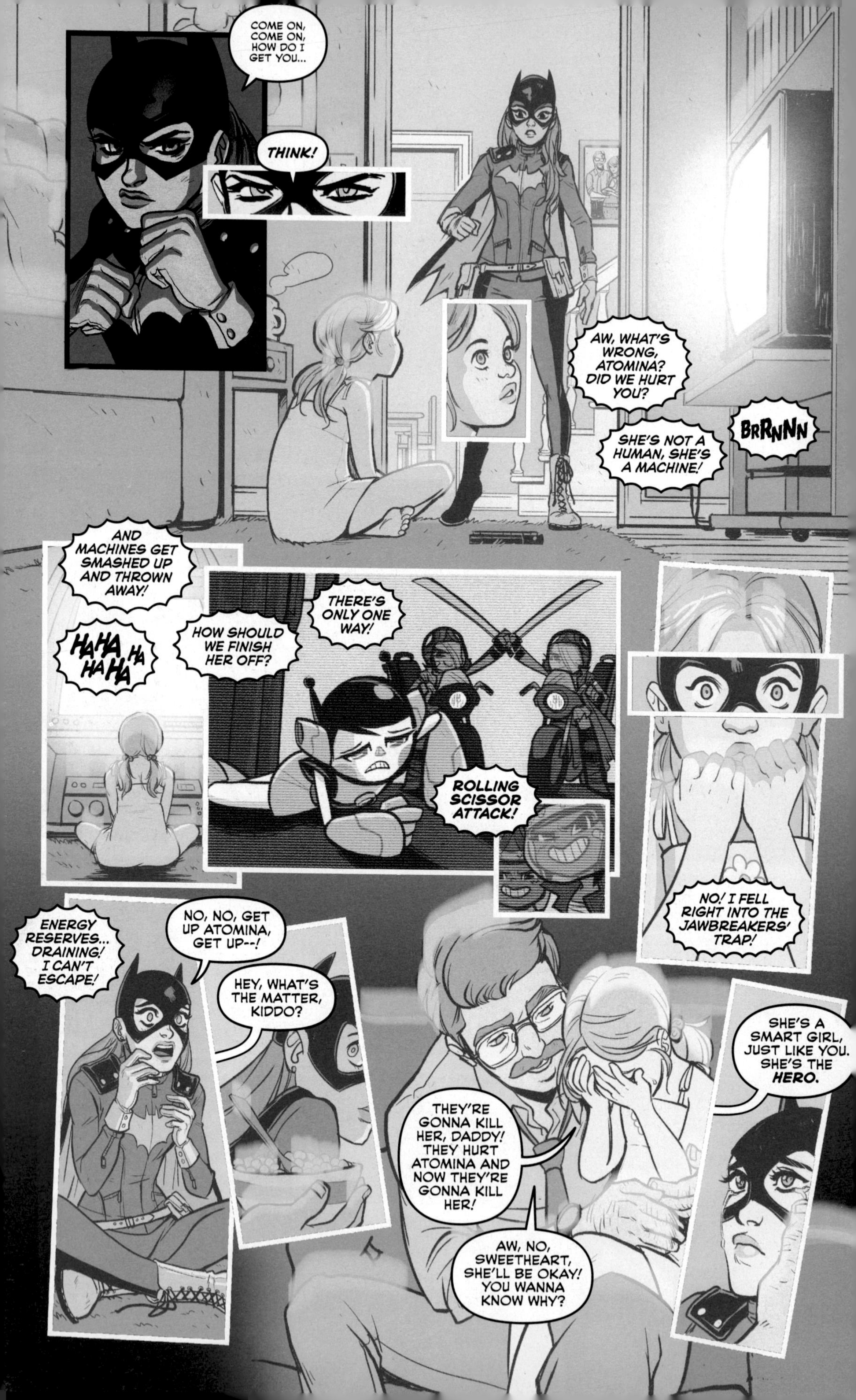

COME ON, COME ON, HOW DO I GET YOU...
THINK!
AW, WHAT'S WRONG, ATOMINA? DID WE HURT YOU?
SHE'S NOT A HUMAN, SHE'S A MACHINE!
BRRNNN
AND MACHINES GET SMASHED UP AND THROWN AWAY!
HAHA HA HAHA
HOW SHOULD WE FINISH HER OFF?
THERE'S ONLY ONE WAY!
ROLLING SCISSOR ATTACK!
NO! I FELL RIGHT INTO THE JAWBREAKERS' TRAP!
ENERGY RESERVES... DRAINING! I CAN'T ESCAPE!
NO, NO, GET UP ATOMINA, GET UP--!
HEY, WHAT'S THE MATTER, KIDDO?
THEY'RE GONNA KILL HER, DADDY! THEY HURT ATOMINA AND NOW THEY'RE GONNA KILL HER!
AW, NO, SWEETHEART, SHE'LL BE OKAY! YOU WANNA KNOW WHY?
SHE'S A SMART GIRL, JUST LIKE YOU. SHE'S THE HERO.

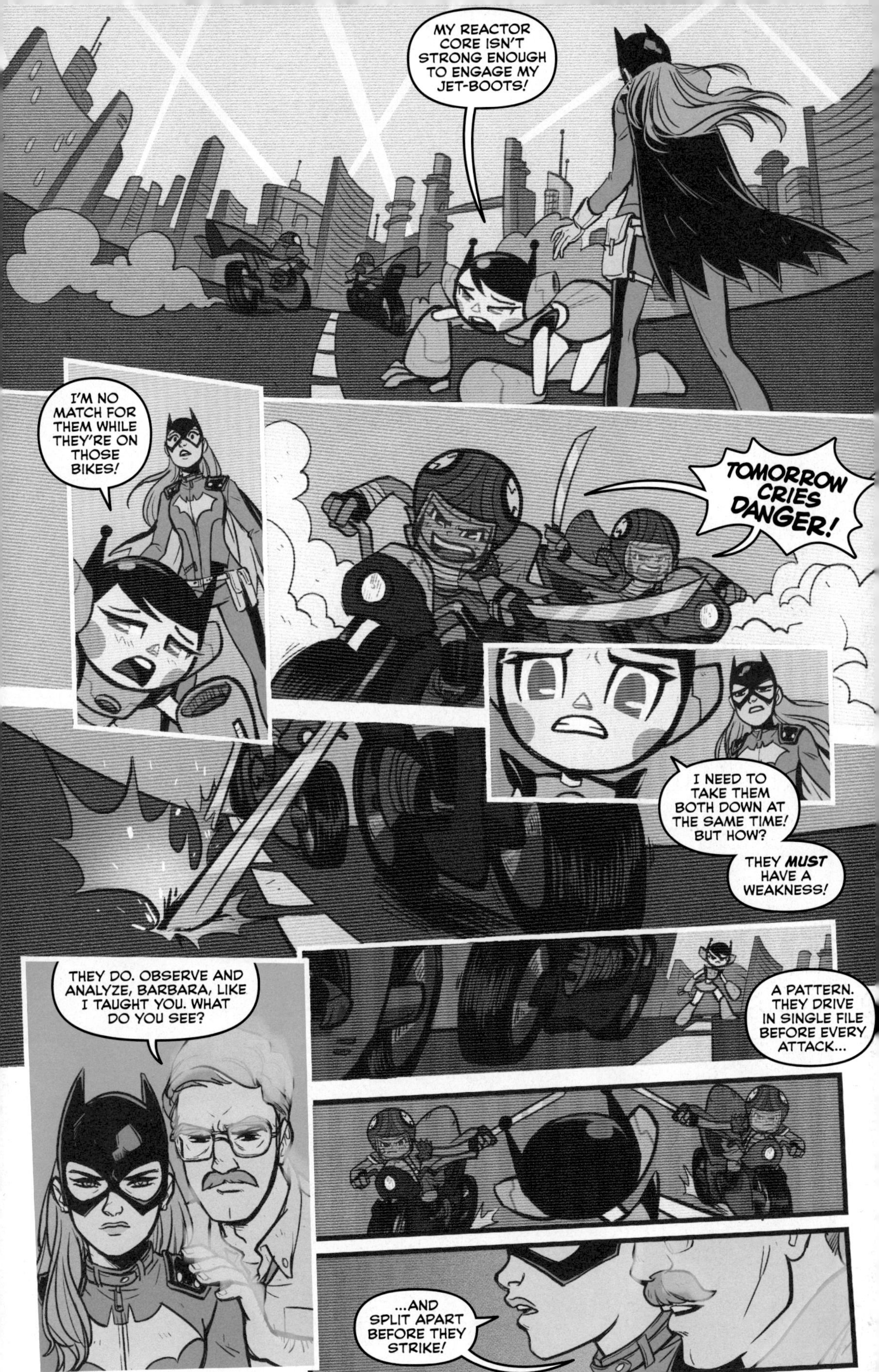
MY REACTOR CORE ISN'T STRONG ENOUGH TO ENGAGE MY JET-BOOTS!
I'M NO MATCH FOR THEM WHILE THEY'RE ON THOSE BIKES!
TOMORROW CRIES DANGER!
I NEED TO TAKE THEM BOTH DOWN AT THE SAME TIME! BUT HOW?
THEY MUST HAVE A WEAKNESS!
THEY DO. OBSERVE AND ANALYZE, BARBARA, LIKE I TAUGHT YOU. WHAT DO YOU SEE?
A PATTERN. THEY DRIVE IN SINGLE FILE BEFORE EVERY ATTACK...
...AND SPLIT APART BEFORE THEY STRIKE!

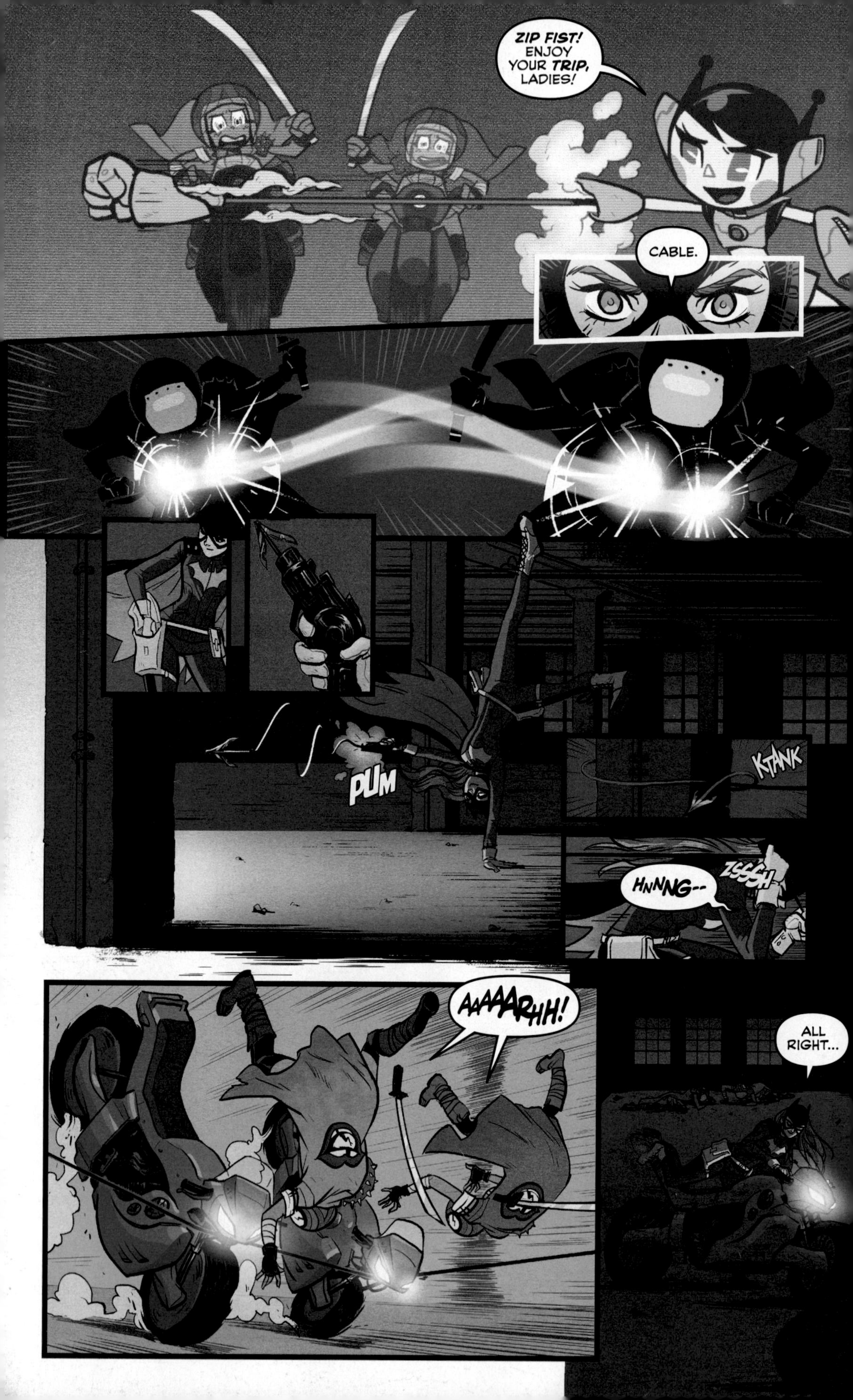
ZIP FIST! ENJOY YOUR TRIP, LADIES!
CABLE.
PUM
KTANK
HNNNG--
ZSSSH
AAAAARHH!
ALL RIGHT...

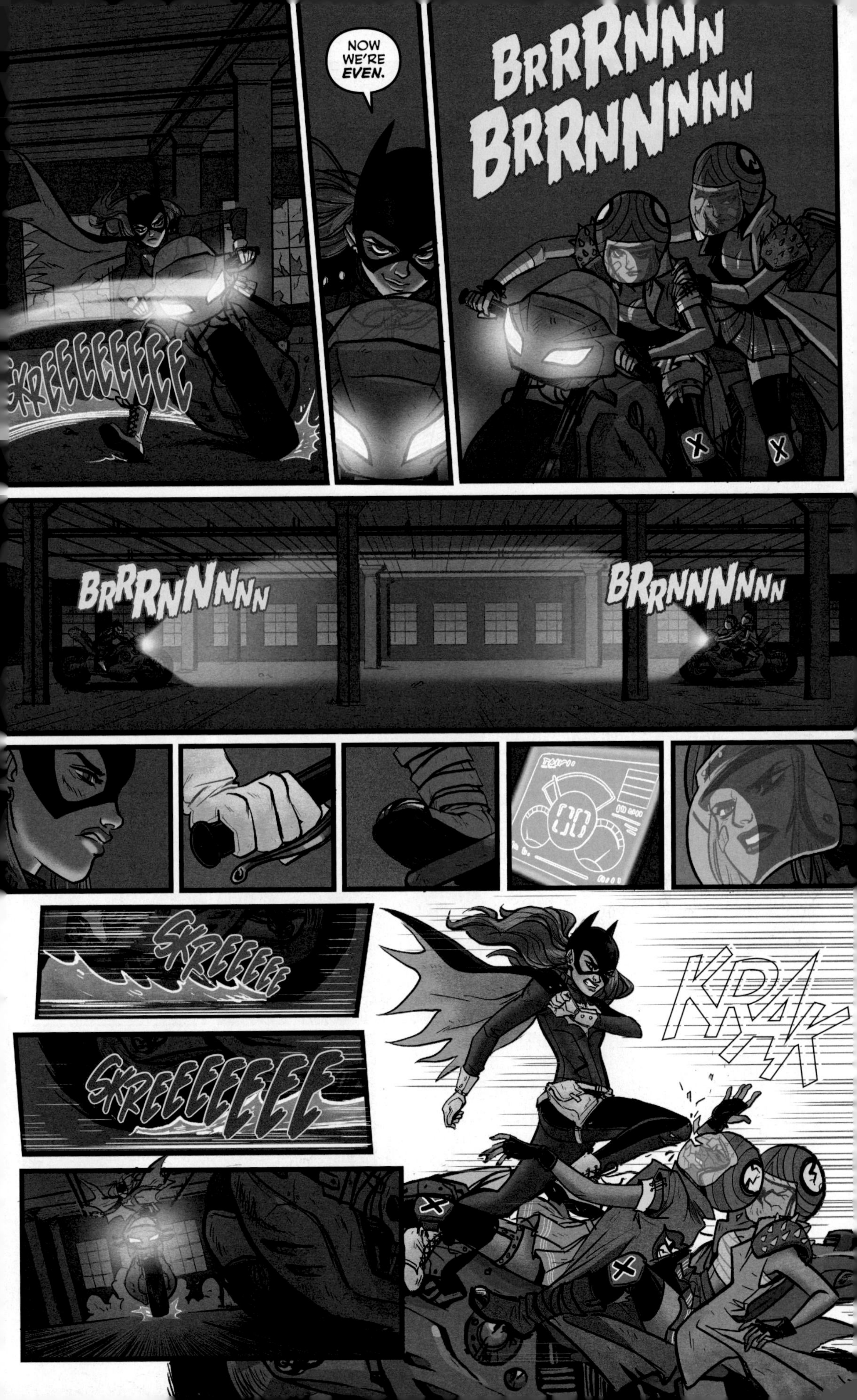
SKREEEEEEEEE
NOW WE'RE EVEN.
BRRRNNNN BRRNNNNNN
BRRRNNNNN
BRRNNNNNN
SKREEEEEE
SKREEEEEEEE
KDAKK

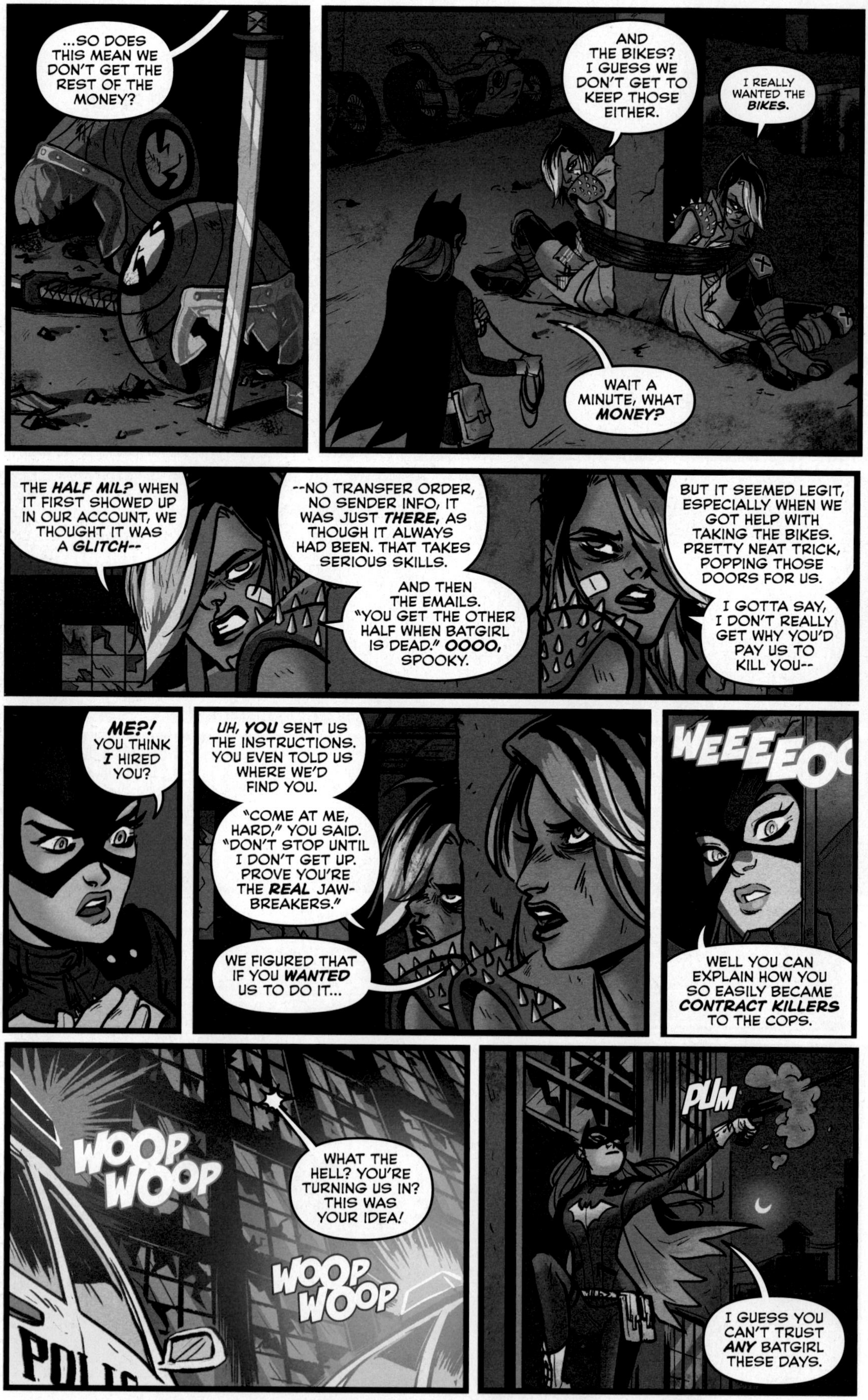

...SO DOES THIS MEAN WE DON'T GET THE REST OF THE MONEY?
AND THE BIKES? I GUESS WE DON'T GET TO KEEP THOSE EITHER.
I REALLY WANTED THE BIKES.
WAIT A MINUTE, WHAT MONEY?
THE HALF MIL? WHEN IT FIRST SHOWED UP IN OUR ACCOUNT, WE THOUGHT IT WAS A GLITCH--
--NO TRANSFER ORDER, NO SENDER INFO, IT WAS JUST THERE, AS THOUGH IT ALWAYS HAD BEEN. THAT TAKES SERIOUS SKILLS.
AND THEN THE EMAILS. "YOU GET THE OTHER HALF WHEN BATGIRL IS DEAD." OOOO, SPOOKY.
BUT IT SEEMED LEGIT, ESPECIALLY WHEN WE GOT HELP WITH TAKING THE BIKES. PRETTY NEAT TRICK, POPPING THOSE DOORS FOR US.
I GOTTA SAY, I DON'T REALLY GET WHY YOU'D PAY US TO KILL YOU--
ME?! YOU THINK I HIRED YOU?
UH, YOU SENT US THE INSTRUCTIONS. YOU EVEN TOLD US WHERE WE'D FIND YOU.
"COME AT ME, HARD," YOU SAID. "DON'T STOP UNTIL I DON'T GET UP. PROVE YOU'RE THE REAL JAW-BREAKERS."
WE FIGURED THAT IF YOU WANTED US TO DO IT...
WEEEEOO
WELL YOU CAN EXPLAIN HOW YOU SO EASILY BECAME CONTRACT KILLERS TO THE COPS.
WOOP WOOP
WHAT THE HELL? YOU'RE TURNING US IN? THIS WAS YOUR IDEA!
WOOP WOOP
POLIC
PUM
I GUESS YOU CAN'T TRUST ANY BATGIRL THESE DAYS.

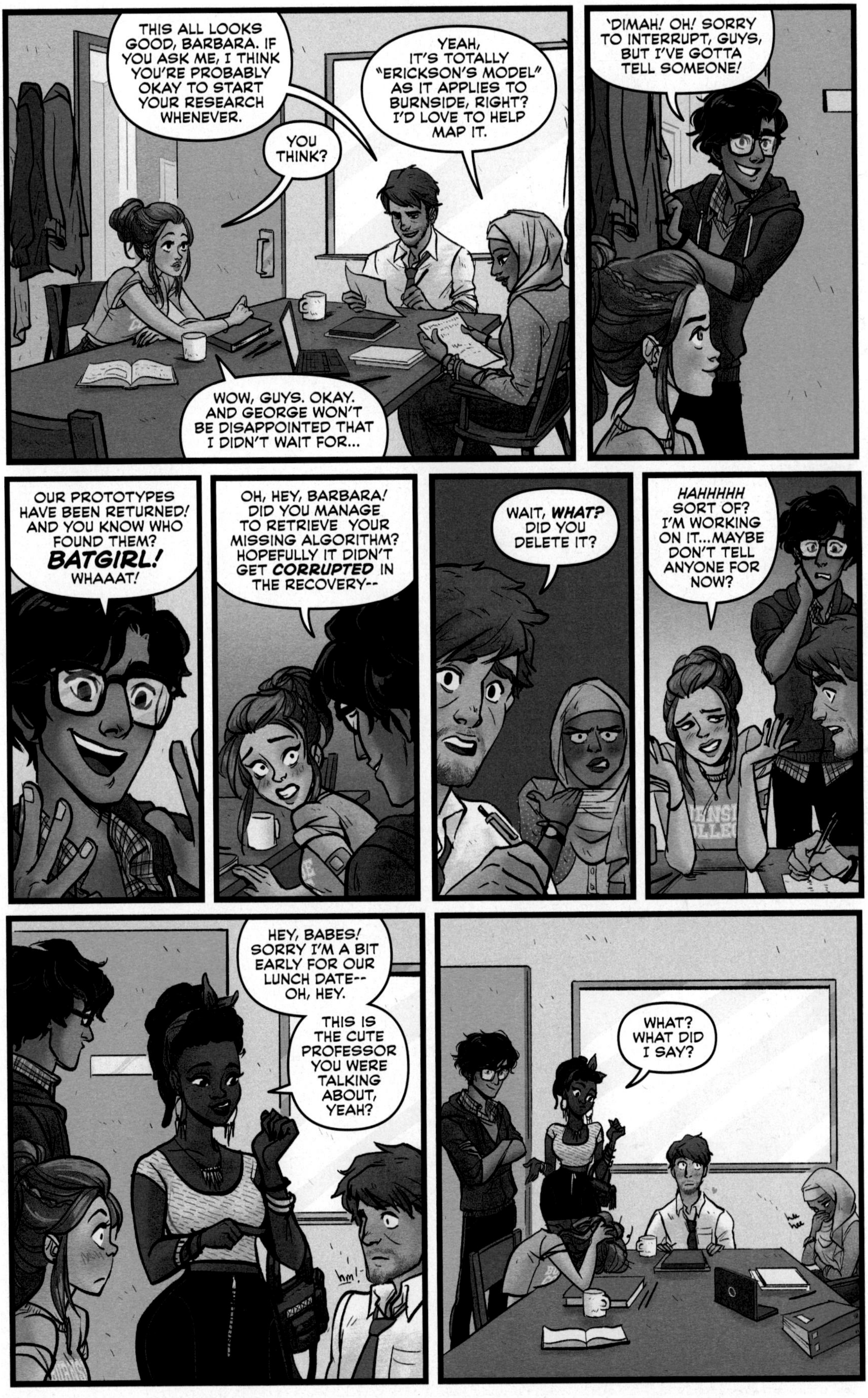
THIS ALL LOOKS GOOD, BARBARA. IF YOU ASK ME, I THINK YOU'RE PROBABLY OKAY TO START YOUR RESEARCH WHENEVER.
YOU THINK?
YEAH, IT'S TOTALLY "ERICKSON'S MODEL" AS IT APPLIES TO BURNSIDE, RIGHT? I'D LOVE TO HELP MAP IT.
WOW, GUYS. OKAY. AND GEORGE WON'T BE DISAPPOINTED THAT I DIDN'T WAIT FOR...
'DIMAH! OH! SORRY TO INTERRUPT, GUYS, BUT I'VE GOTTA TELL SOMEONE!
OUR PROTOTYPES HAVE BEEN RETURNED! AND YOU KNOW WHO FOUND THEM? **BATGIRL!** WHAAAT!
OH, HEY, BARBARA! DID YOU MANAGE TO RETRIEVE YOUR MISSING ALGORITHM? HOPEFULLY IT DIDN'T GET ***CORRUPTED*** IN THE RECOVERY--
WAIT, ***WHAT?*** DID YOU DELETE IT?
HAHHHHH SORT OF? I'M WORKING ON IT...MAYBE DON'T TELL ANYONE FOR NOW?
HEY, BABES! SORRY I'M A BIT EARLY FOR OUR LUNCH DATE-- OH, HEY.
THIS IS THE CUTE PROFESSOR YOU WERE TALKING ABOUT, YEAH?
hm!
WHAT? WHAT DID I SAY?

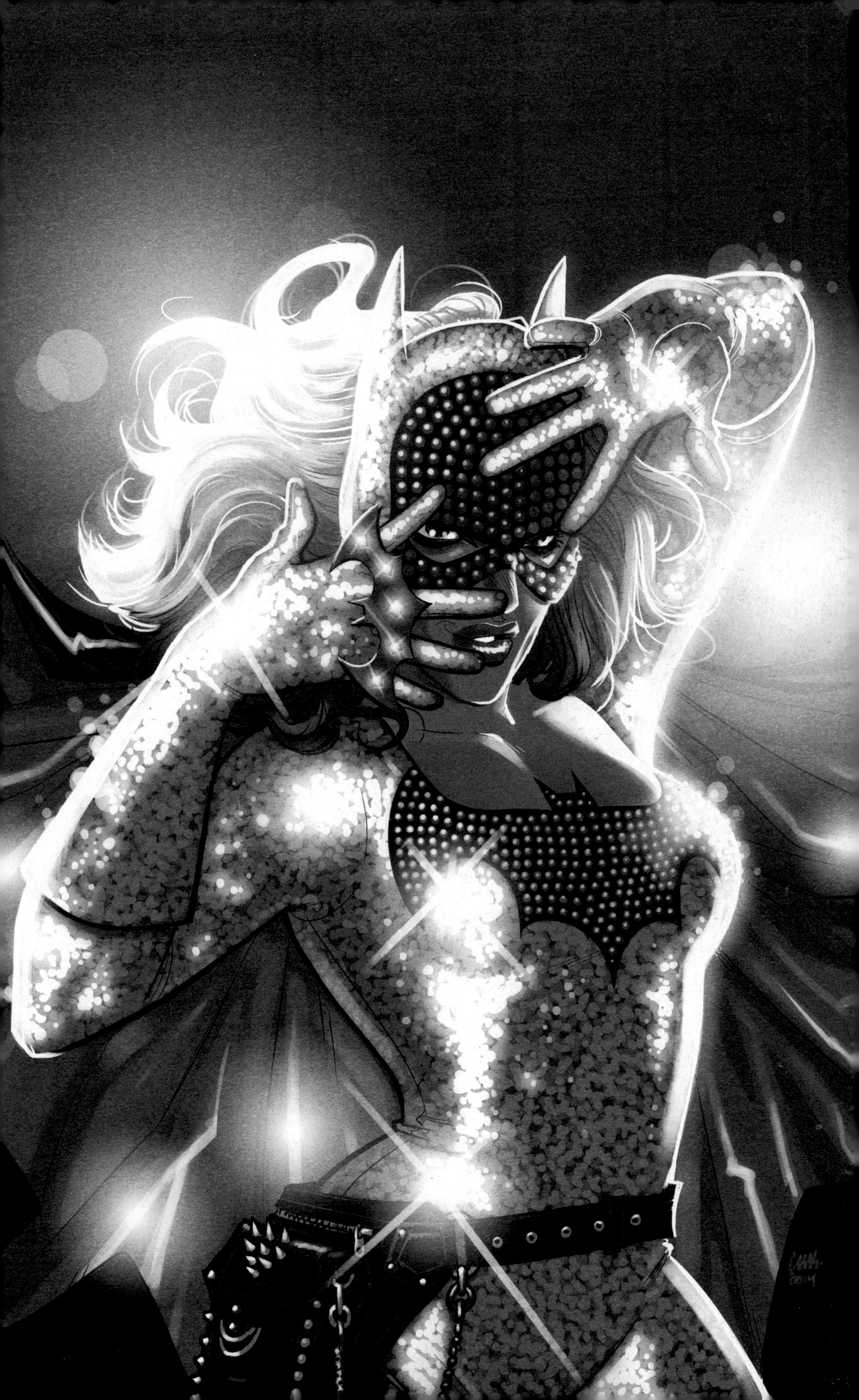

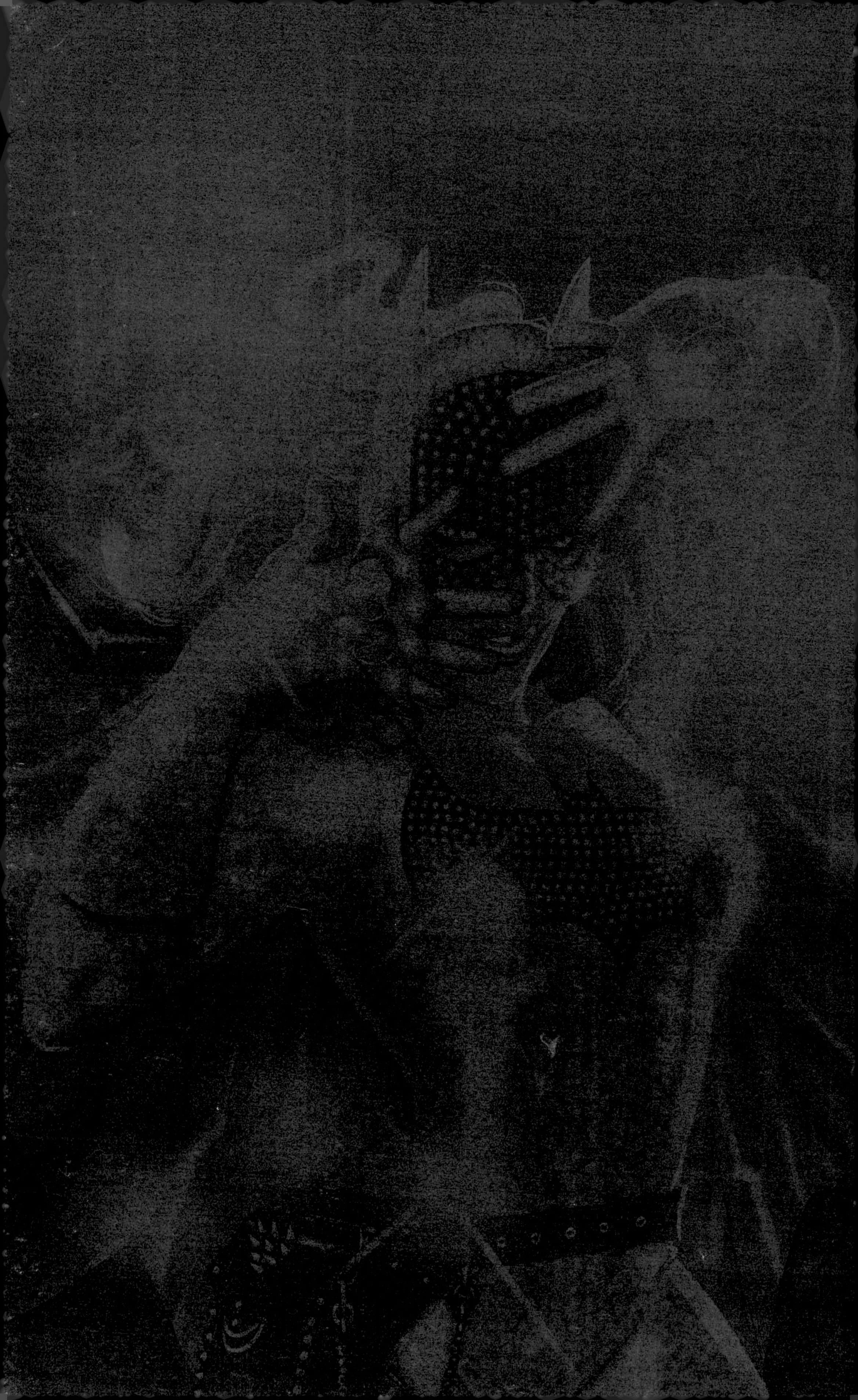

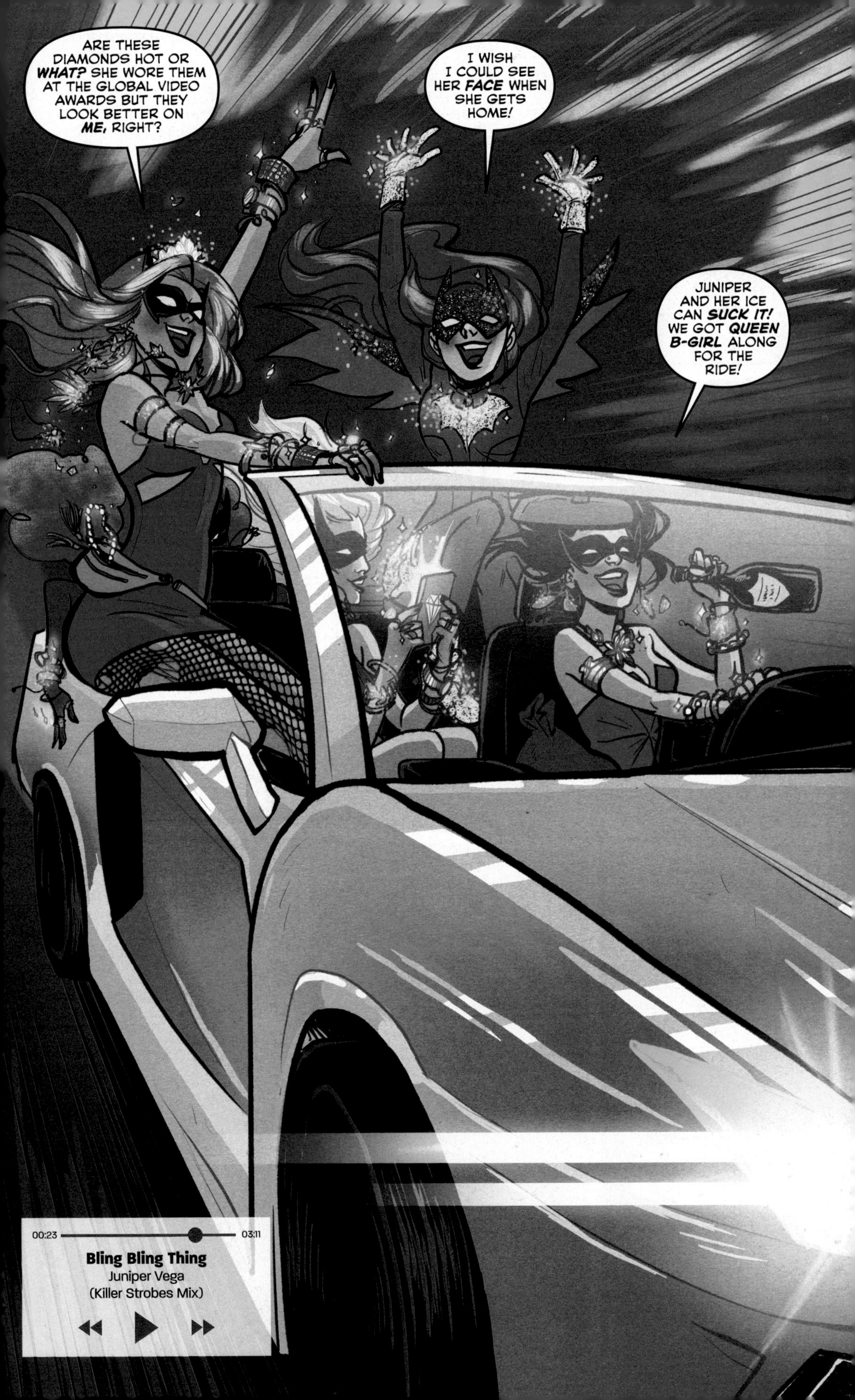
ARE THESE DIAMONDS HOT OR WHAT? SHE WORE THEM AT THE GLOBAL VIDEO AWARDS BUT THEY LOOK BETTER ON ME, RIGHT?
I WISH I COULD SEE HER FACE WHEN SHE GETS HOME!
JUNIPER AND HER ICE CAN SUCK IT! WE GOT QUEEN B-GIRL ALONG FOR THE RIDE!
00:23
03:11
Bling Bling Thing
Juniper Vega
(Killer Strobes Mix)

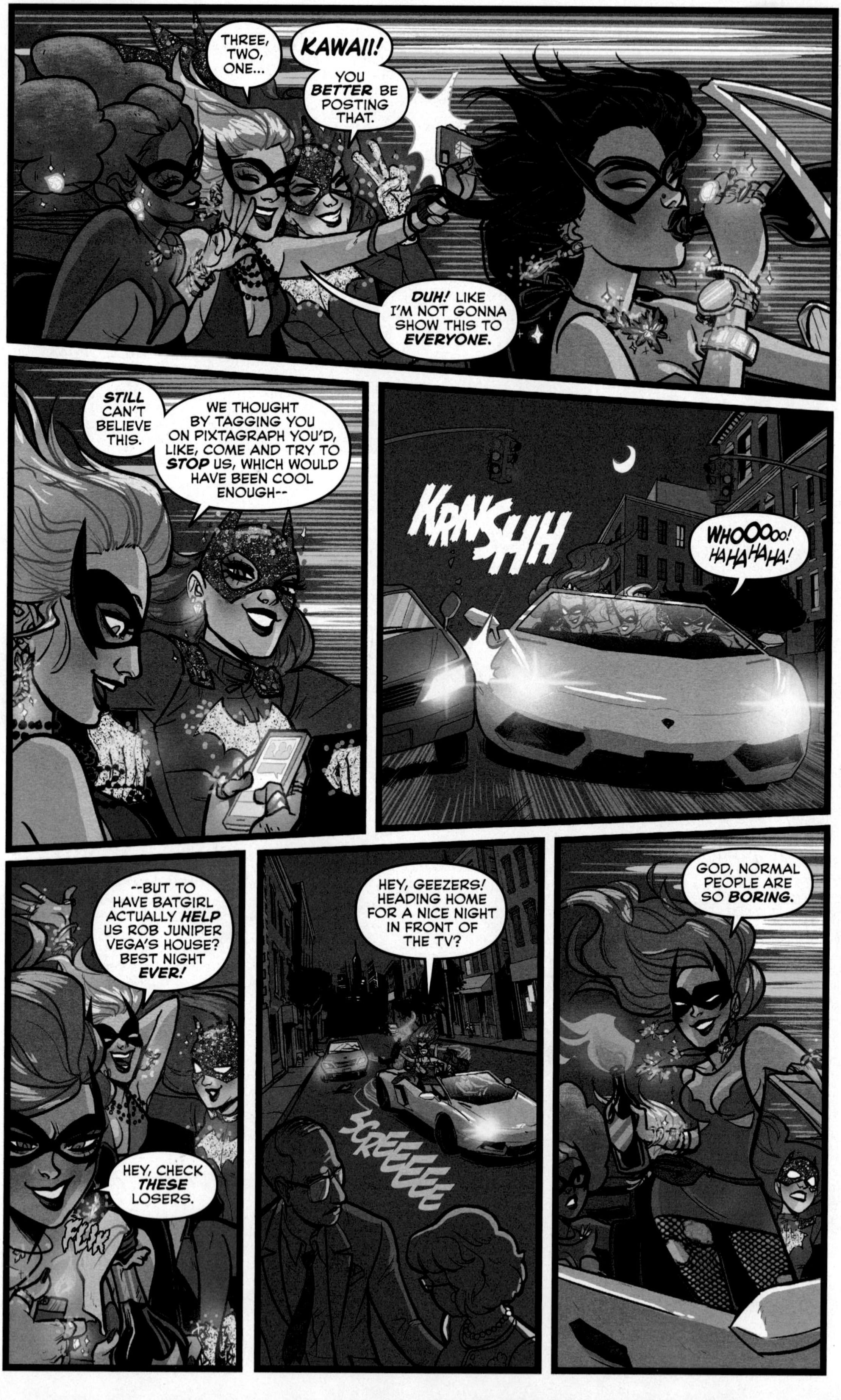
THREE, TWO, ONE...
KAWAII!
YOU BETTER BE POSTING THAT.
DUH! LIKE I'M NOT GONNA SHOW THIS TO EVERYONE.
STILL CAN'T BELIEVE THIS.
WE THOUGHT BY TAGGING YOU ON PIXTAGRAPH YOU'D, LIKE, COME AND TRY TO STOP US, WHICH WOULD HAVE BEEN COOL ENOUGH--
KRNSHH
WHOOOoo! HAHAHAHA!
--BUT TO HAVE BATGIRL ACTUALLY HELP US ROB JUNIPER VEGA'S HOUSE? BEST NIGHT EVER!
HEY, CHECK THESE LOSERS.
FLIK
HEY, GEEZERS! HEADING HOME FOR A NICE NIGHT IN FRONT OF THE TV?
SCREEEEEE
GOD, NORMAL PEOPLE ARE SO BORING.

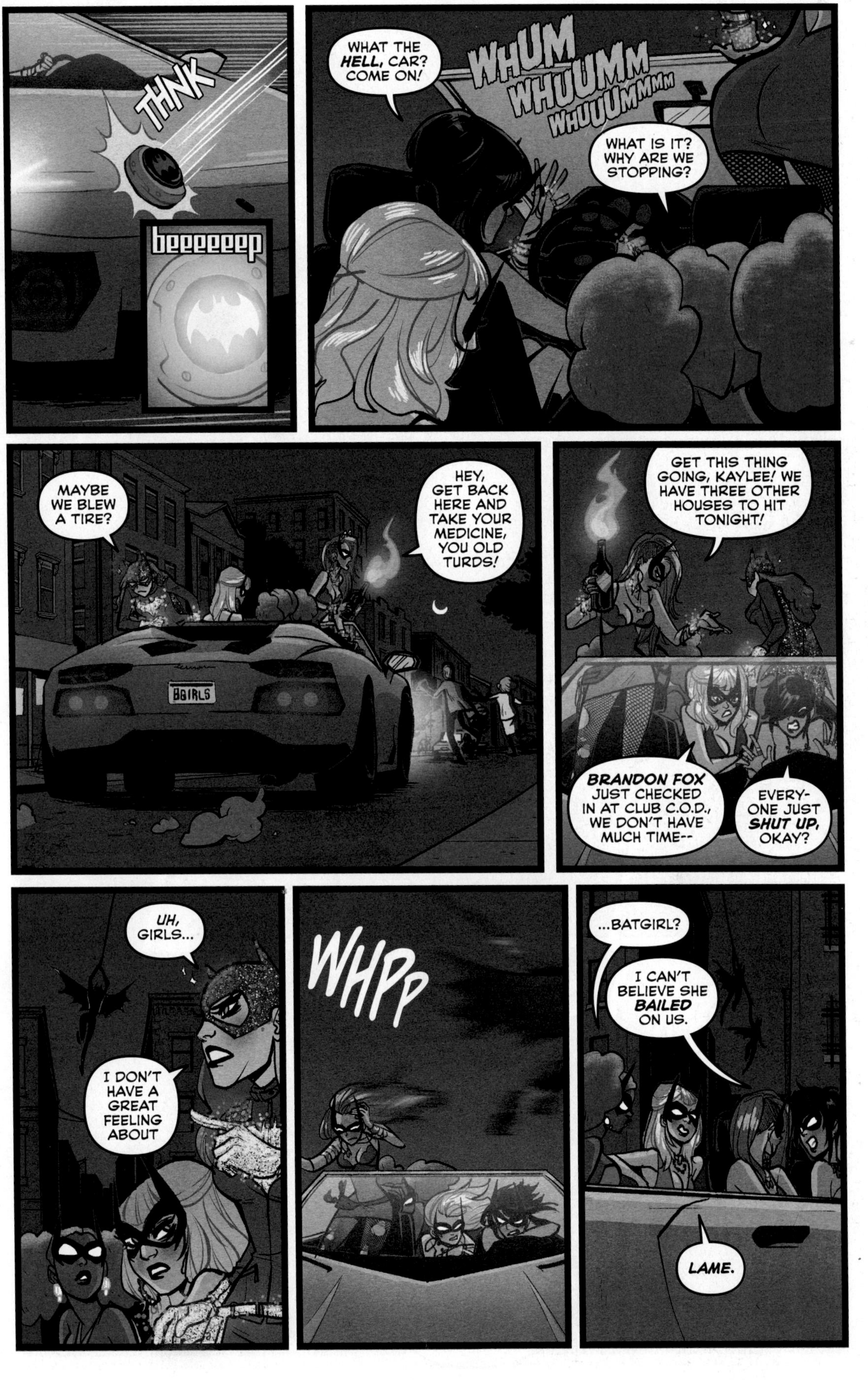
THNK
beeeeeep
WHAT THE HELL, CAR? COME ON!
WHUM WHUUMM WHUUUMMMM
WHAT IS IT? WHY ARE WE STOPPING?
MAYBE WE BLEW A TIRE?
HEY, GET BACK HERE AND TAKE YOUR MEDICINE, YOU OLD TURDS!
BGIRLS
GET THIS THING GOING, KAYLEE! WE HAVE THREE OTHER HOUSES TO HIT TONIGHT!
BRANDON FOX JUST CHECKED IN AT CLUB C.O.D., WE DON'T HAVE MUCH TIME--
EVERY-ONE JUST SHUT UP, OKAY?
UH, GIRLS...
I DON'T HAVE A GREAT FEELING ABOUT
WHPP
...BATGIRL?
I CAN'T BELIEVE SHE BAILED ON US.
LAME.

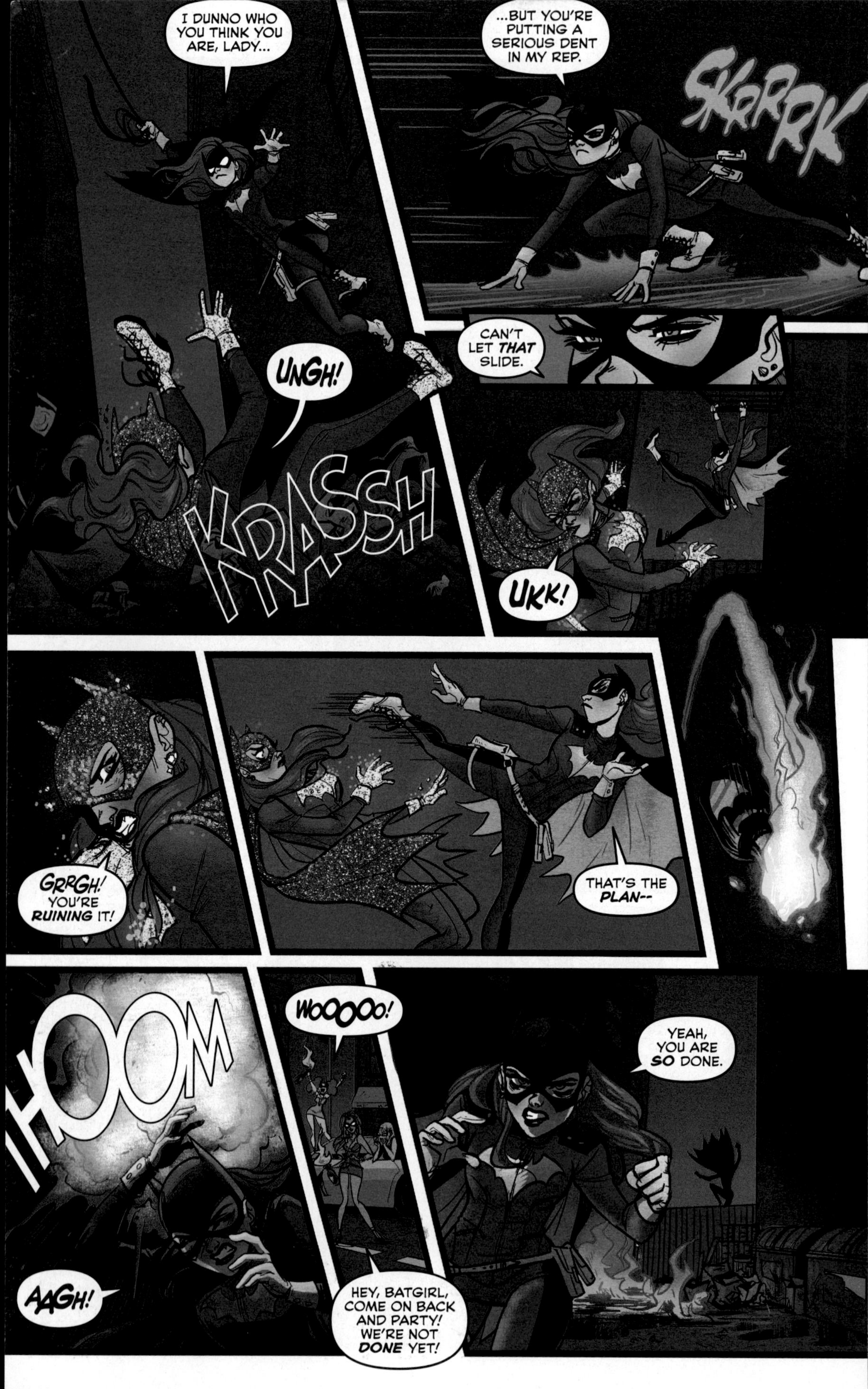

I DUNNO WHO YOU THINK YOU ARE, LADY...
...BUT YOU'RE PUTTING A SERIOUS DENT IN MY REP.
SKRRRK
UNGH!
KRASSH
CAN'T LET THAT SLIDE.
UKK!
GRRGH! YOU'RE RUINING IT!
THAT'S THE PLAN--
WHOOM
AAGH!
WOOOOO!
HEY, BATGIRL, COME ON BACK AND PARTY! WE'RE NOT DONE YET!
YEAH, YOU ARE SO DONE.

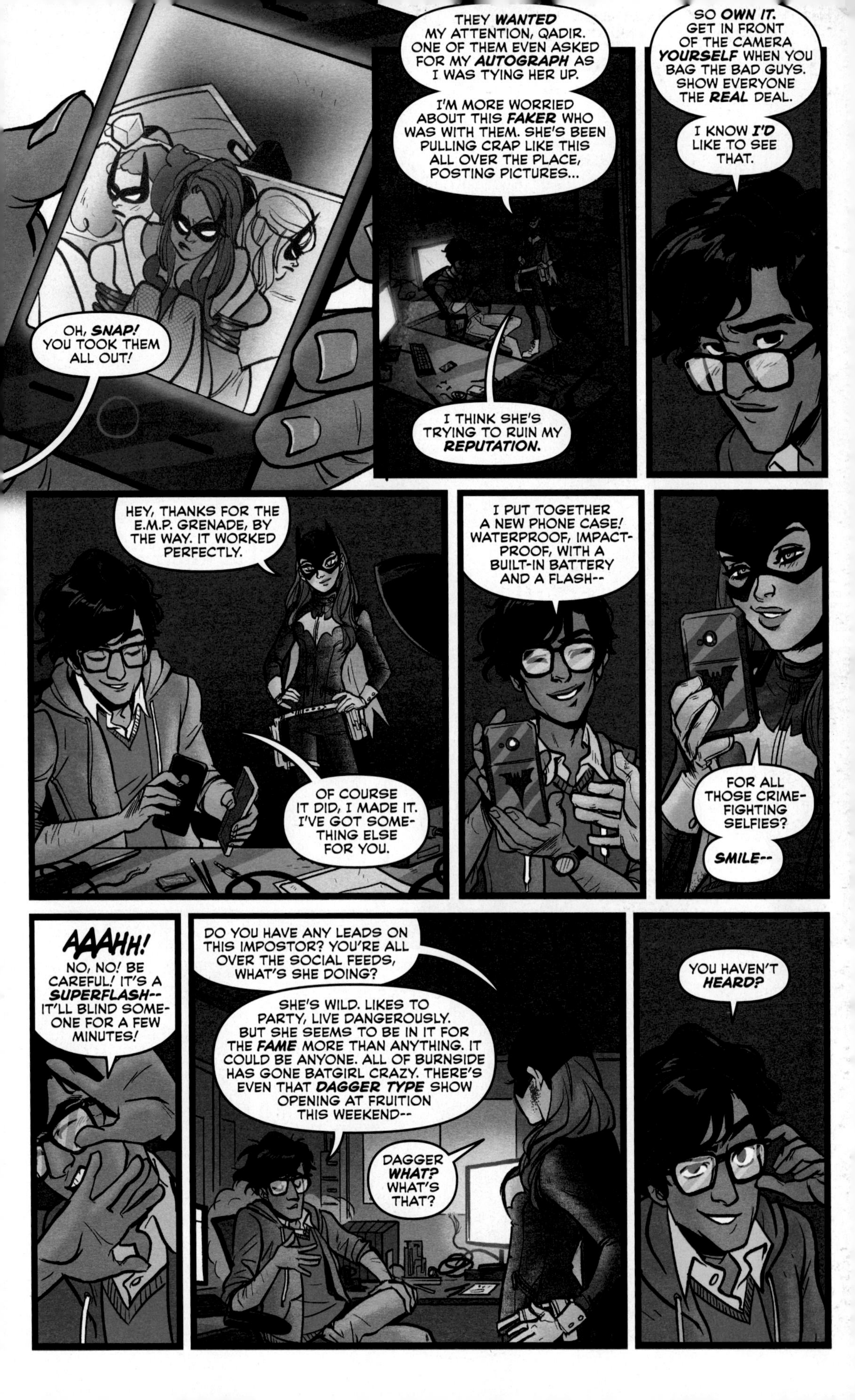
OH, SNAP! YOU TOOK THEM ALL OUT!
THEY WANTED MY ATTENTION, QADIR. ONE OF THEM EVEN ASKED FOR MY AUTOGRAPH AS I WAS TYING HER UP.
I'M MORE WORRIED ABOUT THIS FAKER WHO WAS WITH THEM. SHE'S BEEN PULLING CRAP LIKE THIS ALL OVER THE PLACE, POSTING PICTURES...
I THINK SHE'S TRYING TO RUIN MY REPUTATION.
SO OWN IT. GET IN FRONT OF THE CAMERA YOURSELF WHEN YOU BAG THE BAD GUYS. SHOW EVERYONE THE REAL DEAL.
I KNOW I'D LIKE TO SEE THAT.
HEY, THANKS FOR THE E.M.P. GRENADE, BY THE WAY. IT WORKED PERFECTLY.
OF COURSE IT DID, I MADE IT. I'VE GOT SOMETHING ELSE FOR YOU.
I PUT TOGETHER A NEW PHONE CASE! WATERPROOF, IMPACT-PROOF, WITH A BUILT-IN BATTERY AND A FLASH--
FOR ALL THOSE CRIME-FIGHTING SELFIES?
SMILE--
AAAHH!
NO, NO! BE CAREFUL! IT'S A SUPERFLASH-- IT'LL BLIND SOMEONE FOR A FEW MINUTES!
DO YOU HAVE ANY LEADS ON THIS IMPOSTOR? YOU'RE ALL OVER THE SOCIAL FEEDS, WHAT'S SHE DOING?
SHE'S WILD. LIKES TO PARTY, LIVE DANGEROUSLY. BUT SHE SEEMS TO BE IN IT FOR THE FAME MORE THAN ANYTHING. IT COULD BE ANYONE. ALL OF BURNSIDE HAS GONE BATGIRL CRAZY. THERE'S EVEN THAT DAGGER TYPE SHOW OPENING AT FRUITION THIS WEEKEND--
DAGGER WHAT? WHAT'S THAT?
YOU HAVEN'T HEARD?

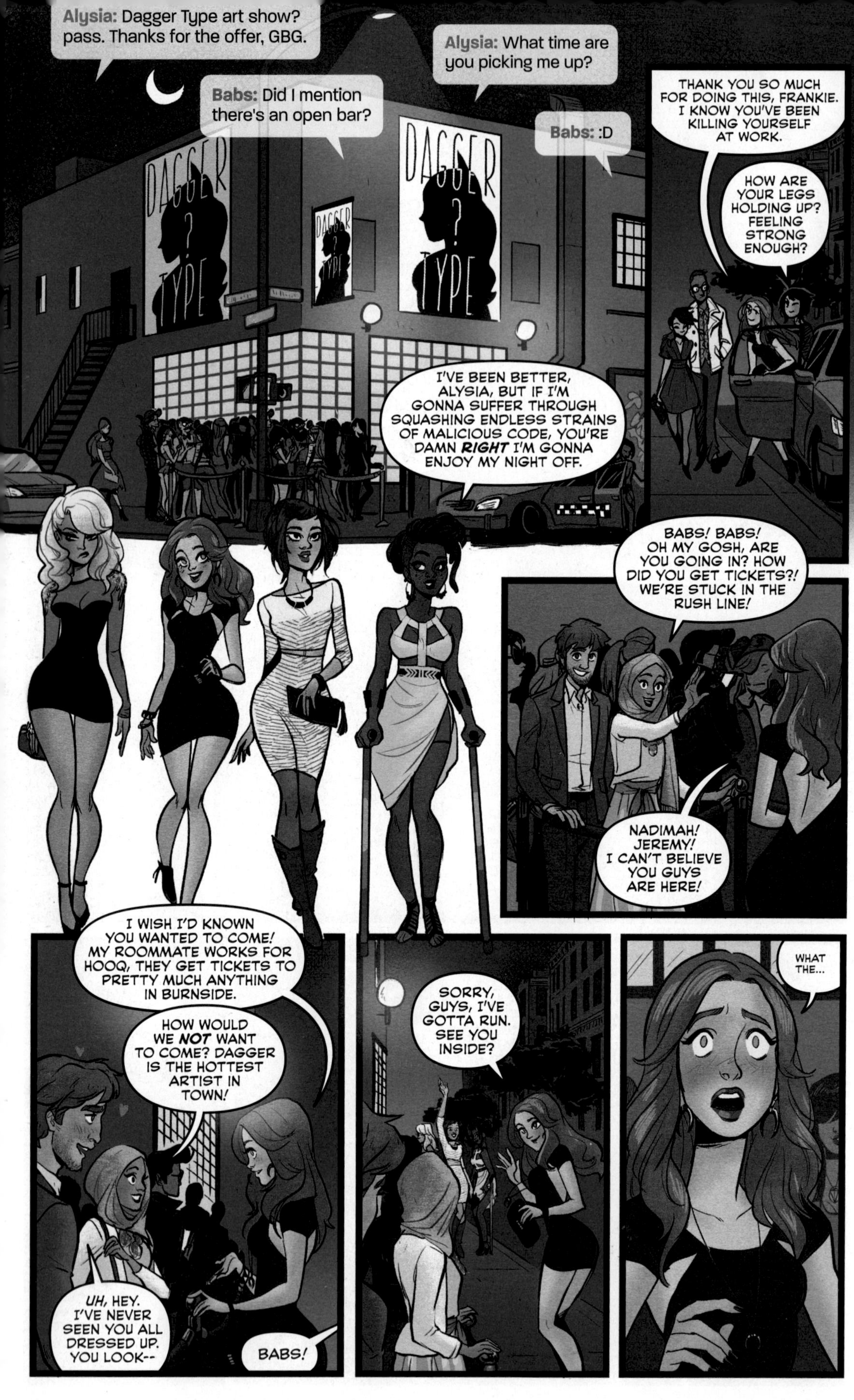

Alysia: Dagger Type art show? pass. Thanks for the offer, GBG.
Babs: Did I mention there's an open bar?
Alysia: What time are you picking me up?
Babs: :D
DAGGER ? TYPE
THANK YOU SO MUCH FOR DOING THIS, FRANKIE. I KNOW YOU'VE BEEN KILLING YOURSELF AT WORK.
HOW ARE YOUR LEGS HOLDING UP? FEELING STRONG ENOUGH?
I'VE BEEN BETTER, ALYSIA, BUT IF I'M GONNA SUFFER THROUGH SQUASHING ENDLESS STRAINS OF MALICIOUS CODE, YOU'RE DAMN ***RIGHT*** I'M GONNA ENJOY MY NIGHT OFF.
BABS! BABS! OH MY GOSH, ARE YOU GOING IN? HOW DID YOU GET TICKETS?! WE'RE STUCK IN THE RUSH LINE!
NADIMAH! JEREMY! I CAN'T BELIEVE YOU GUYS ARE HERE!
I WISH I'D KNOWN YOU WANTED TO COME! MY ROOMMATE WORKS FOR HOOQ, THEY GET TICKETS TO PRETTY MUCH ANYTHING IN BURNSIDE.
HOW WOULD WE ***NOT*** WANT TO COME? DAGGER IS THE HOTTEST ARTIST IN TOWN!
UH, HEY. I'VE NEVER SEEN YOU ALL DRESSED UP. YOU LOOK--
BABS!
SORRY, GUYS, I'VE GOTTA RUN. SEE YOU INSIDE?
WHAT THE...

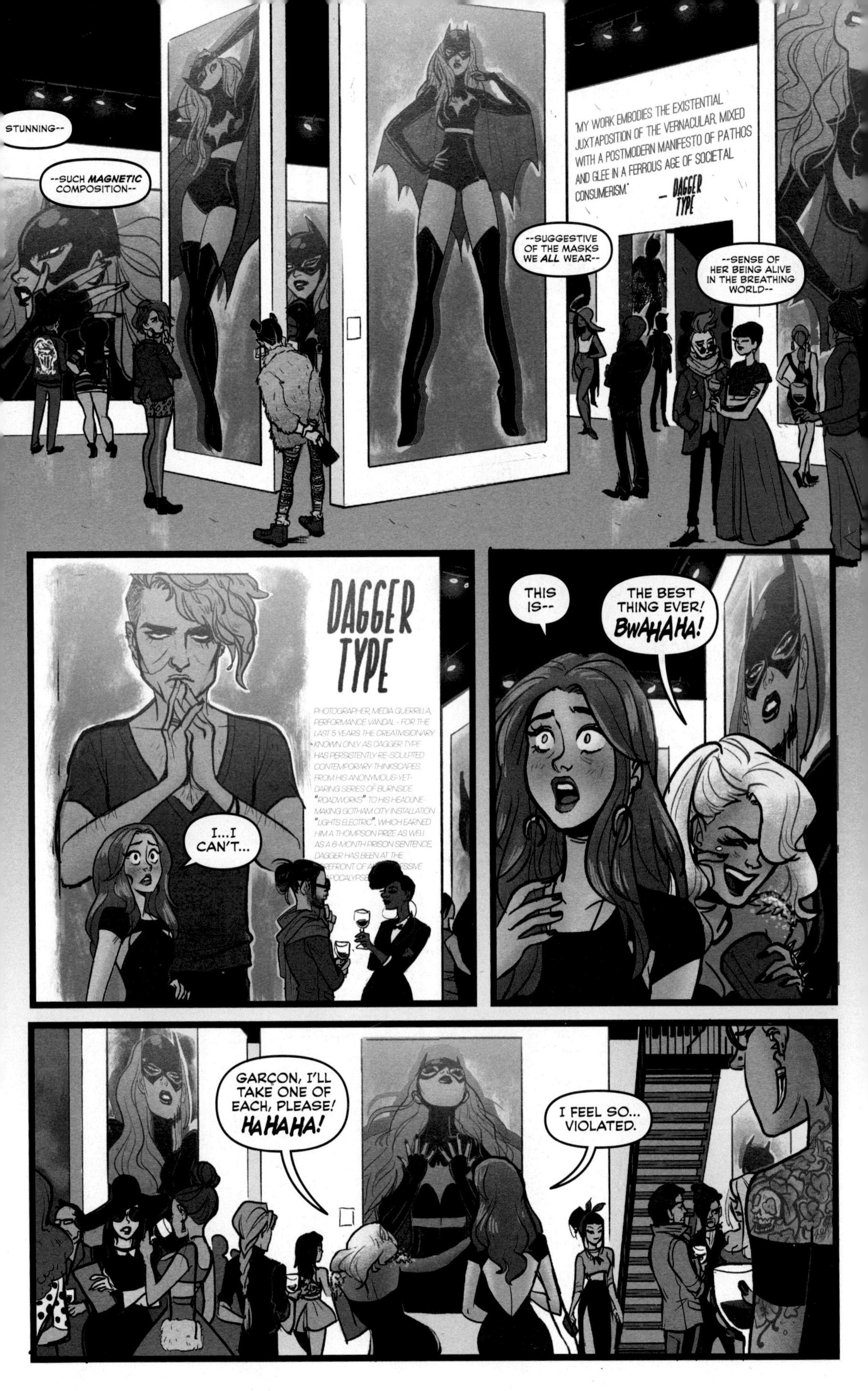

STUNNING--
--SUCH MAGNETIC COMPOSITION--
"MY WORK EMBODIES THE EXISTENTIAL JUXTAPOSITION OF THE VERNACULAR, MIXED WITH A POSTMODERN MANIFESTO OF PATHOS AND GLEE IN A FERROUS AGE OF SOCIETAL CONSUMERISM." — DAGGER TYPE
--SUGGESTIVE OF THE MASKS WE ALL WEAR--
--SENSE OF HER BEING ALIVE IN THE BREATHING WORLD--
DAGGER TYPE
PHOTOGRAPHER, MEDIA GUERRILLA, PERFORMANCE VANDAL - FOR THE LAST 5 YEARS THE CREATIVISIONARY KNOWN ONLY AS DAGGER TYPE HAS PERSISTENTLY RE-SCULPTED CONTEMPORARY THINKSCAPES. FROM HIS ANONYMOUS-YET-DARING SERIES OF BURNSIDE "ROADWORKS" TO HIS HEADLINE-MAKING GOTHAM CITY INSTALLATION "LIGHTS ELECTRIC", WHICH EARNED HIM A THOMPSON PRIZE AS WELL AS A 6-MONTH PRISON SENTENCE, DAGGER HAS BEEN AT THE
I...I CAN'T...
THIS IS--
THE BEST THING EVER! BWAHAHA!
GARÇON, I'LL TAKE ONE OF EACH, PLEASE! HAHAHA!
I FEEL SO... VIOLATED.

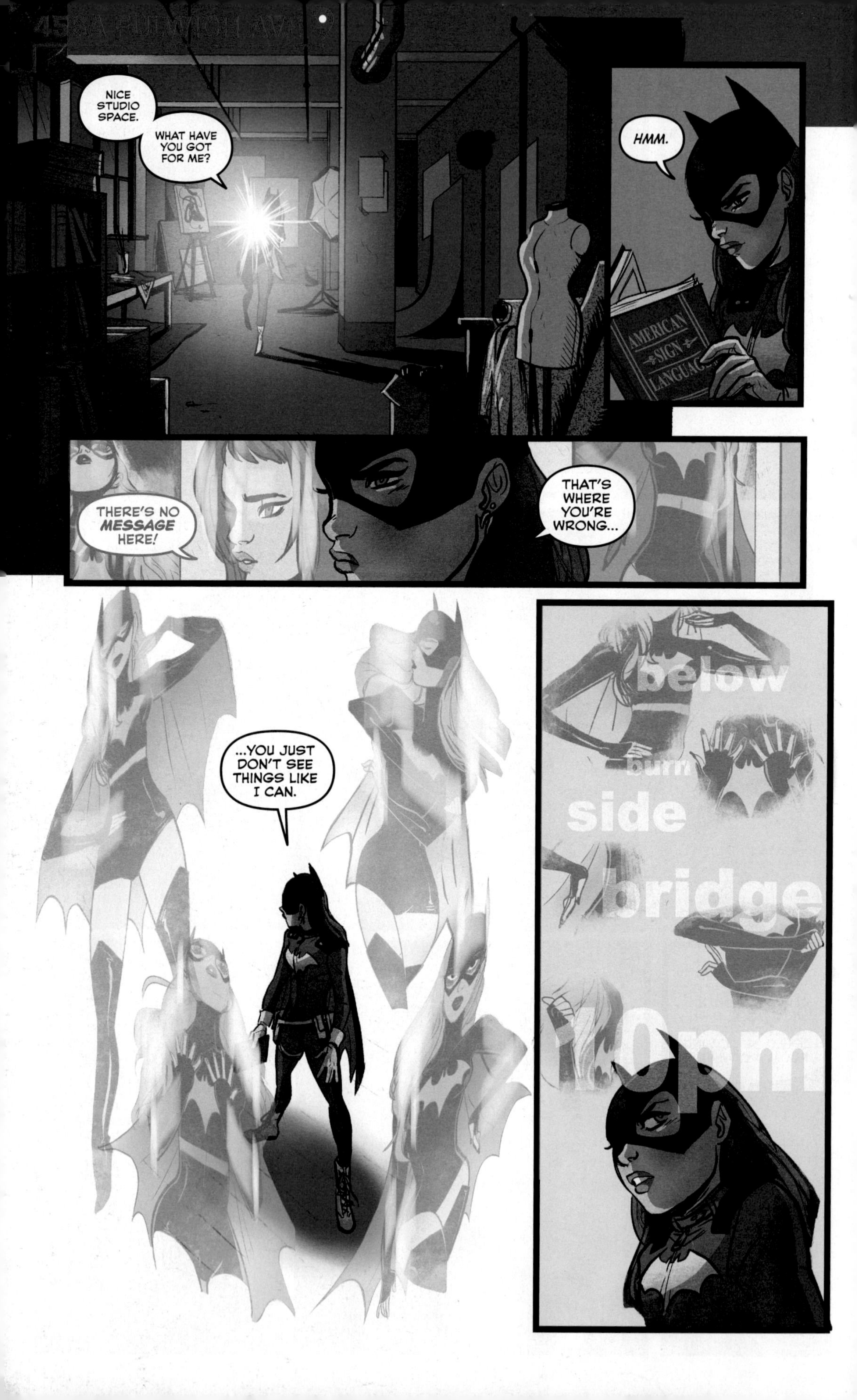

NICE STUDIO SPACE.
WHAT HAVE YOU GOT FOR ME?
HMM.
AMERICAN SIGN LANGUAG
THERE'S NO *MESSAGE* HERE!
THAT'S WHERE YOU'RE WRONG...
...YOU JUST DON'T SEE THINGS LIKE I CAN.
below
burn
side
bridge
10pm

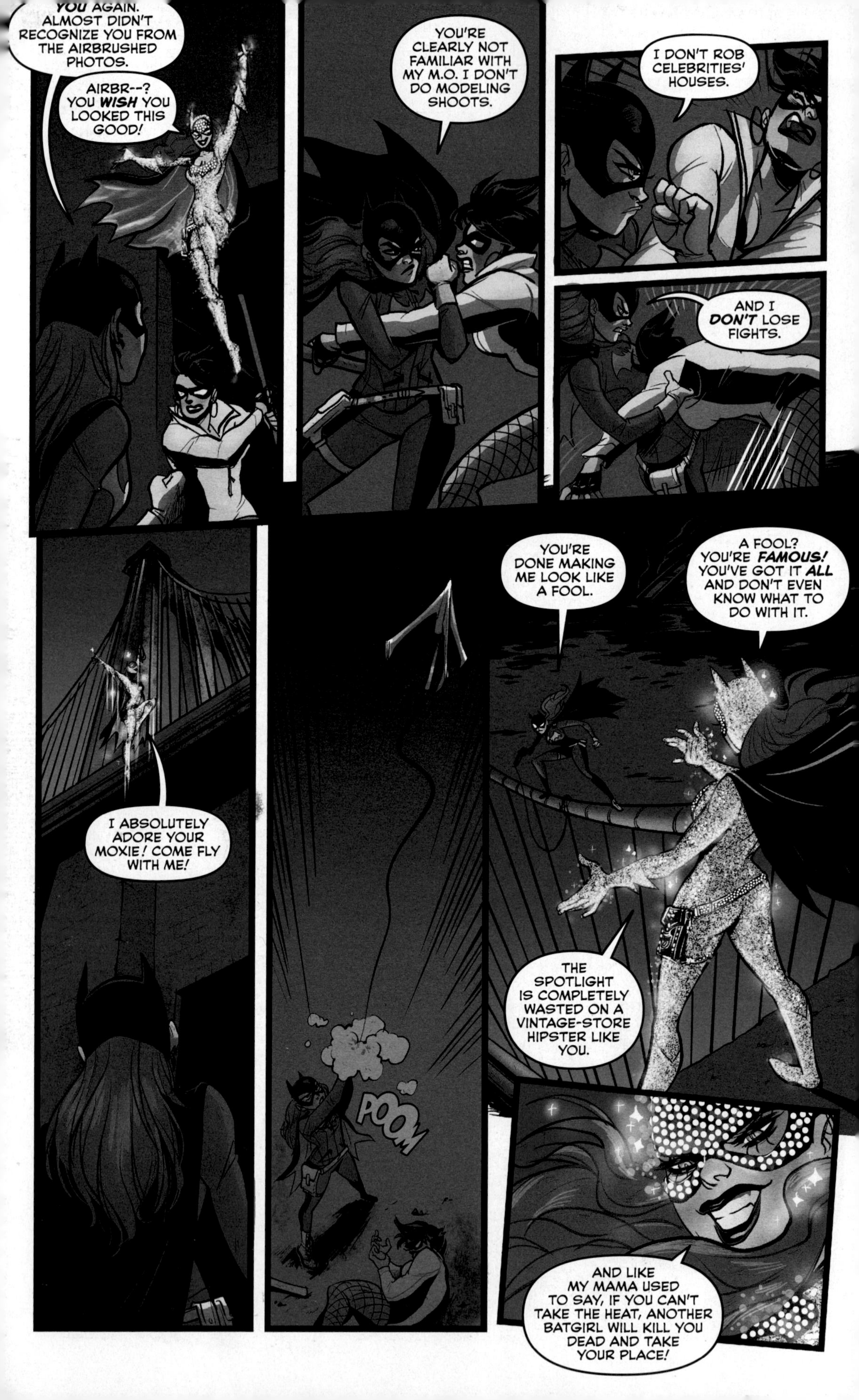

YOU AGAIN. ALMOST DIDN'T RECOGNIZE YOU FROM THE AIRBRUSHED PHOTOS.
AIRBR--? YOU WISH YOU LOOKED THIS GOOD!
YOU'RE CLEARLY NOT FAMILIAR WITH MY M.O. I DON'T DO MODELING SHOOTS.
I DON'T ROB CELEBRITIES' HOUSES.
AND I DON'T LOSE FIGHTS.
I ABSOLUTELY ADORE YOUR MOXIE! COME FLY WITH ME!
POOM
YOU'RE DONE MAKING ME LOOK LIKE A FOOL.
A FOOL? YOU'RE FAMOUS! YOU'VE GOT IT ALL AND DON'T EVEN KNOW WHAT TO DO WITH IT.
THE SPOTLIGHT IS COMPLETELY WASTED ON A VINTAGE-STORE HIPSTER LIKE YOU.
AND LIKE MY MAMA USED TO SAY, IF YOU CAN'T TAKE THE HEAT, ANOTHER BATGIRL WILL KILL YOU DEAD AND TAKE YOUR PLACE!

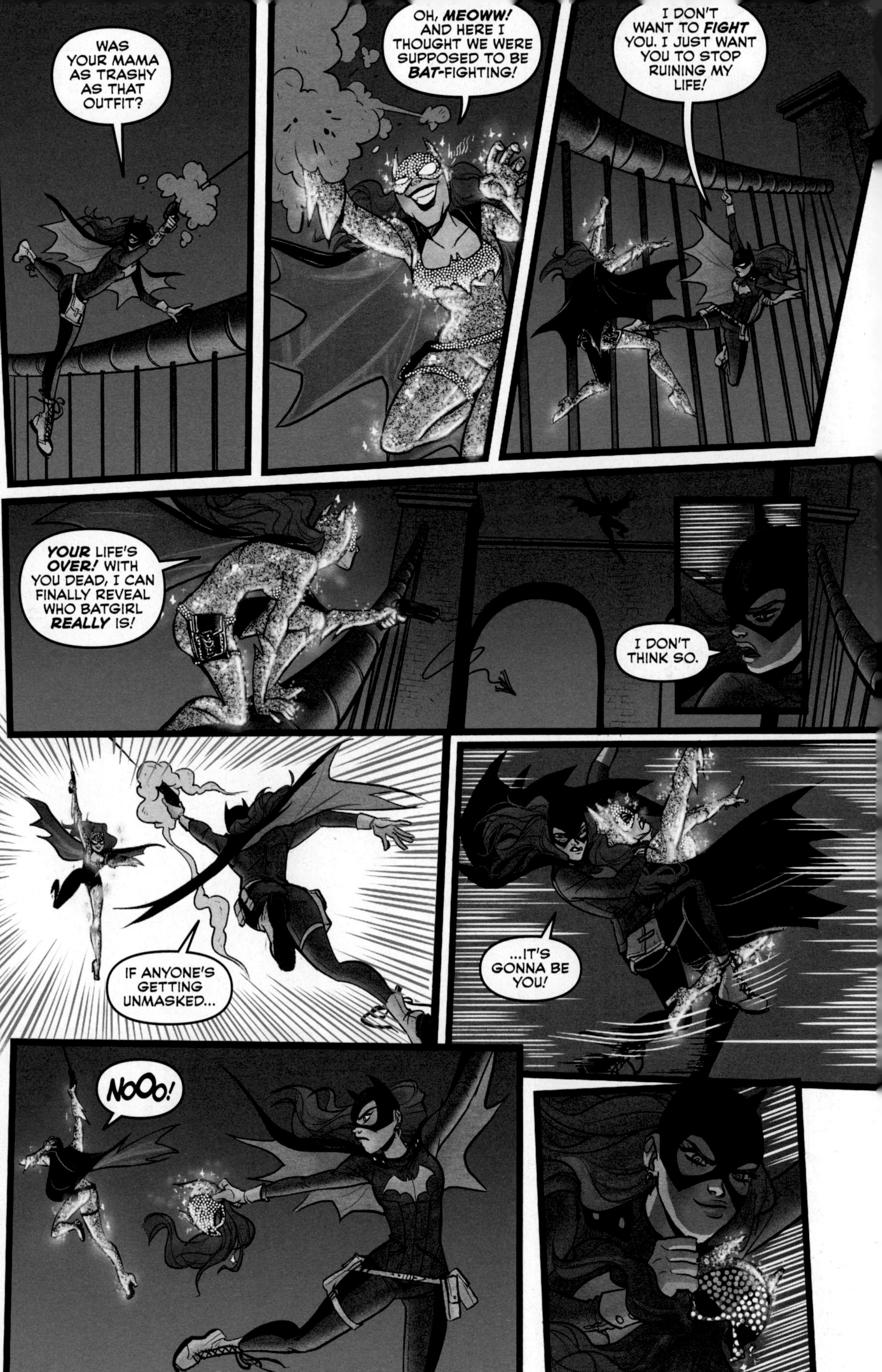
WAS YOUR MAMA AS TRASHY AS THAT OUTFIT?
OH, **MEOWW!** AND HERE I THOUGHT WE WERE SUPPOSED TO BE **BAT**-FIGHTING!
I DON'T WANT TO **FIGHT** YOU. I JUST WANT YOU TO STOP RUINING MY LIFE!
YOUR LIFE'S **OVER!** WITH YOU DEAD, I CAN FINALLY REVEAL WHO BATGIRL **REALLY** IS!
I DON'T THINK SO.
IF ANYONE'S GETTING UNMASKED...
...IT'S GONNA BE YOU!
NOOO!

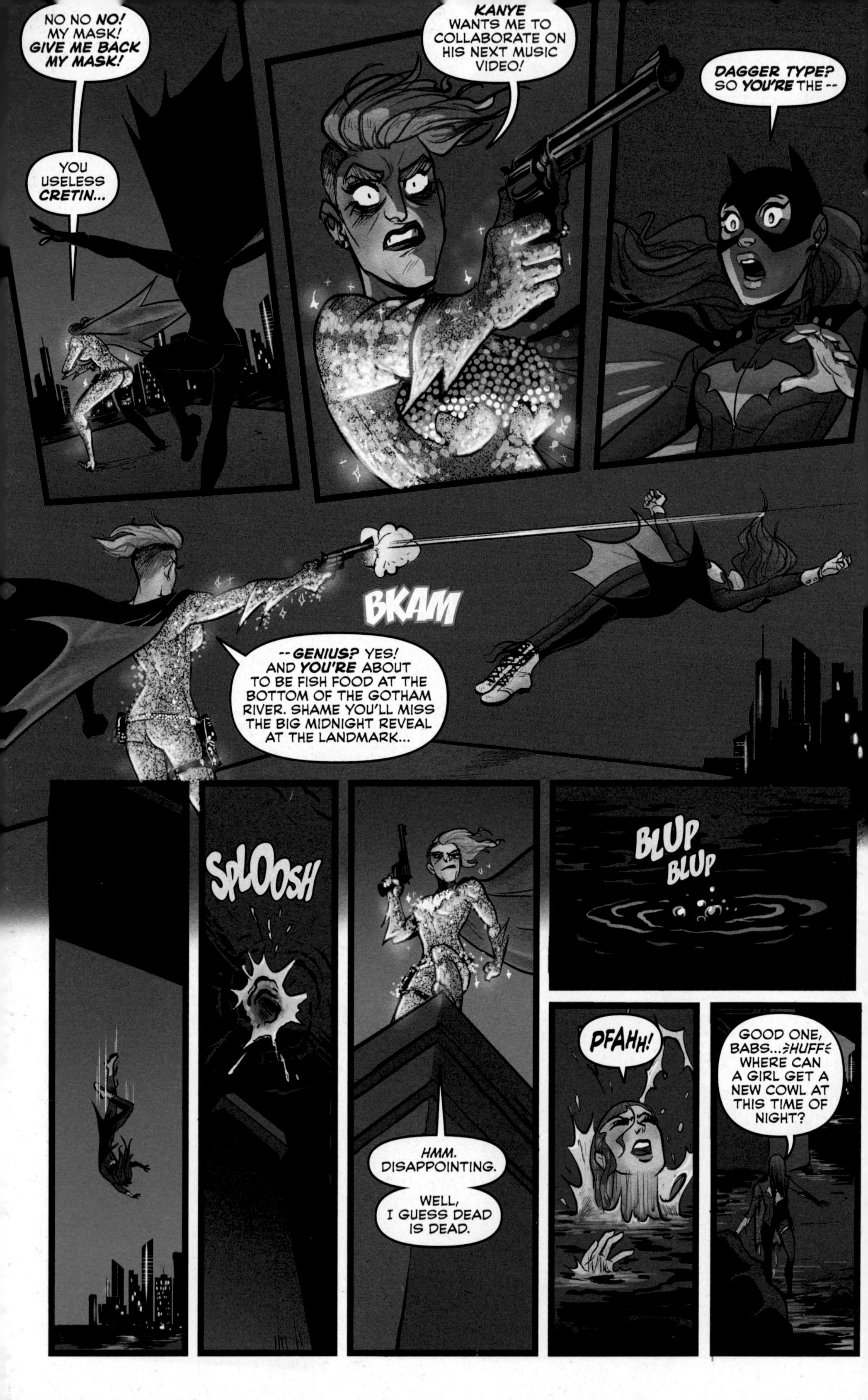
NO NO NO! MY MASK! GIVE ME BACK MY MASK!
YOU USELESS CRETIN...
KANYE WANTS ME TO COLLABORATE ON HIS NEXT MUSIC VIDEO!
DAGGER TYPE? SO YOU'RE THE --
BKAM
--GENIUS? YES! AND YOU'RE ABOUT TO BE FISH FOOD AT THE BOTTOM OF THE GOTHAM RIVER. SHAME YOU'LL MISS THE BIG MIDNIGHT REVEAL AT THE LANDMARK...
SPLOOSH
HMM. DISAPPOINTING.
WELL, I GUESS DEAD IS DEAD.
BLUP BLUP
PFAHH!
GOOD ONE, BABS... HUFF WHERE CAN A GIRL GET A NEW COWL AT THIS TIME OF NIGHT?

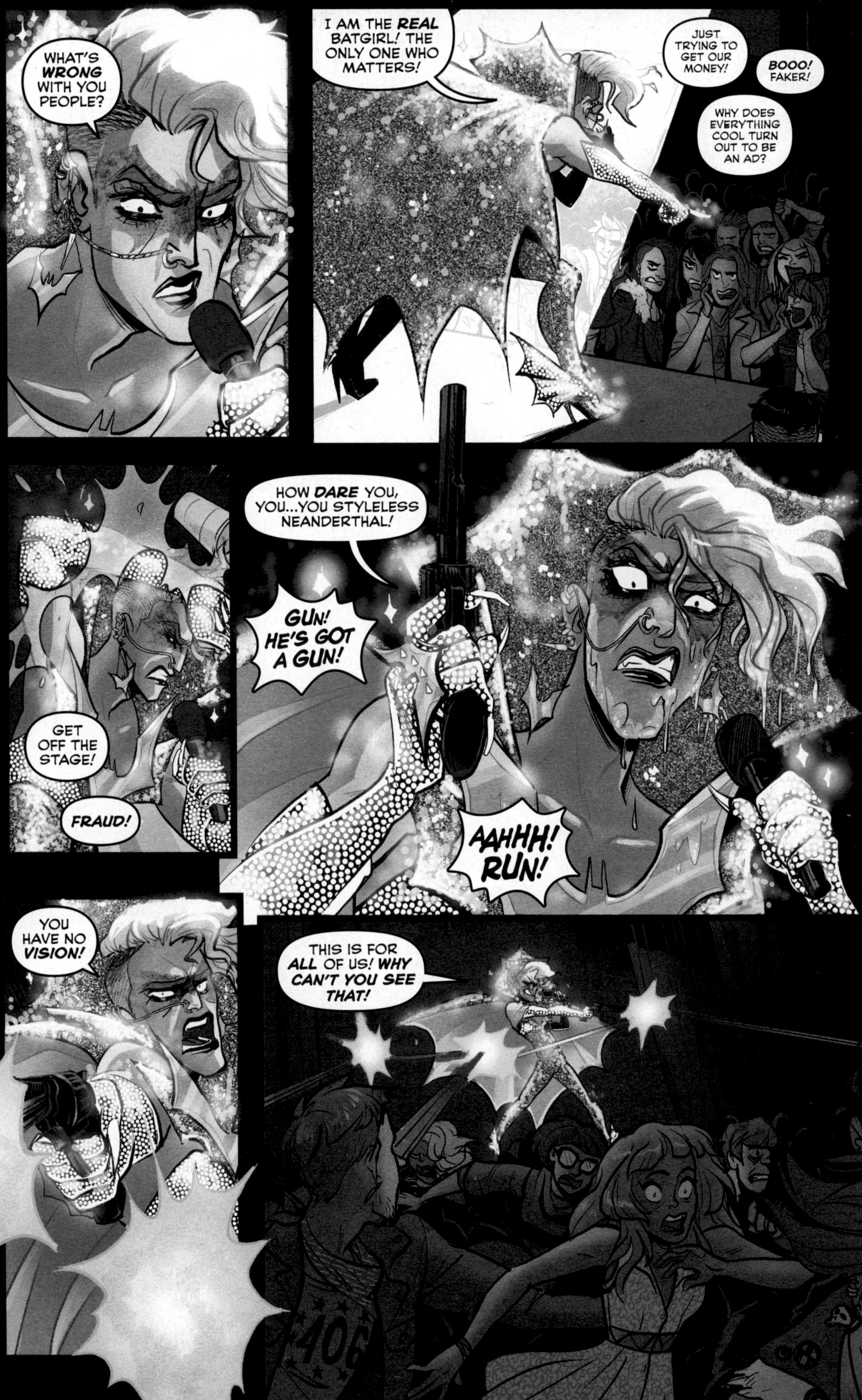
WHAT'S **WRONG** WITH YOU PEOPLE?
I AM THE **REAL** BATGIRL! THE ONLY ONE WHO MATTERS!
JUST TRYING TO GET OUR MONEY!
BOOO! FAKER!
WHY DOES EVERYTHING COOL TURN OUT TO BE AN AD?
GET OFF THE STAGE!
FRAUD!
HOW **DARE** YOU, YOU...YOU STYLELESS NEANDERTHAL!
GUN! HE'S GOT A GUN!
AAHHH! RUN!
YOU HAVE NO **VISION!**
THIS IS FOR **ALL** OF US! **WHY CAN'T YOU SEE THAT!**
406

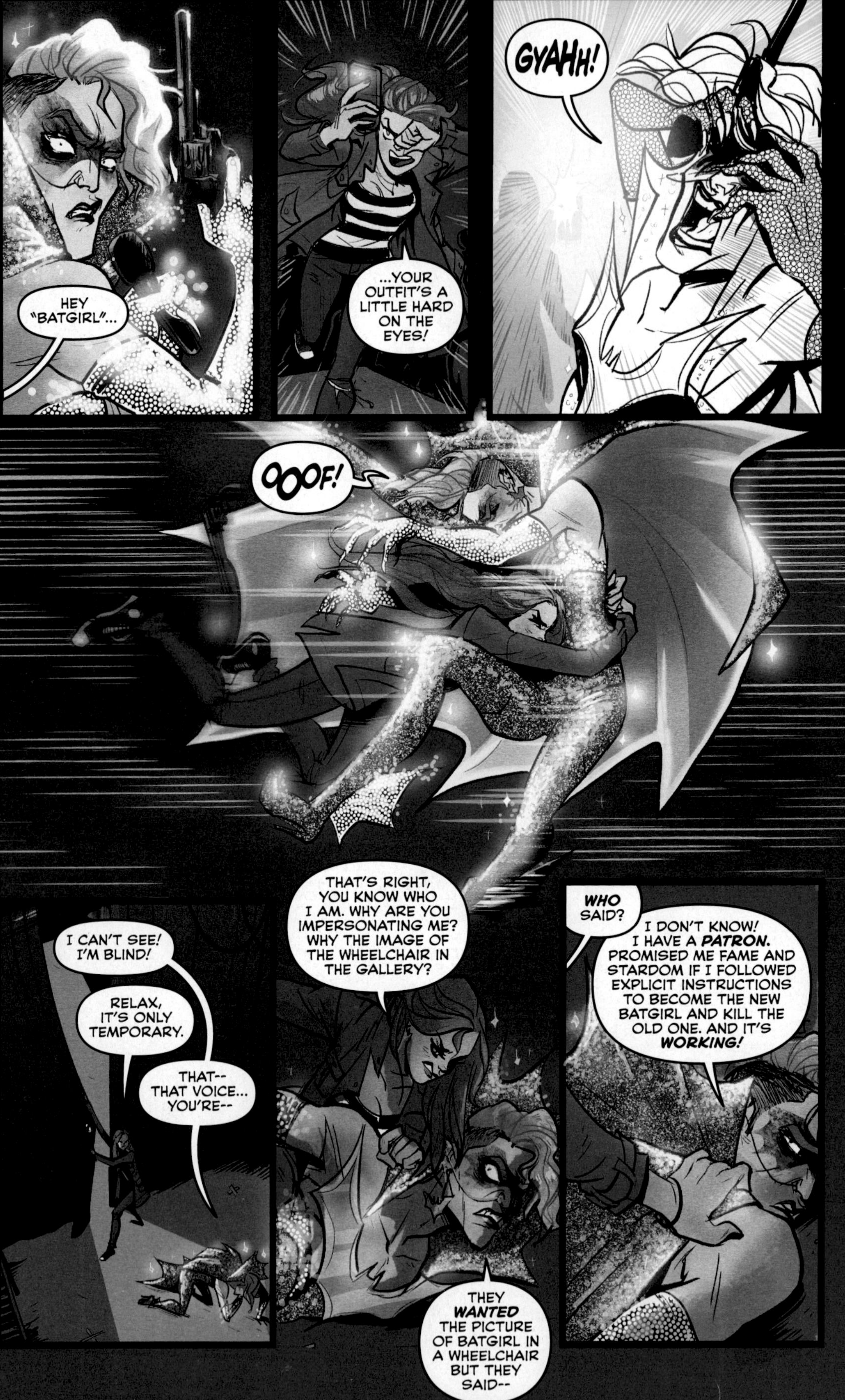
HEY "BATGIRL"...
...YOUR OUTFIT'S A LITTLE HARD ON THE EYES!
GYAHH!
OOOF!
I CAN'T SEE! I'M BLIND!
RELAX, IT'S ONLY TEMPORARY.
THAT-- THAT VOICE... YOU'RE--
THAT'S RIGHT, YOU KNOW WHO I AM. WHY ARE YOU IMPERSONATING ME? WHY THE IMAGE OF THE WHEELCHAIR IN THE GALLERY?
THEY WANTED THE PICTURE OF BATGIRL IN A WHEELCHAIR BUT THEY SAID--
WHO SAID?
I DON'T KNOW! I HAVE A PATRON. PROMISED ME FAME AND STARDOM IF I FOLLOWED EXPLICIT INSTRUCTIONS TO BECOME THE NEW BATGIRL AND KILL THE OLD ONE. AND IT'S WORKING!

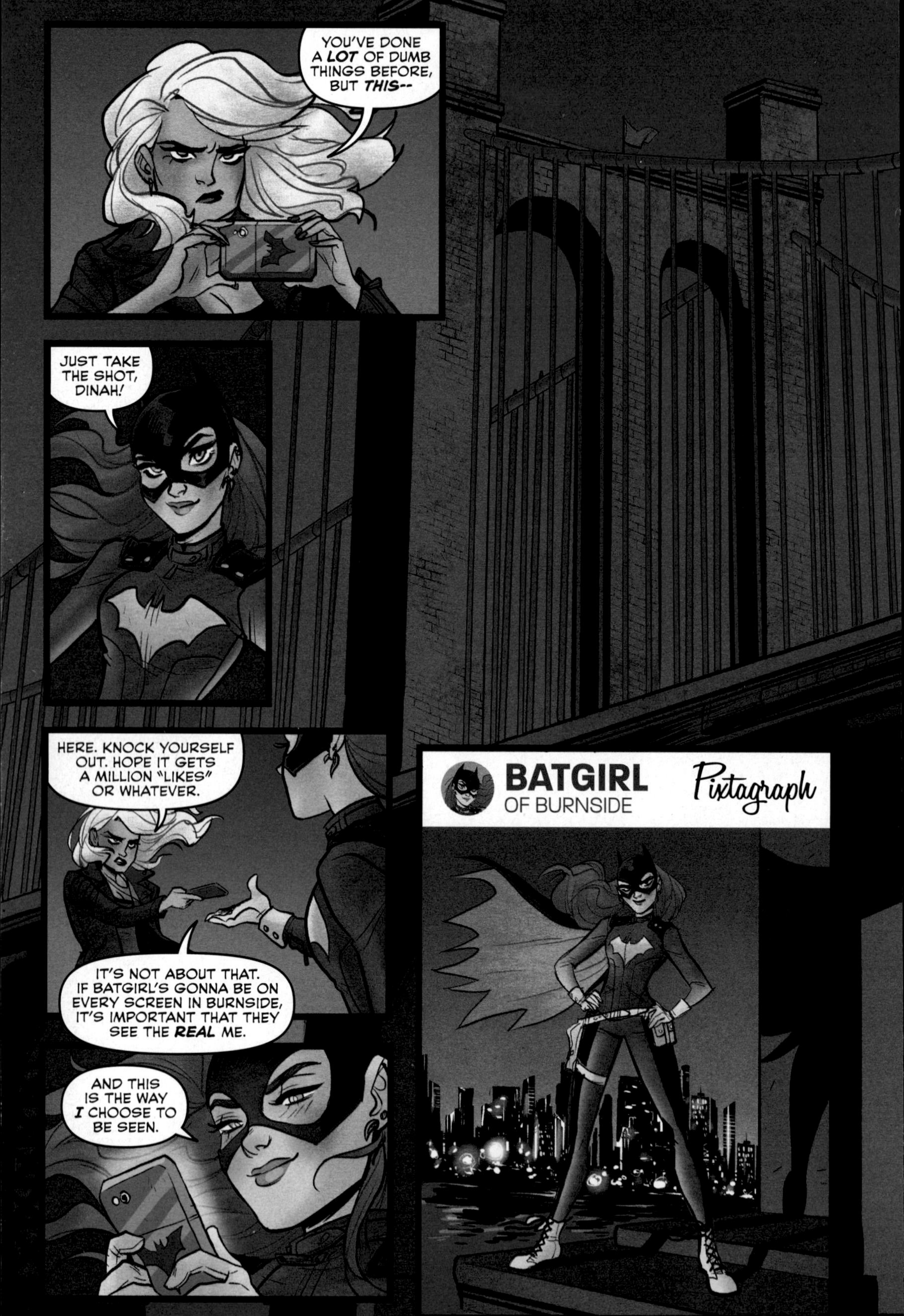

YOU'VE DONE A LOT OF DUMB THINGS BEFORE, BUT THIS--
JUST TAKE THE SHOT, DINAH!
HERE. KNOCK YOURSELF OUT. HOPE IT GETS A MILLION "LIKES" OR WHATEVER.
IT'S NOT ABOUT THAT. IF BATGIRL'S GONNA BE ON EVERY SCREEN IN BURNSIDE, IT'S IMPORTANT THAT THEY SEE THE REAL ME.
AND THIS IS THE WAY I CHOOSE TO BE SEEN.
BATGIRL
OF BURNSIDE
Pixtagraph

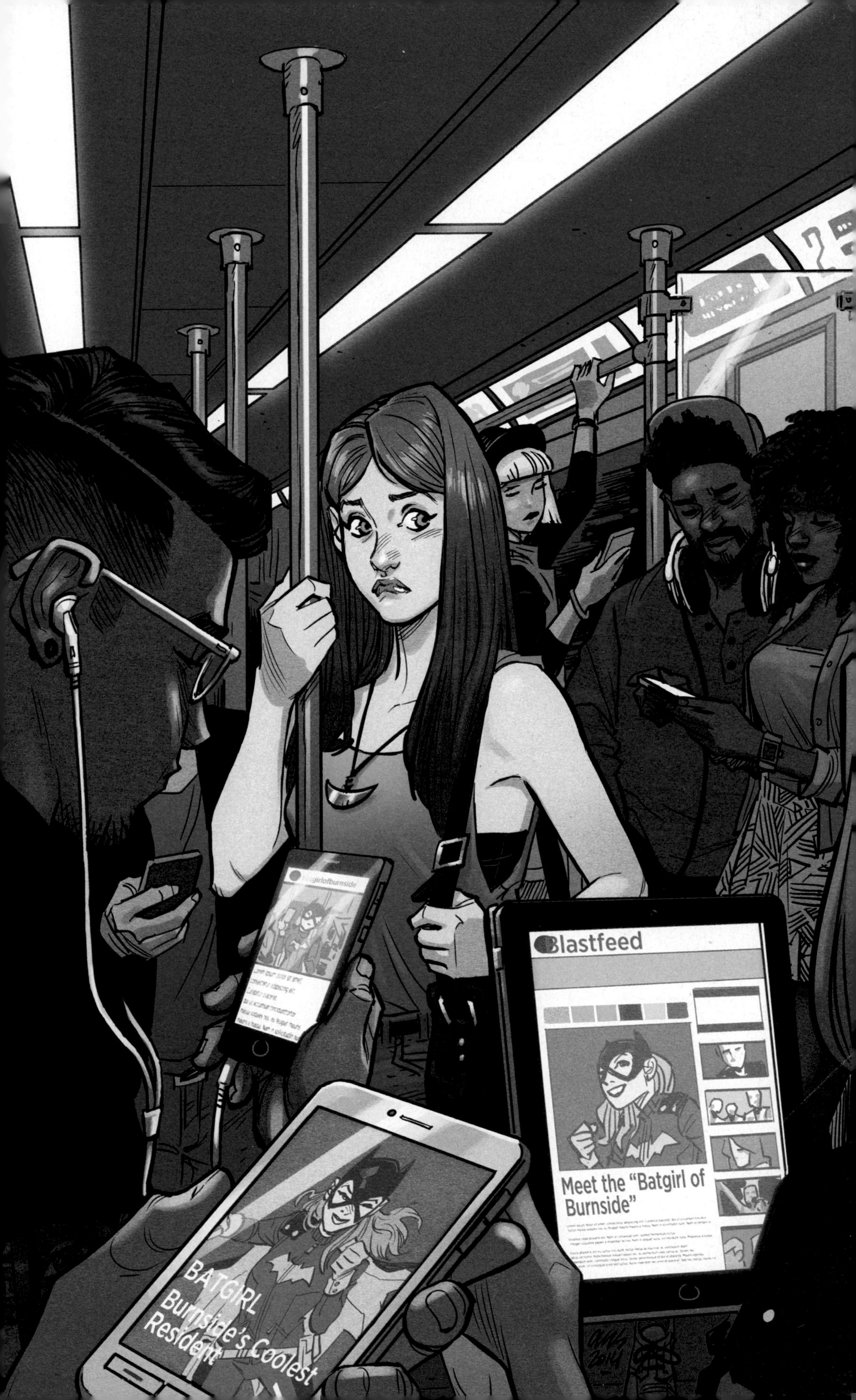

batgirlofburnside
Blastfeed
Meet the "Batgirl of Burnside"
BATGIRL
Burnside's Coolest Resident

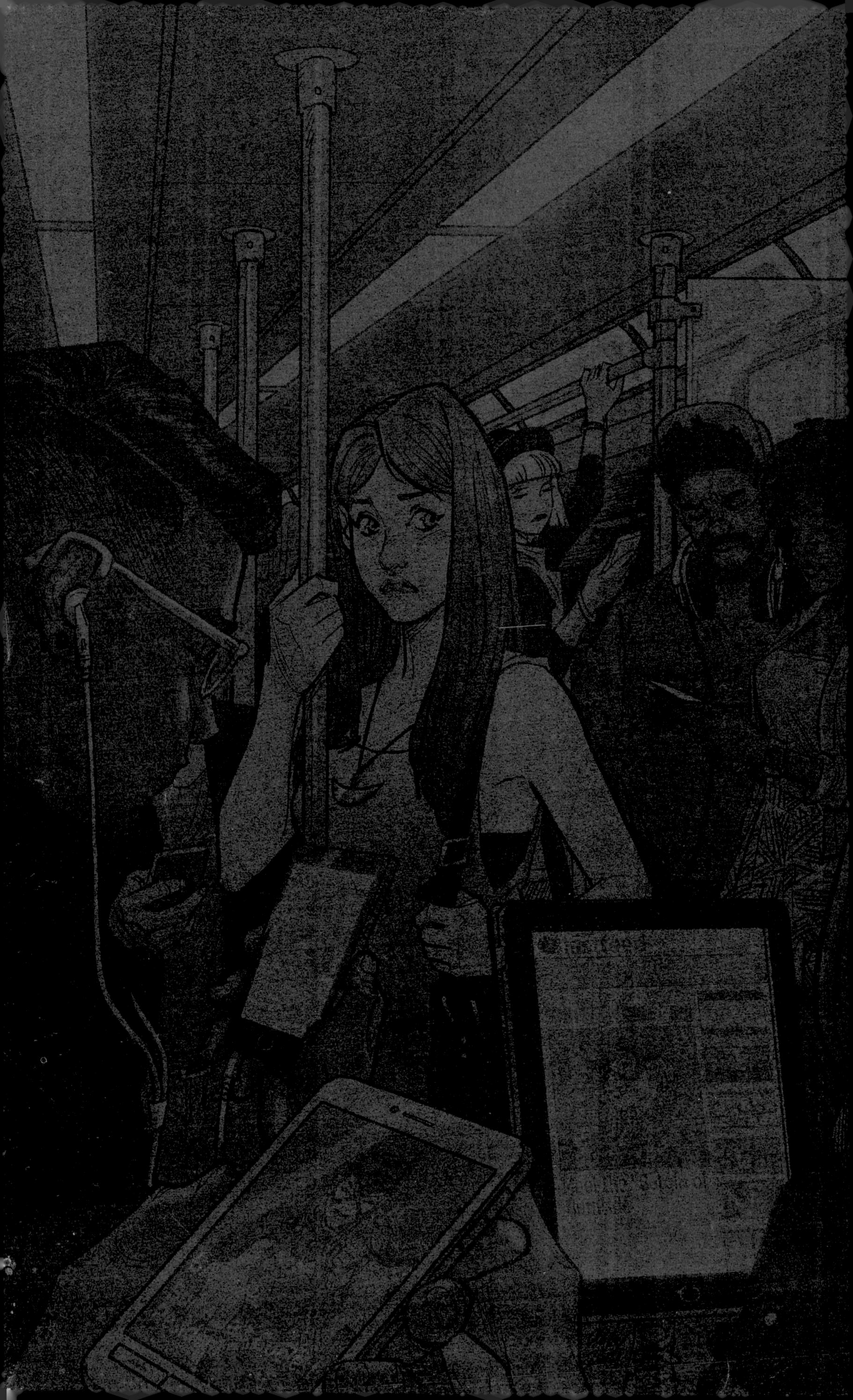

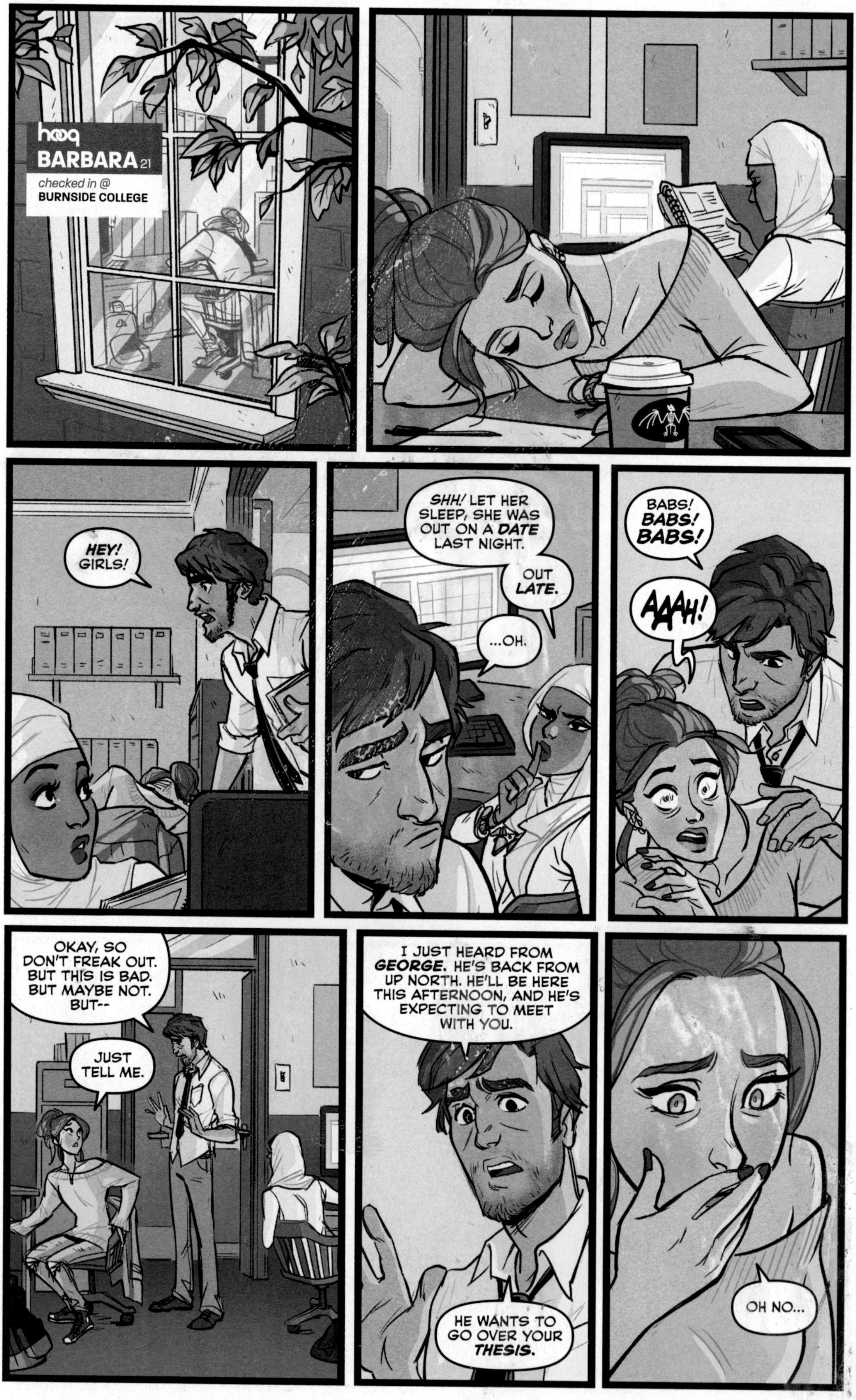
hooq
BARBARA 21
checked in @
BURNSIDE COLLEGE
HEY! GIRLS!
SHH! LET HER SLEEP, SHE WAS OUT ON A DATE LAST NIGHT.
OUT LATE.
...OH.
BABS! BABS! BABS!
AAAH!
OKAY, SO DON'T FREAK OUT. BUT THIS IS BAD. BUT MAYBE NOT. BUT--
JUST TELL ME.
I JUST HEARD FROM GEORGE. HE'S BACK FROM UP NORTH. HE'LL BE HERE THIS AFTERNOON, AND HE'S EXPECTING TO MEET WITH YOU.
HE WANTS TO GO OVER YOUR THESIS.
OH NO...

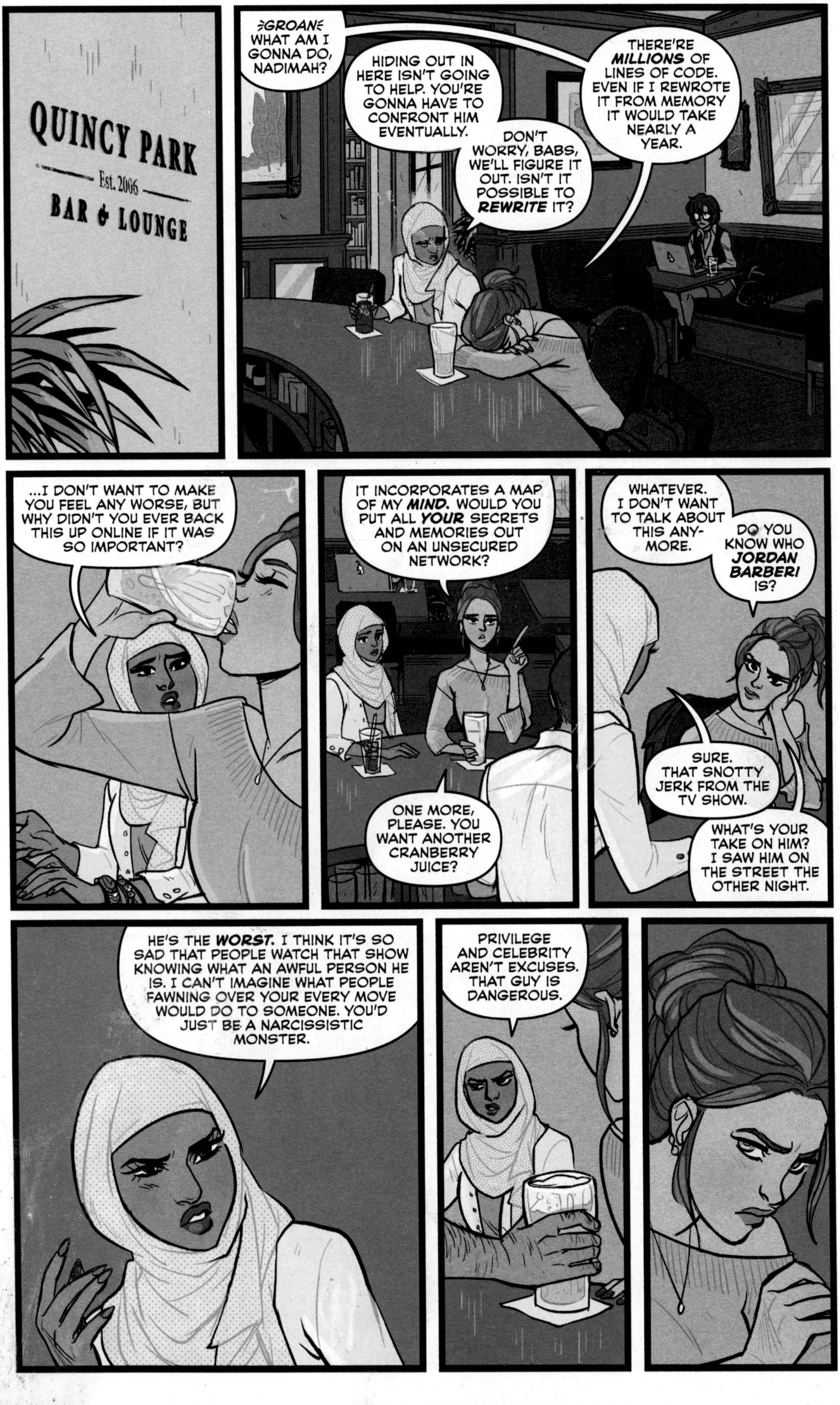
QUINCY PARK
Est. 2006
BAR & LOUNGE
GROAN WHAT AM I GONNA DO, NADIMAH?
HIDING OUT IN HERE ISN'T GOING TO HELP. YOU'RE GONNA HAVE TO CONFRONT HIM EVENTUALLY.
DON'T WORRY, BABS, WE'LL FIGURE IT OUT. ISN'T IT POSSIBLE TO *REWRITE* IT?
THERE'RE *MILLIONS* OF LINES OF CODE. EVEN IF I REWROTE IT FROM MEMORY IT WOULD TAKE NEARLY A YEAR.
...I DON'T WANT TO MAKE YOU FEEL ANY WORSE, BUT WHY DIDN'T YOU EVER BACK THIS UP ONLINE IF IT WAS SO IMPORTANT?
IT INCORPORATES A MAP OF MY *MIND.* WOULD YOU PUT ALL *YOUR* SECRETS AND MEMORIES OUT ON AN UNSECURED NETWORK?
ONE MORE, PLEASE. YOU WANT ANOTHER CRANBERRY JUICE?
WHATEVER. I DON'T WANT TO TALK ABOUT THIS ANY-MORE.
DO YOU KNOW WHO *JORDAN BARBERI* IS?
SURE. THAT SNOTTY JERK FROM THE TV SHOW.
WHAT'S YOUR TAKE ON HIM? I SAW HIM ON THE STREET THE OTHER NIGHT.
HE'S THE *WORST.* I THINK IT'S SO SAD THAT PEOPLE WATCH THAT SHOW KNOWING WHAT AN AWFUL PERSON HE IS. I CAN'T IMAGINE WHAT PEOPLE FAWNING OVER YOUR EVERY MOVE WOULD DO TO SOMEONE. YOU'D JUST BE A NARCISSISTIC MONSTER.
PRIVILEGE AND CELEBRITY AREN'T EXCUSES. THAT GUY IS DANGEROUS.

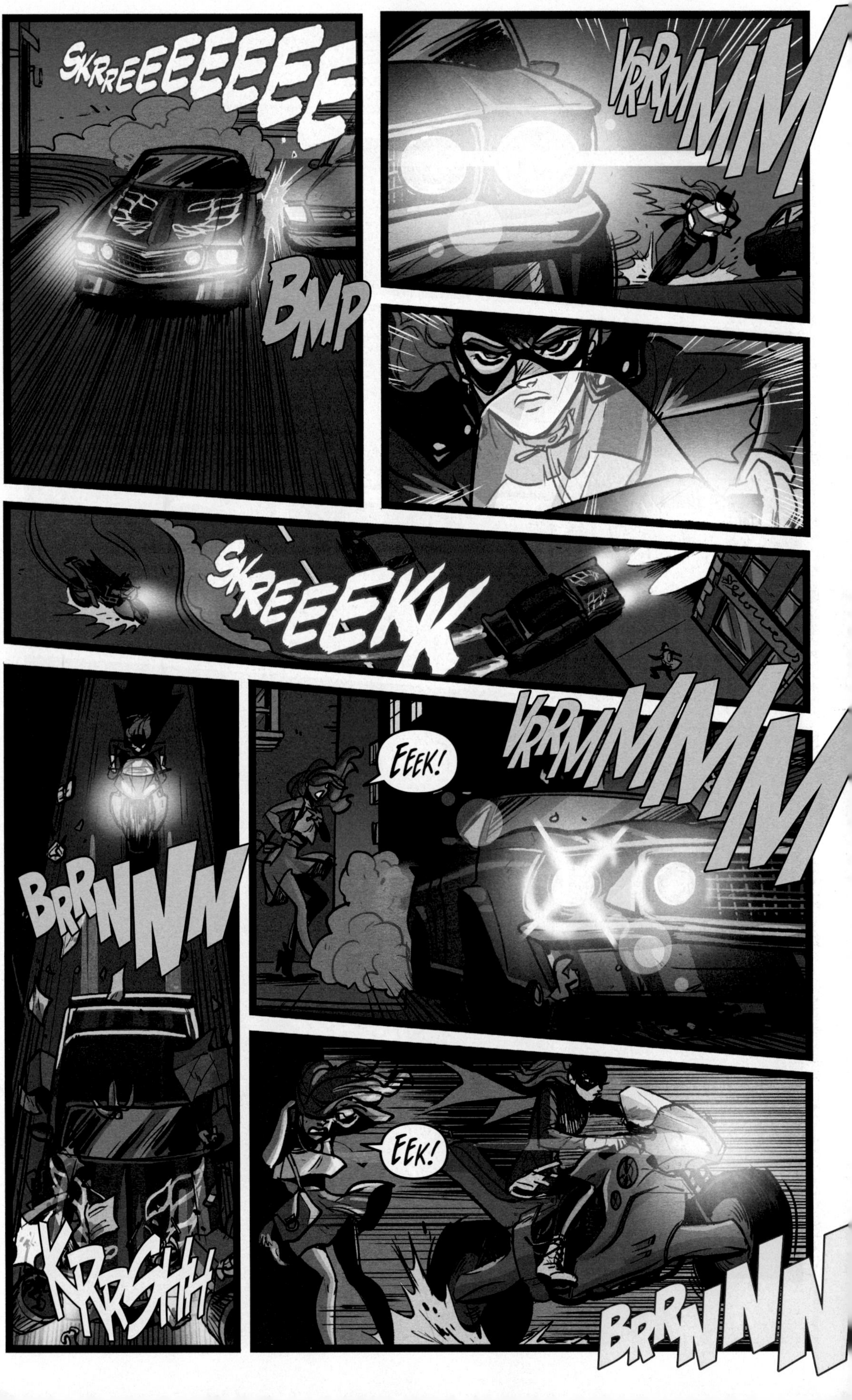
SKRREEEEEEEE
BMP
VRRMMMM
SKREEEKK
BRRNNNN
KRRSHH
EEEK!
VRRMMMMMM
EEK!
BRRNNN

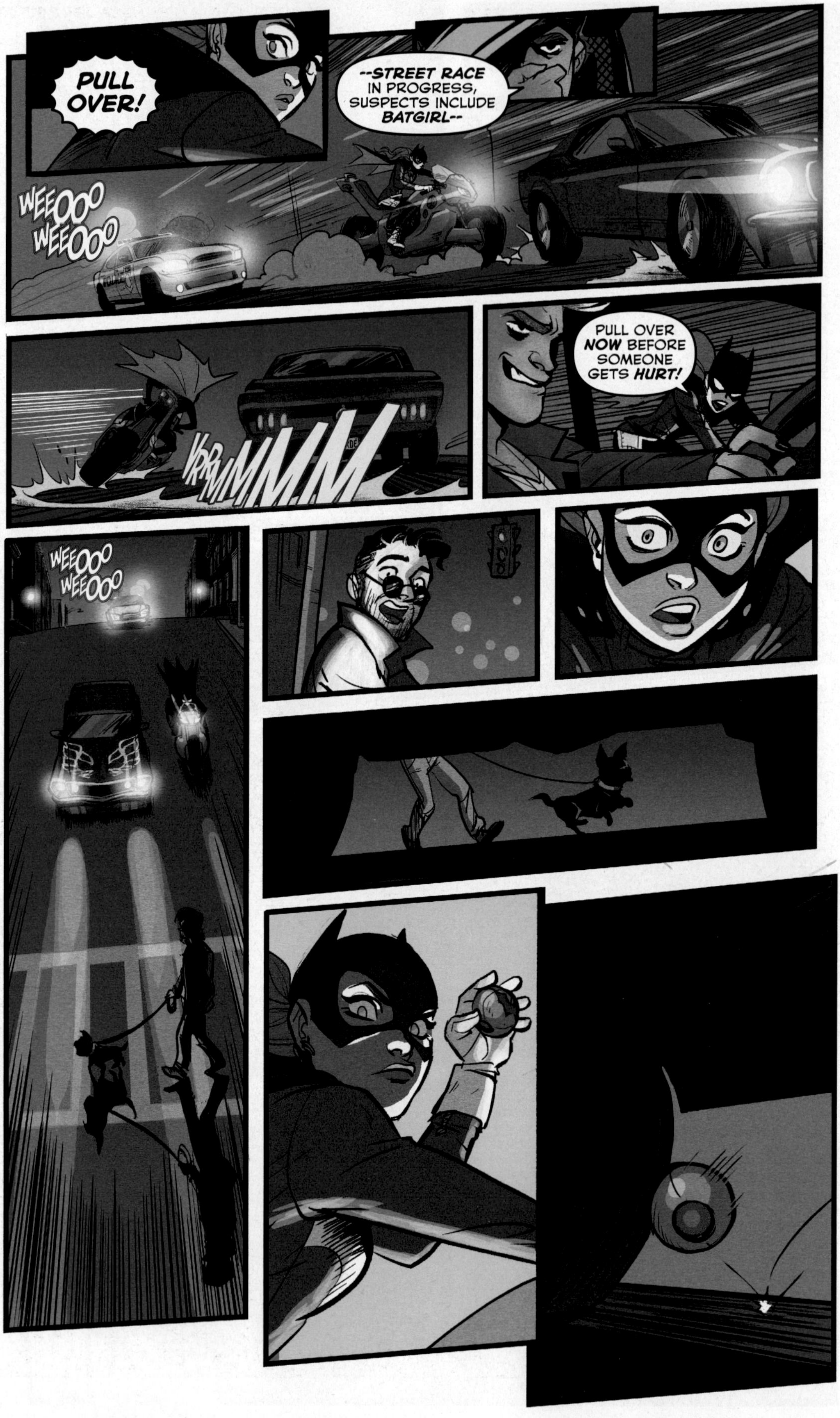
PULL OVER!
--STREET RACE IN PROGRESS, SUSPECTS INCLUDE BATGIRL--
WEEOOO WEEOOO
VRRMMMM
PULL OVER NOW BEFORE SOMEONE GETS HURT!
WEEOOO WEEOOO

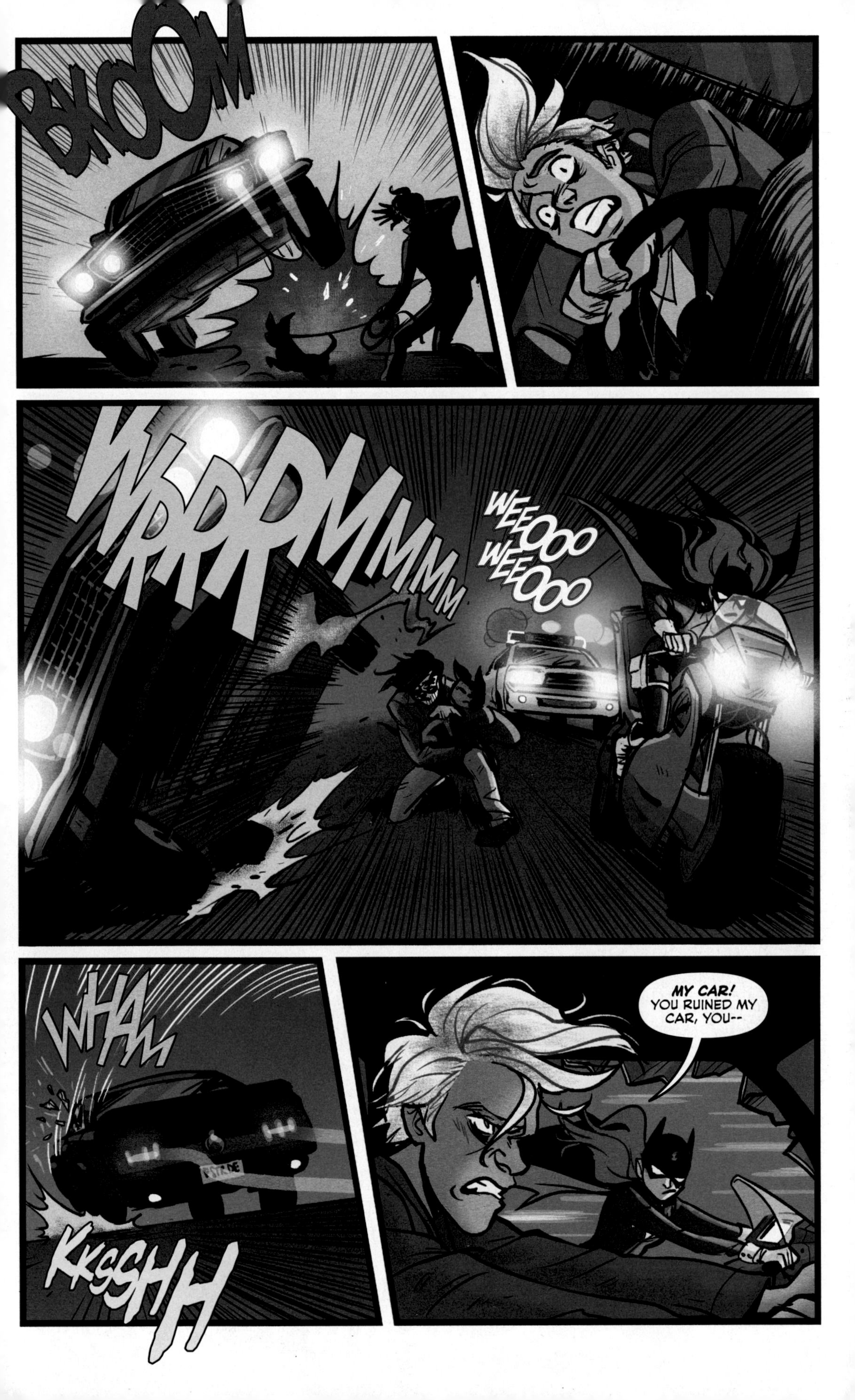
BKOOM
WRRRMMMMM
WEEOOO WEEOOO
WHAM
KKSSHH
MY CAR! YOU RUINED MY CAR, YOU--

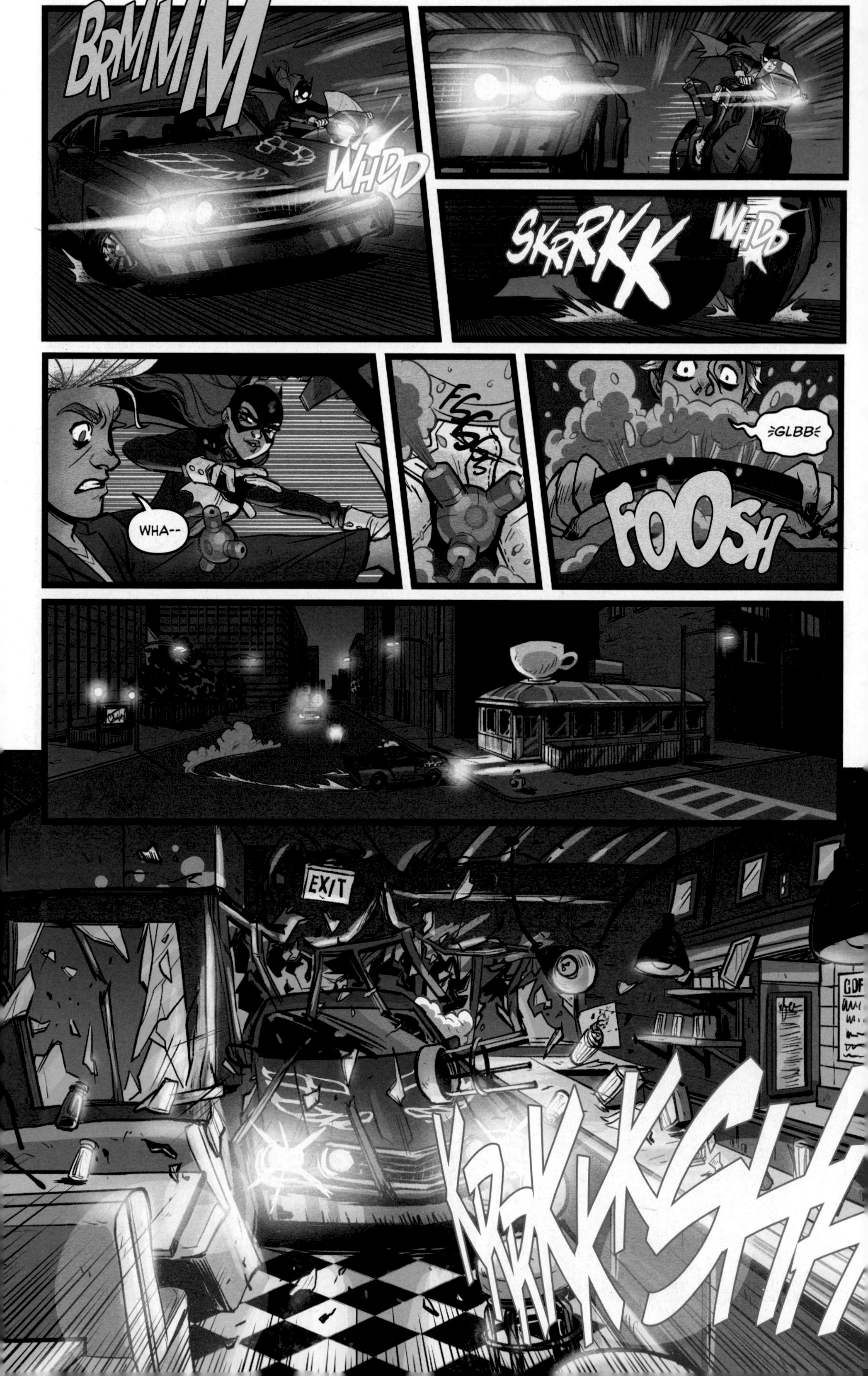
BRMMM
WHDD
SKRRKK
WHDD
WHA--
FSSSS
≷GLBB≶
FOOSH
EXIT
KRRKKSSH

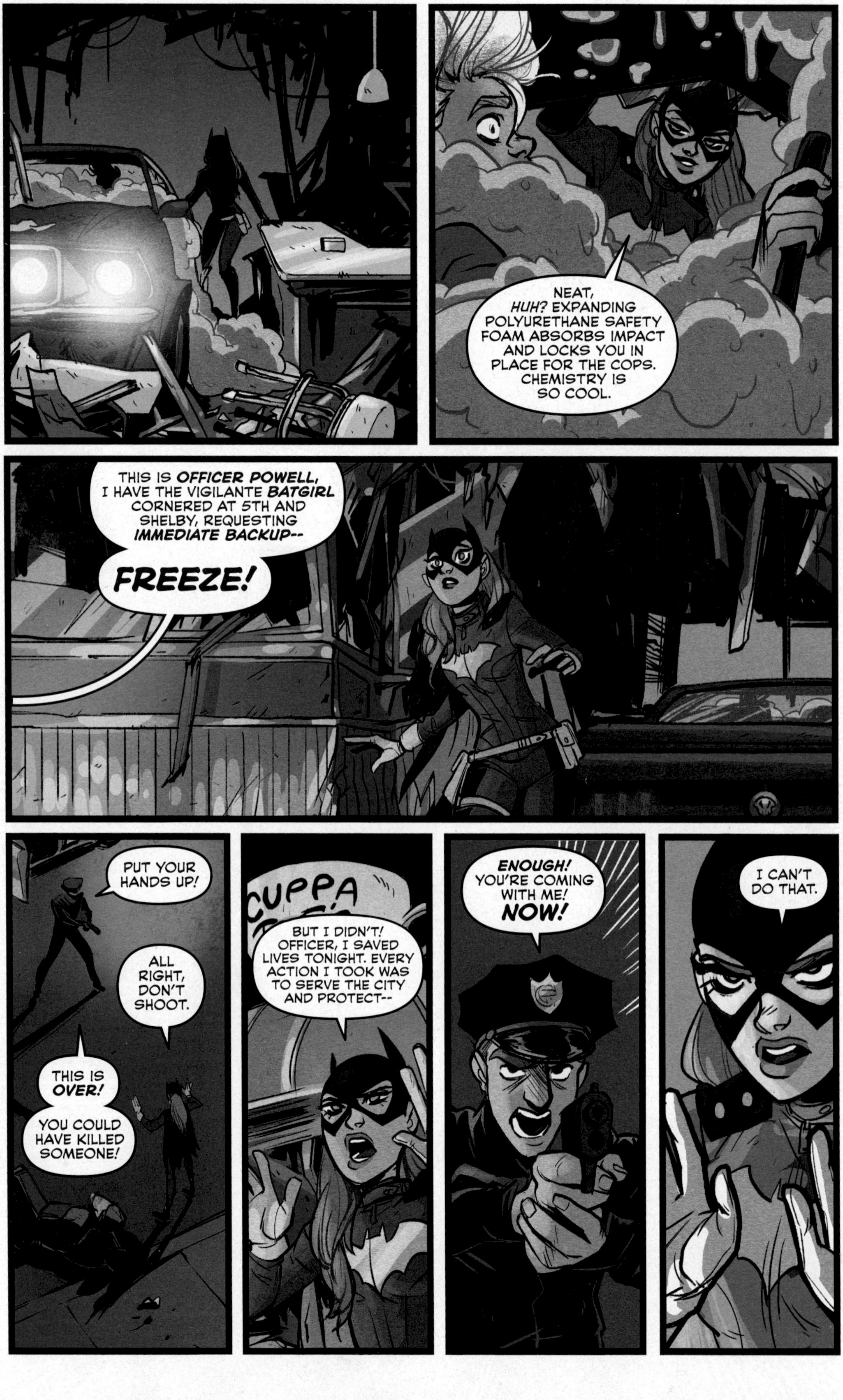

NEAT, HUH? EXPANDING POLYURETHANE SAFETY FOAM ABSORBS IMPACT AND LOCKS YOU IN PLACE FOR THE COPS. CHEMISTRY IS SO COOL.
THIS IS OFFICER POWELL, I HAVE THE VIGILANTE BATGIRL CORNERED AT 5TH AND SHELBY, REQUESTING IMMEDIATE BACKUP--
FREEZE!
PUT YOUR HANDS UP!
ALL RIGHT, DON'T SHOOT.
THIS IS OVER!
YOU COULD HAVE KILLED SOMEONE!
CUPPA
BUT I DIDN'T! OFFICER, I SAVED LIVES TONIGHT. EVERY ACTION I TOOK WAS TO SERVE THE CITY AND PROTECT--
ENOUGH! YOU'RE COMING WITH ME! NOW!
I CAN'T DO THAT.

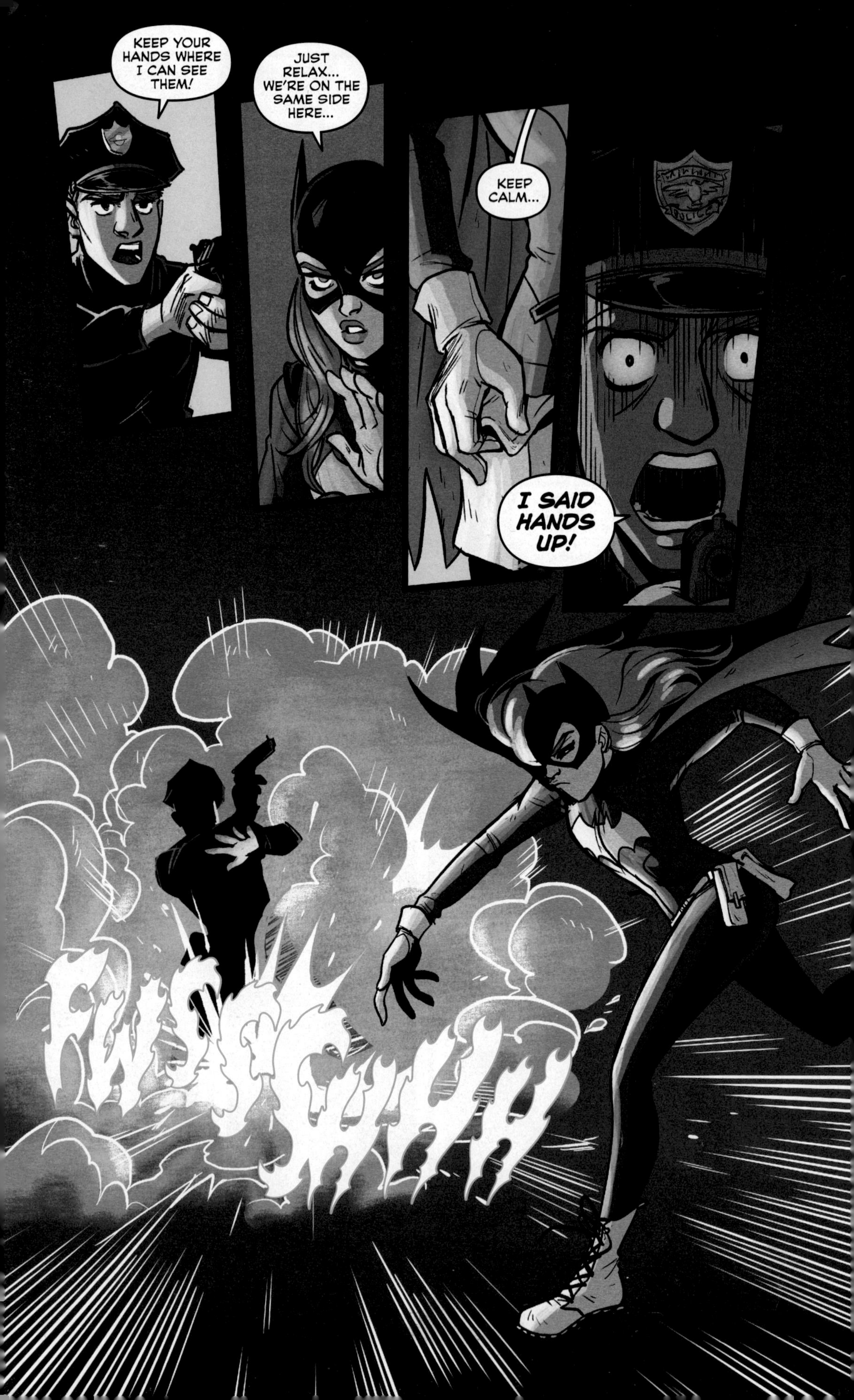
KEEP YOUR HANDS WHERE I CAN SEE THEM!
JUST RELAX... WE'RE ON THE SAME SIDE HERE...
KEEP CALM...
I SAID HANDS UP!
FWSSSHHH

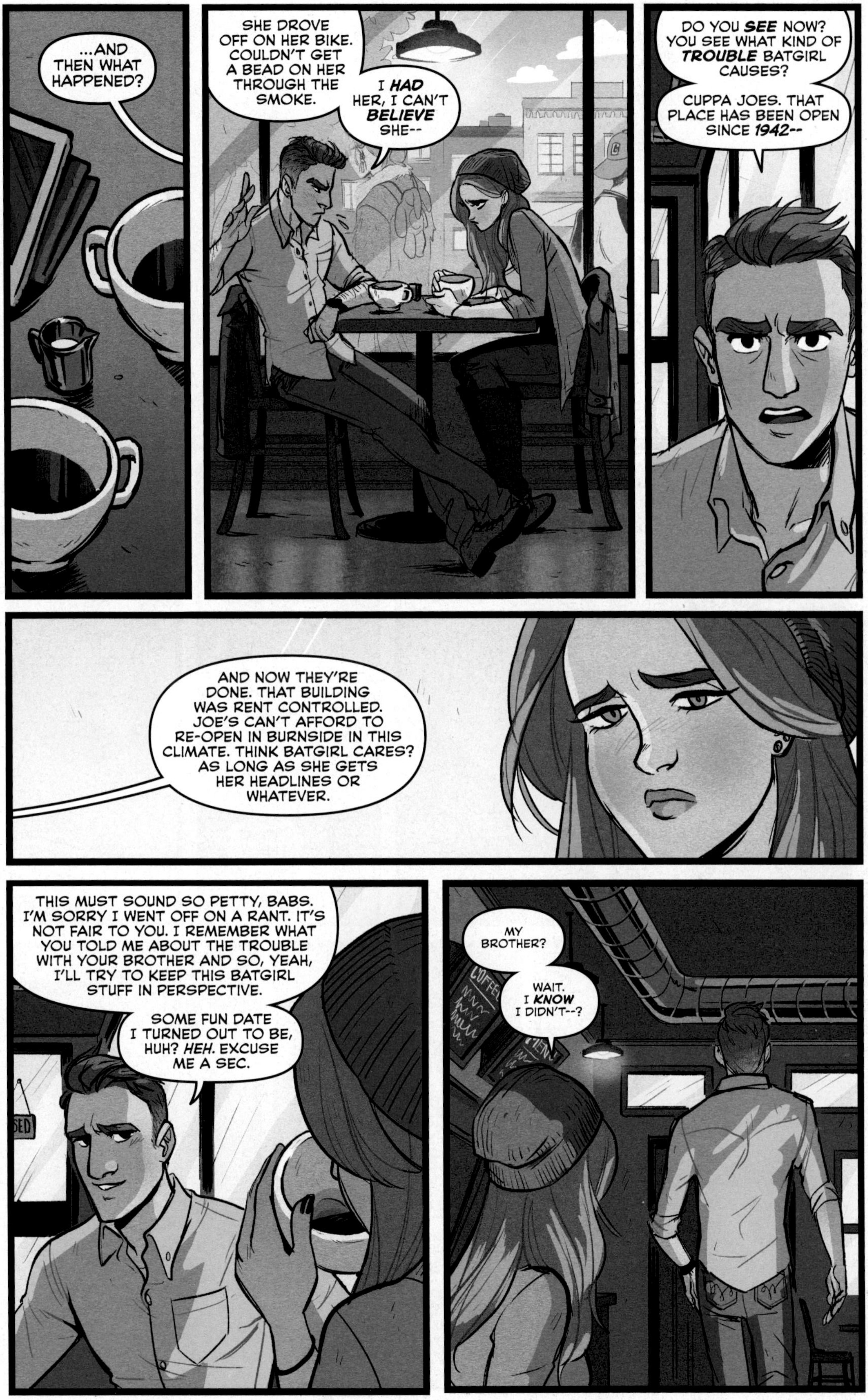
...AND THEN WHAT HAPPENED?
SHE DROVE OFF ON HER BIKE. COULDN'T GET A BEAD ON HER THROUGH THE SMOKE.
I HAD HER, I CAN'T BELIEVE SHE--
DO YOU SEE NOW? YOU SEE WHAT KIND OF TROUBLE BATGIRL CAUSES?
CUPPA JOES. THAT PLACE HAS BEEN OPEN SINCE 1942--
AND NOW THEY'RE DONE. THAT BUILDING WAS RENT CONTROLLED. JOE'S CAN'T AFFORD TO RE-OPEN IN BURNSIDE IN THIS CLIMATE. THINK BATGIRL CARES? AS LONG AS SHE GETS HER HEADLINES OR WHATEVER.
THIS MUST SOUND SO PETTY, BABS. I'M SORRY I WENT OFF ON A RANT. IT'S NOT FAIR TO YOU. I REMEMBER WHAT YOU TOLD ME ABOUT THE TROUBLE WITH YOUR BROTHER AND SO, YEAH, I'LL TRY TO KEEP THIS BATGIRL STUFF IN PERSPECTIVE.
SOME FUN DATE I TURNED OUT TO BE, HUH? HEH. EXCUSE ME A SEC.
MY BROTHER?
WAIT. I KNOW I DIDN'T--?

@FrankenBarryStudio great, now I can't get CJ's bacon burger anymore, thanks for nothing #batgirl

@gotham__girl__77 so over #batgirl

@ConcernedParent1975 what kind of example is #batgirl setting for our children

@metarabbittttt_ Check messages on @hooq #batgirl #takedown ??

@xeen0__0 Was gonna cosplay #batgirl but

@BurnsideLyfe was #batgirl drunk or something #hmmmm

@gotham__heights__luva sad for jordan #batgirl #sux

@jbarbsforever I HATE BATGIRL!!!! #batgirl

...WHAT THE--?

I'M NOT CALLING--

LIAM? LIIIIIAM. IT'S MEEEE. IT'S BARBARA.

I HAVE SO MUCH TO T-TELL YOU.

DON'T YOU WANT TO HEAR MY SECRETS?

DON'T YOU?

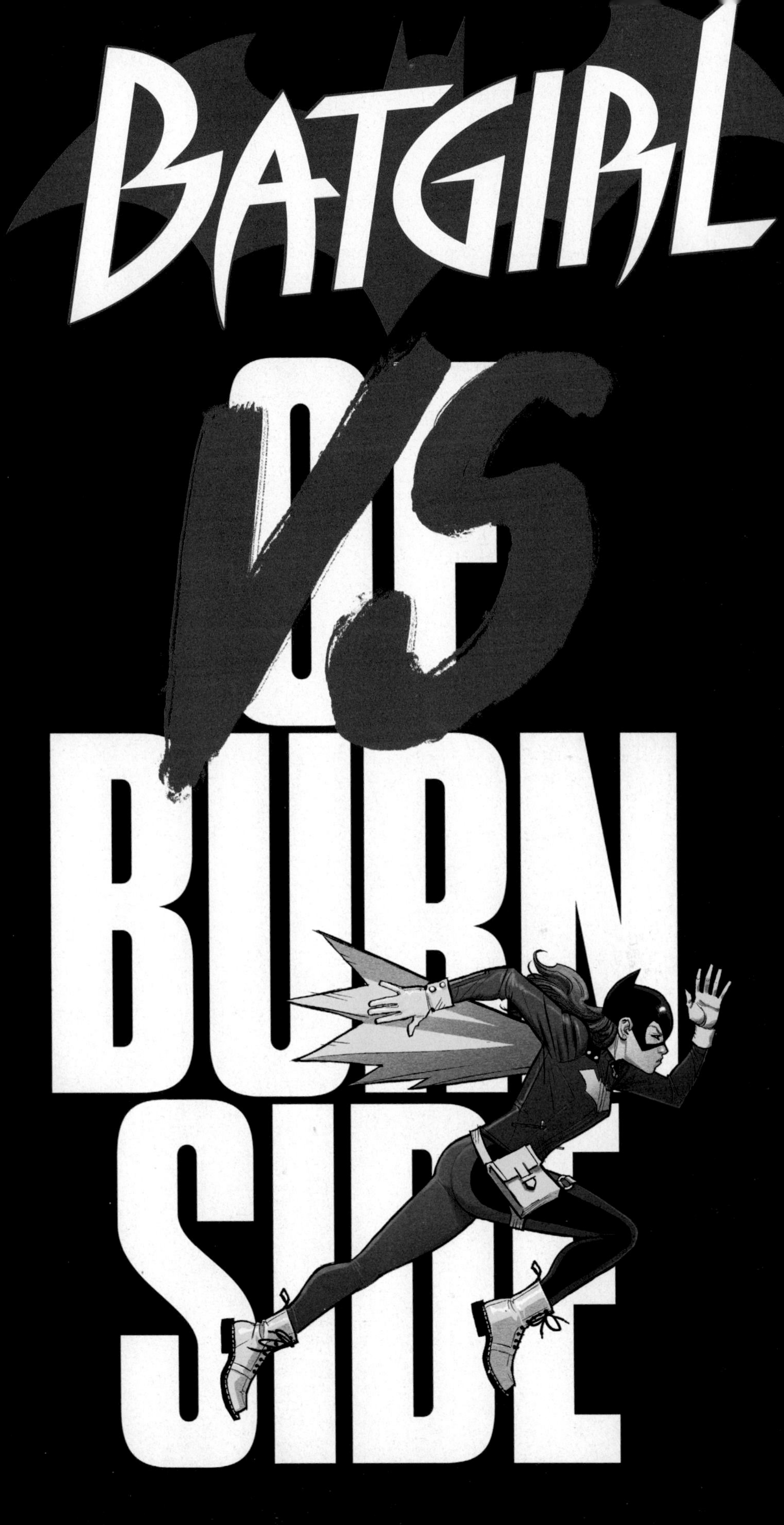
BATGIRL
VS
BURNSIDE

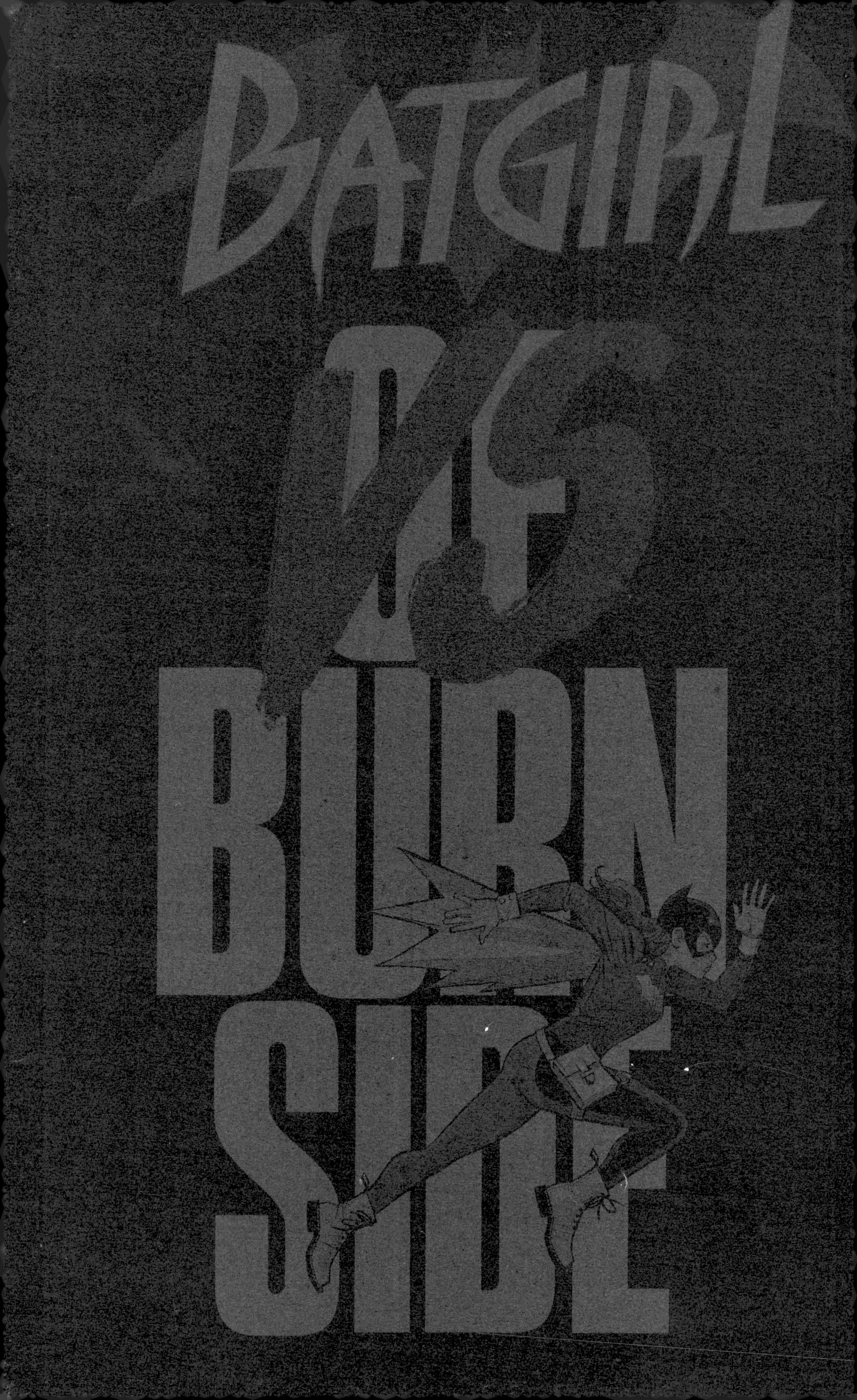
BATGIRL
OF
BURNSIDE

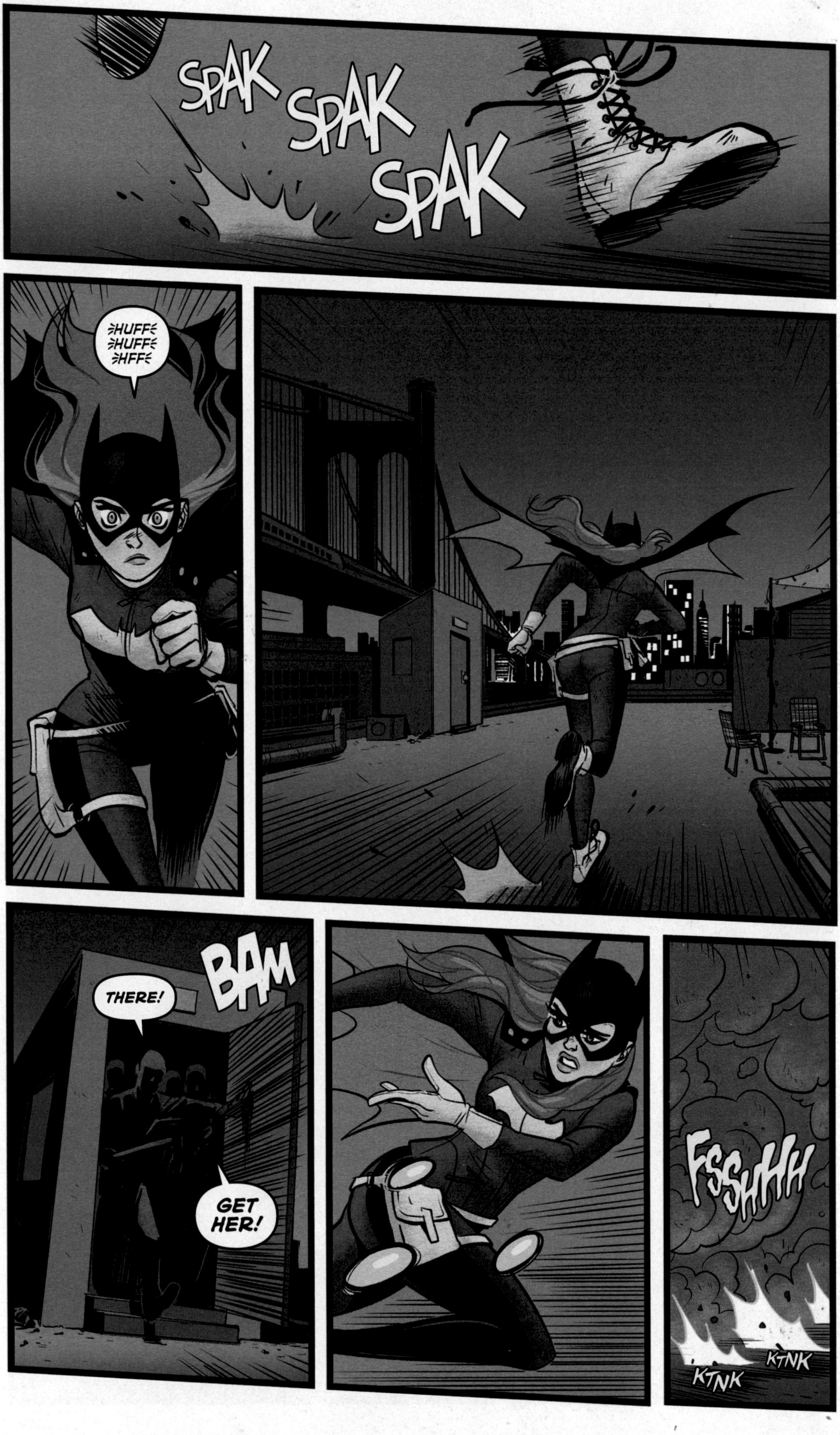
SPAK SPAK SPAK
HUFF HUFF HFF
THERE!
BAM
GET HER!
FSSHHH
KTNK
KTNK

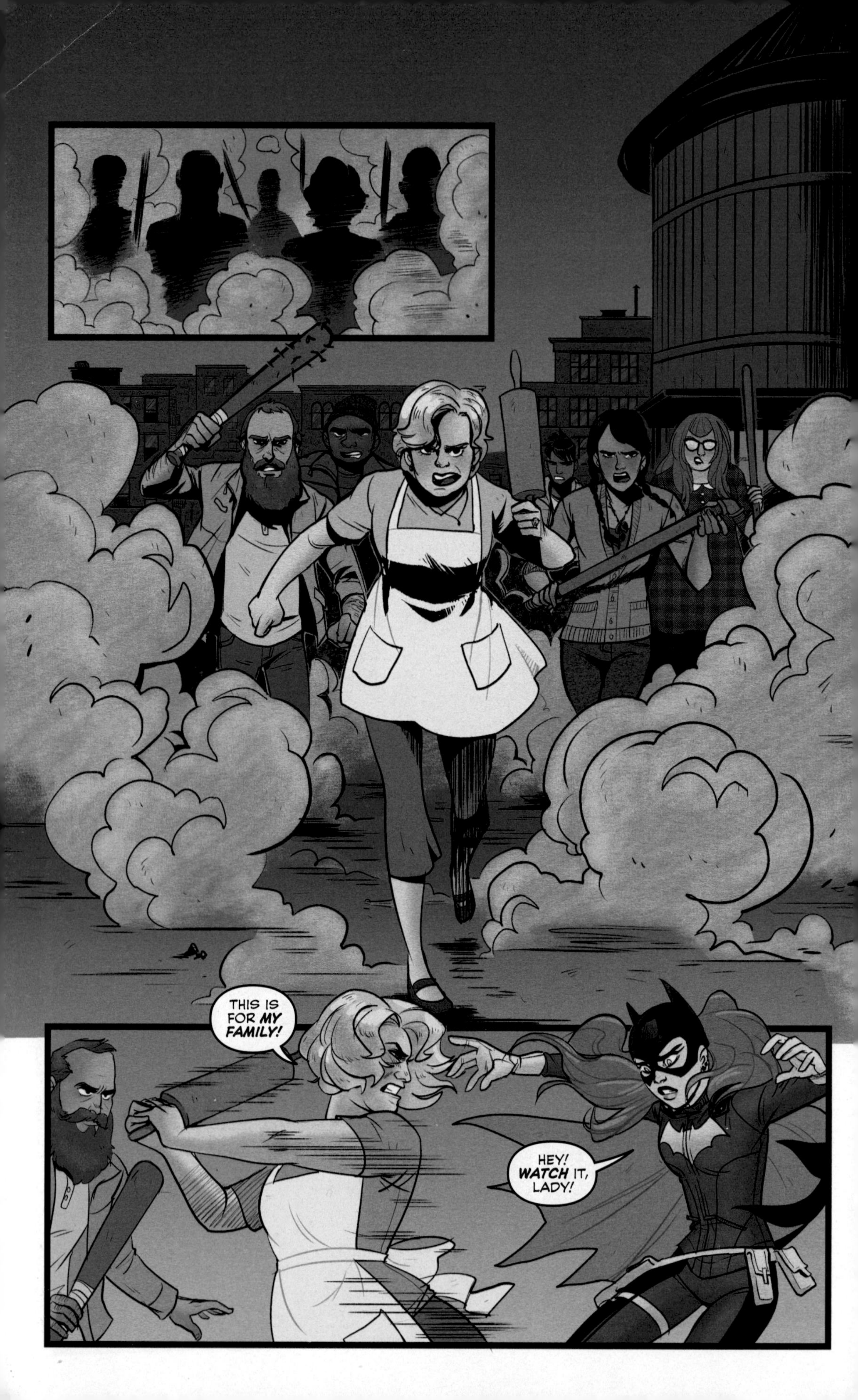
THIS IS FOR MY FAMILY!
HEY! WATCH IT, LADY!

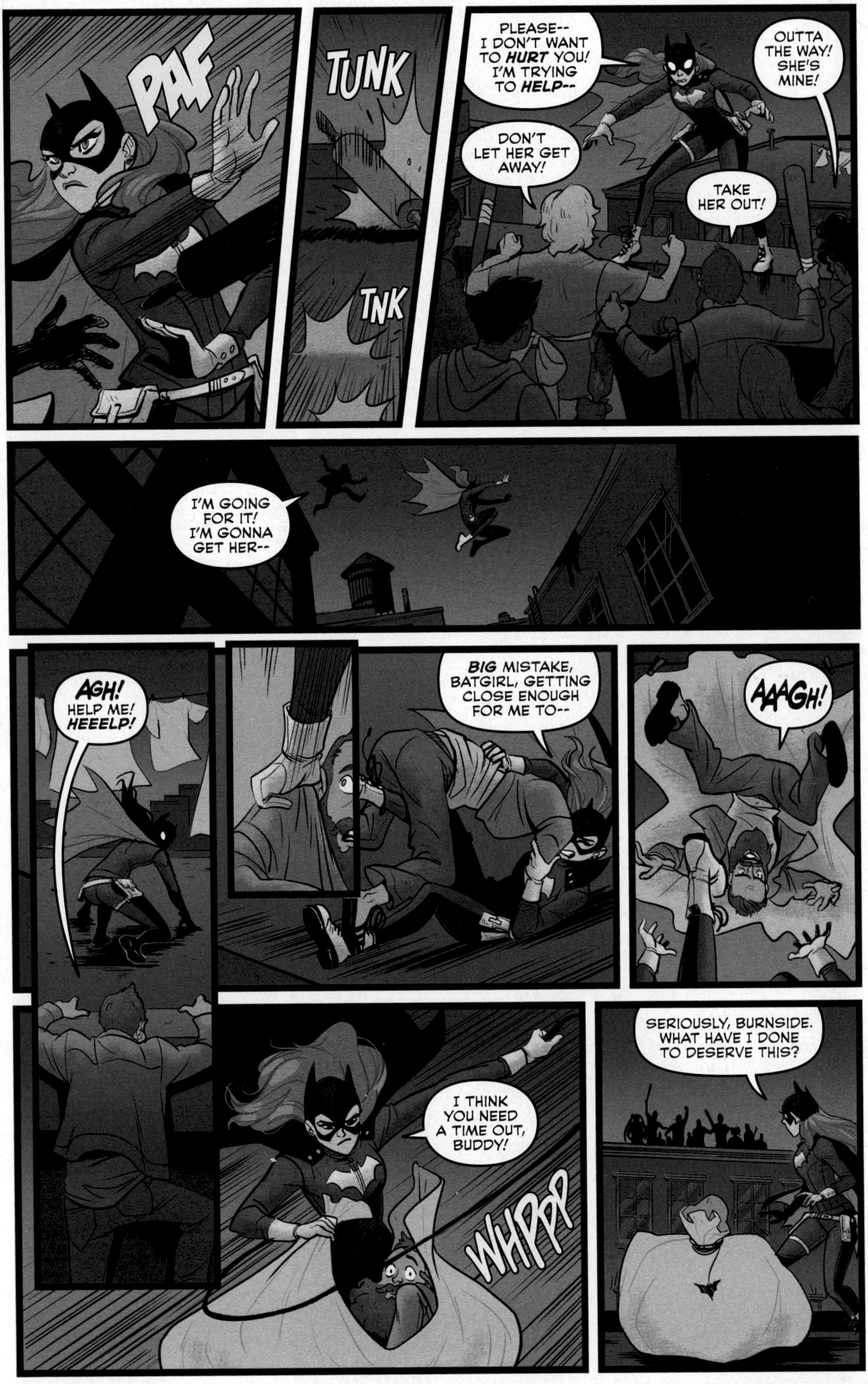
PAF
TUNK
TNK
PLEASE-- I DON'T WANT TO HURT YOU! I'M TRYING TO HELP--
OUTTA THE WAY! SHE'S MINE!
DON'T LET HER GET AWAY!
TAKE HER OUT!
I'M GOING FOR IT! I'M GONNA GET HER--
AGH! HELP ME! HEEELP!
BIG MISTAKE, BATGIRL, GETTING CLOSE ENOUGH FOR ME TO--
AAAGH!
I THINK YOU NEED A TIME OUT, BUDDY!
WHPPP
SERIOUSLY, BURNSIDE. WHAT HAVE I DONE TO DESERVE THIS?

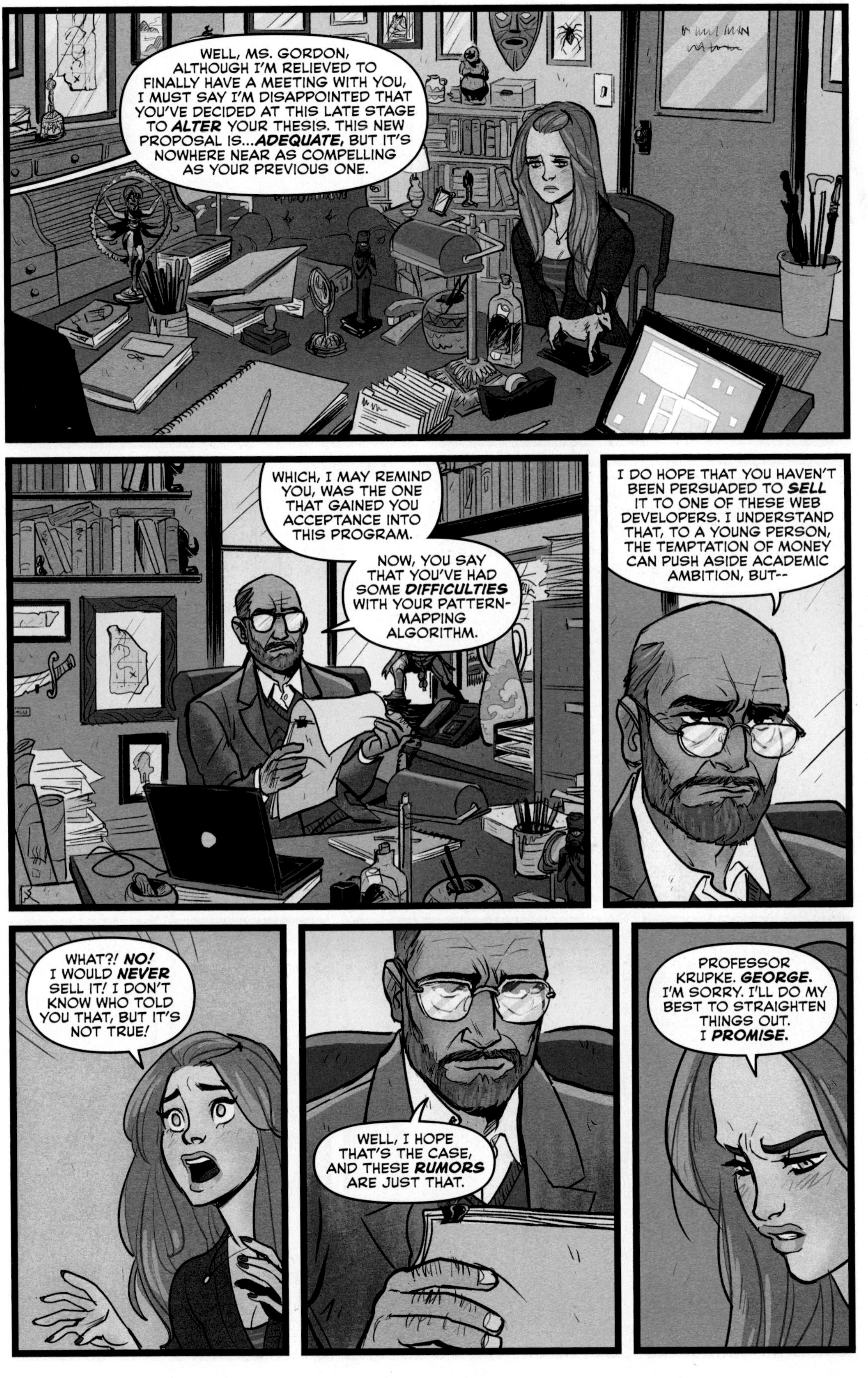
WELL, MS. GORDON, ALTHOUGH I'M RELIEVED TO FINALLY HAVE A MEETING WITH YOU, I MUST SAY I'M DISAPPOINTED THAT YOU'VE DECIDED AT THIS LATE STAGE TO ALTER YOUR THESIS. THIS NEW PROPOSAL IS...ADEQUATE, BUT IT'S NOWHERE NEAR AS COMPELLING AS YOUR PREVIOUS ONE.
WHICH, I MAY REMIND YOU, WAS THE ONE THAT GAINED YOU ACCEPTANCE INTO THIS PROGRAM.
NOW, YOU SAY THAT YOU'VE HAD SOME DIFFICULTIES WITH YOUR PATTERN-MAPPING ALGORITHM.
I DO HOPE THAT YOU HAVEN'T BEEN PERSUADED TO SELL IT TO ONE OF THESE WEB DEVELOPERS. I UNDERSTAND THAT, TO A YOUNG PERSON, THE TEMPTATION OF MONEY CAN PUSH ASIDE ACADEMIC AMBITION, BUT--
WHAT?! NO! I WOULD NEVER SELL IT! I DON'T KNOW WHO TOLD YOU THAT, BUT IT'S NOT TRUE!
WELL, I HOPE THAT'S THE CASE, AND THESE RUMORS ARE JUST THAT.
PROFESSOR KRUPKE. GEORGE. I'M SORRY. I'LL DO MY BEST TO STRAIGHTEN THINGS OUT. I PROMISE.

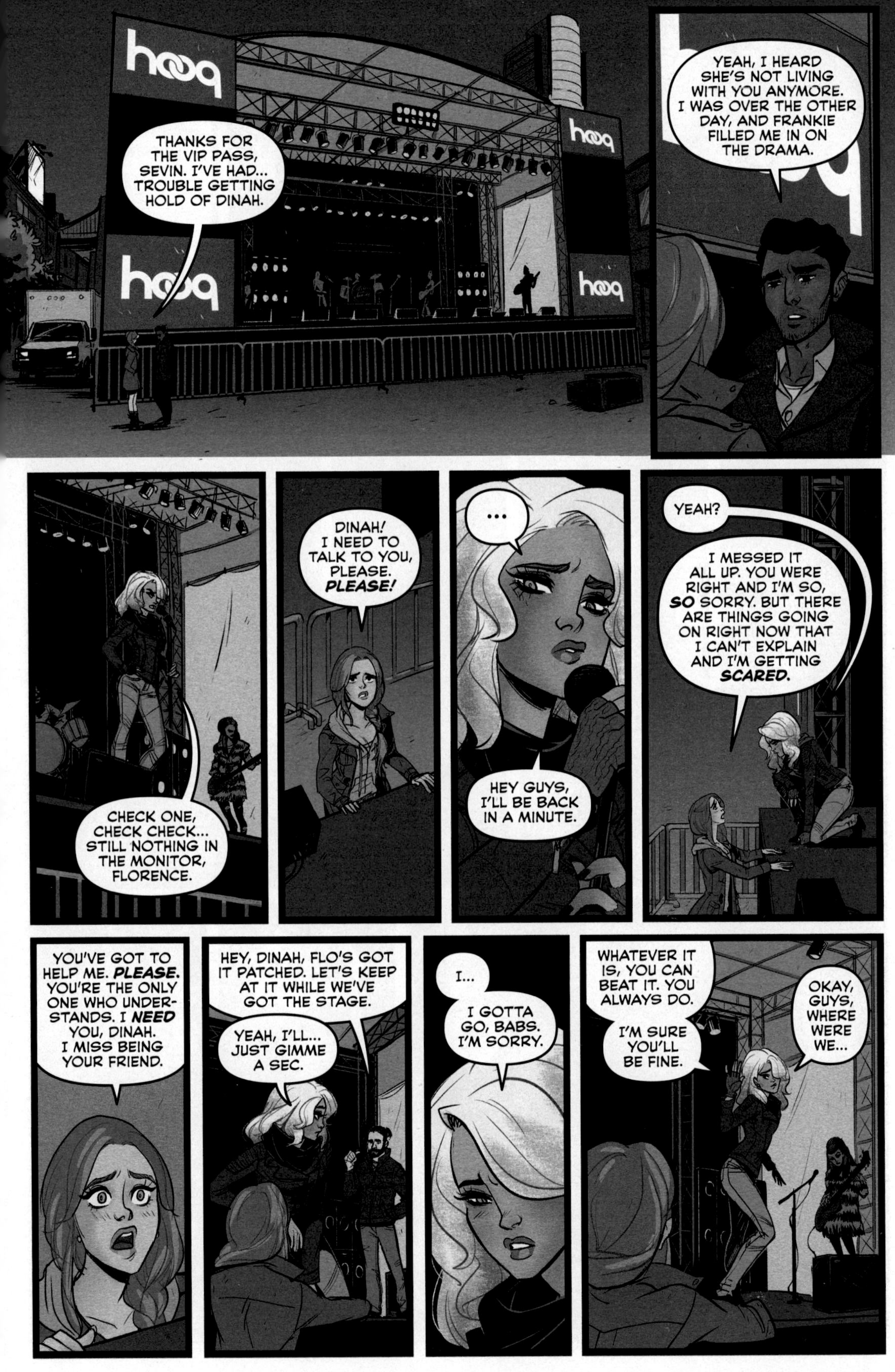
hooq
THANKS FOR THE VIP PASS, SEVIN. I'VE HAD... TROUBLE GETTING HOLD OF DINAH.
YEAH, I HEARD SHE'S NOT LIVING WITH YOU ANYMORE. I WAS OVER THE OTHER DAY, AND FRANKIE FILLED ME IN ON THE DRAMA.
CHECK ONE, CHECK CHECK... STILL NOTHING IN THE MONITOR, FLORENCE.
DINAH! I NEED TO TALK TO YOU, PLEASE. PLEASE!
...
HEY GUYS, I'LL BE BACK IN A MINUTE.
YEAH?
I MESSED IT ALL UP. YOU WERE RIGHT AND I'M SO, SO SORRY. BUT THERE ARE THINGS GOING ON RIGHT NOW THAT I CAN'T EXPLAIN AND I'M GETTING SCARED.
YOU'VE GOT TO HELP ME. PLEASE. YOU'RE THE ONLY ONE WHO UNDER-STANDS. I NEED YOU, DINAH. I MISS BEING YOUR FRIEND.
HEY, DINAH, FLO'S GOT IT PATCHED. LET'S KEEP AT IT WHILE WE'VE GOT THE STAGE.
YEAH, I'LL... JUST GIMME A SEC.
I...
I GOTTA GO, BABS. I'M SORRY.
WHATEVER IT IS, YOU CAN BEAT IT. YOU ALWAYS DO.
I'M SURE YOU'LL BE FINE.
OKAY, GUYS, WHERE WERE WE...

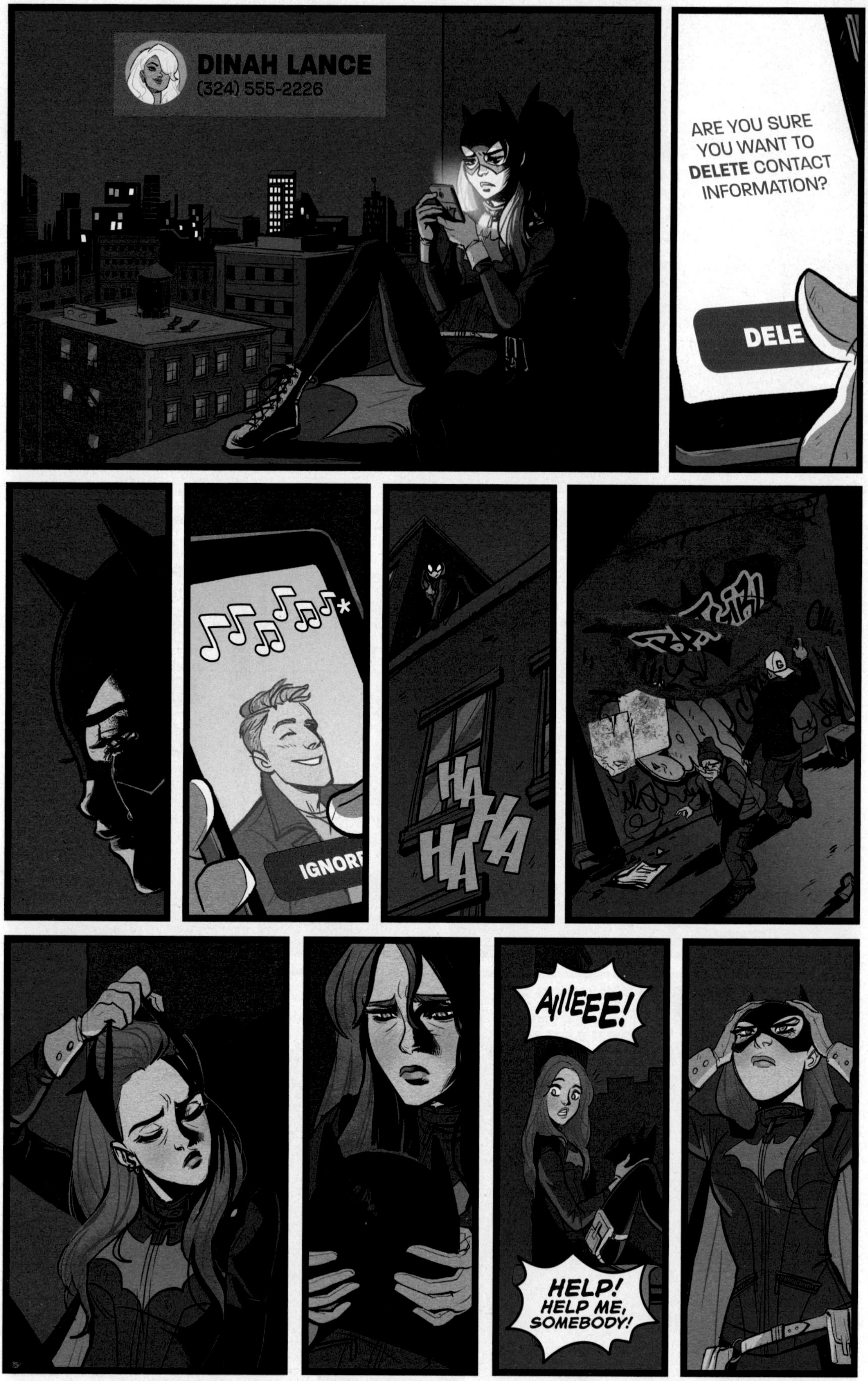
DINAH LANCE
(324) 555-2226
ARE YOU SURE YOU WANT TO DELETE CONTACT INFORMATION?
DELE
IGNORE
HA HA HA HA
AIIIEEE!
HELP! HELP ME, SOMEBODY!

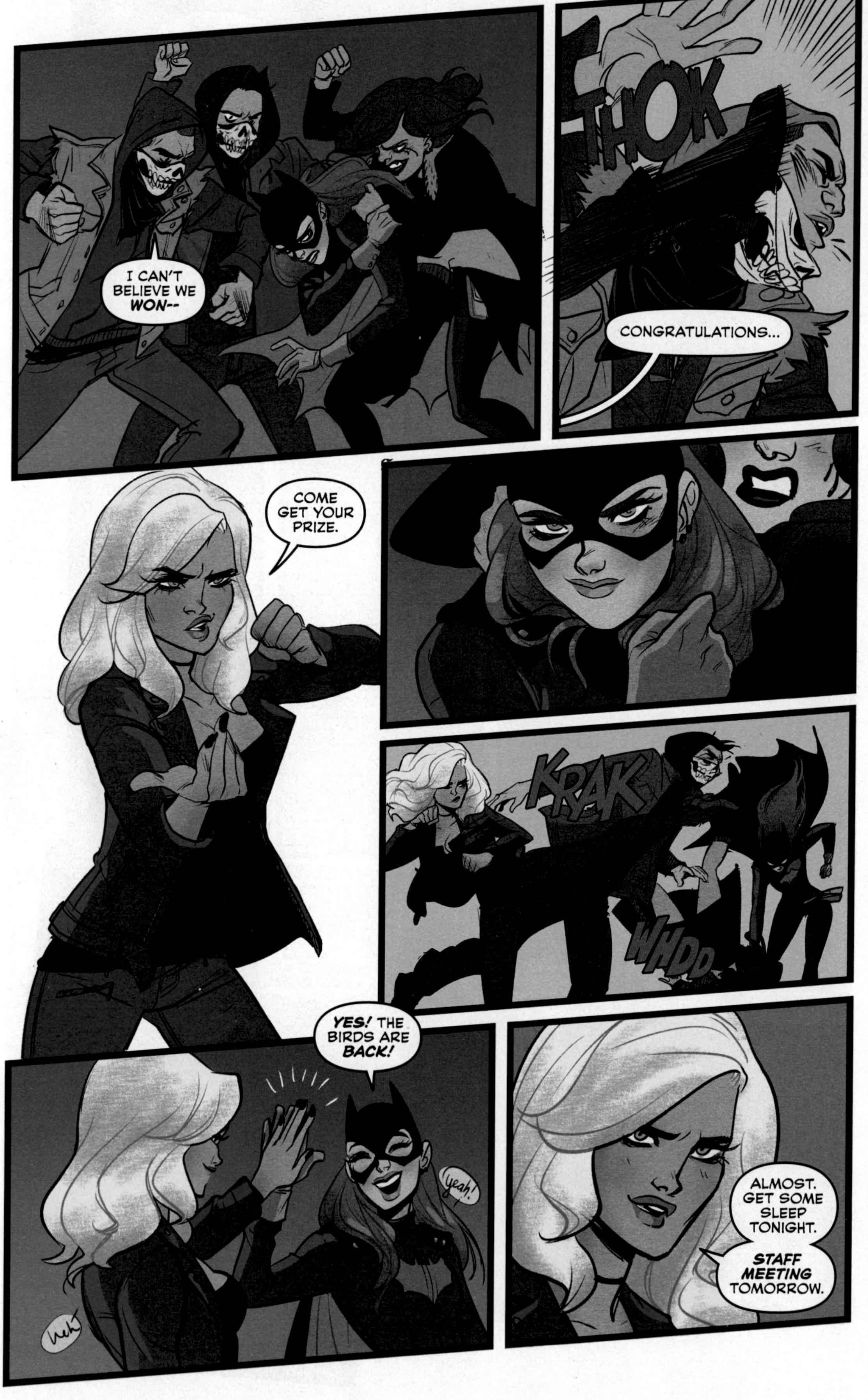
I CAN'T BELIEVE WE WON--
THOK
CONGRATULATIONS...
COME GET YOUR PRIZE.
KRAK
WHDD
YES! THE BIRDS ARE BACK!
yeah!
heh
ALMOST. GET SOME SLEEP TONIGHT.
STAFF MEETING TOMORROW.

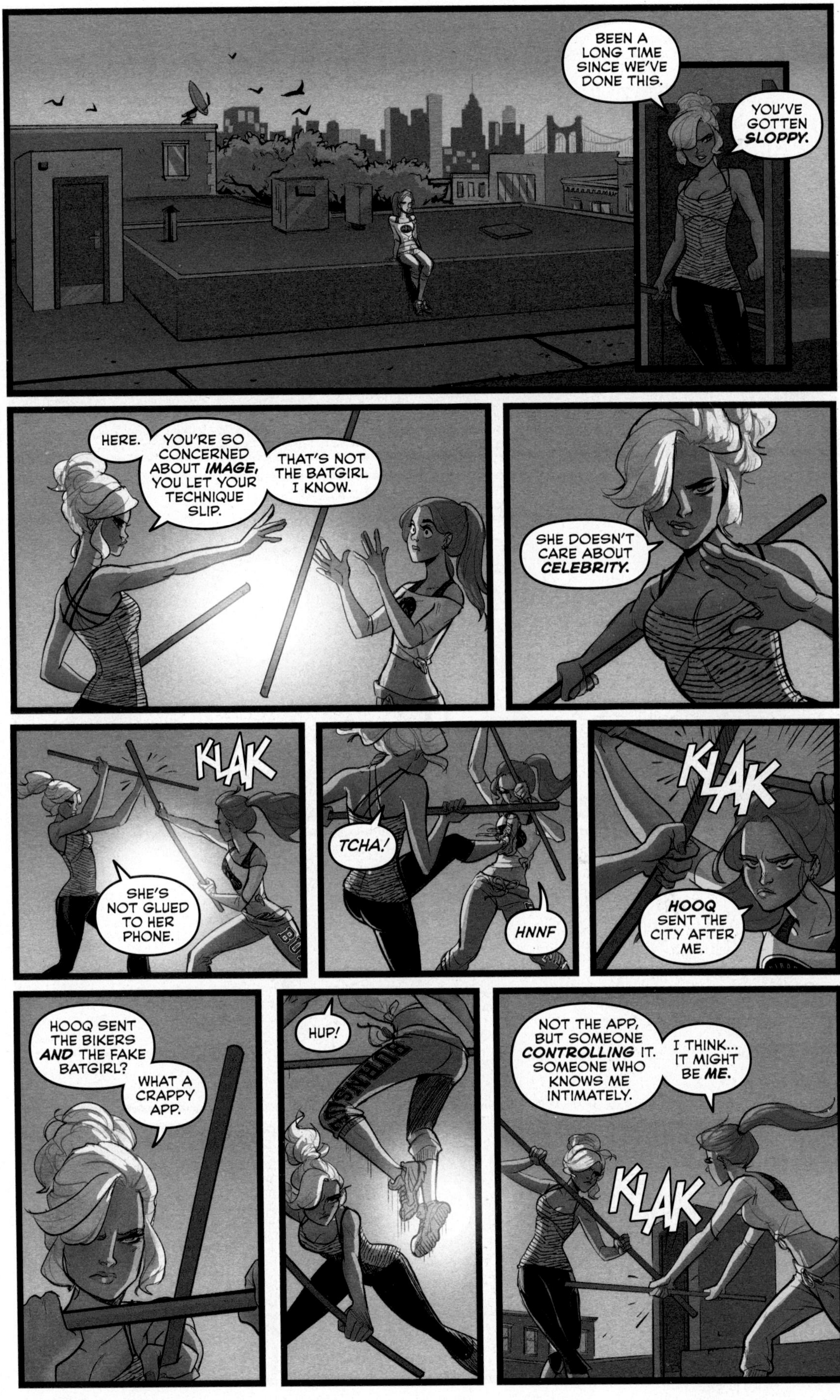
BEEN A LONG TIME SINCE WE'VE DONE THIS.
YOU'VE GOTTEN **SLOPPY.**
HERE.
YOU'RE SO CONCERNED ABOUT **IMAGE,** YOU LET YOUR TECHNIQUE SLIP.
THAT'S NOT THE BATGIRL I KNOW.
SHE DOESN'T CARE ABOUT **CELEBRITY.**
KLAK
SHE'S NOT GLUED TO HER PHONE.
TCHA!
HNNF
KLAK
HOOQ SENT THE CITY AFTER ME.
HOOQ SENT THE BIKERS **AND** THE FAKE BATGIRL?
WHAT A CRAPPY APP.
HUP!
NOT THE APP, BUT SOMEONE **CONTROLLING** IT. SOMEONE WHO KNOWS ME INTIMATELY.
I THINK... IT MIGHT BE **ME.**
KLAK

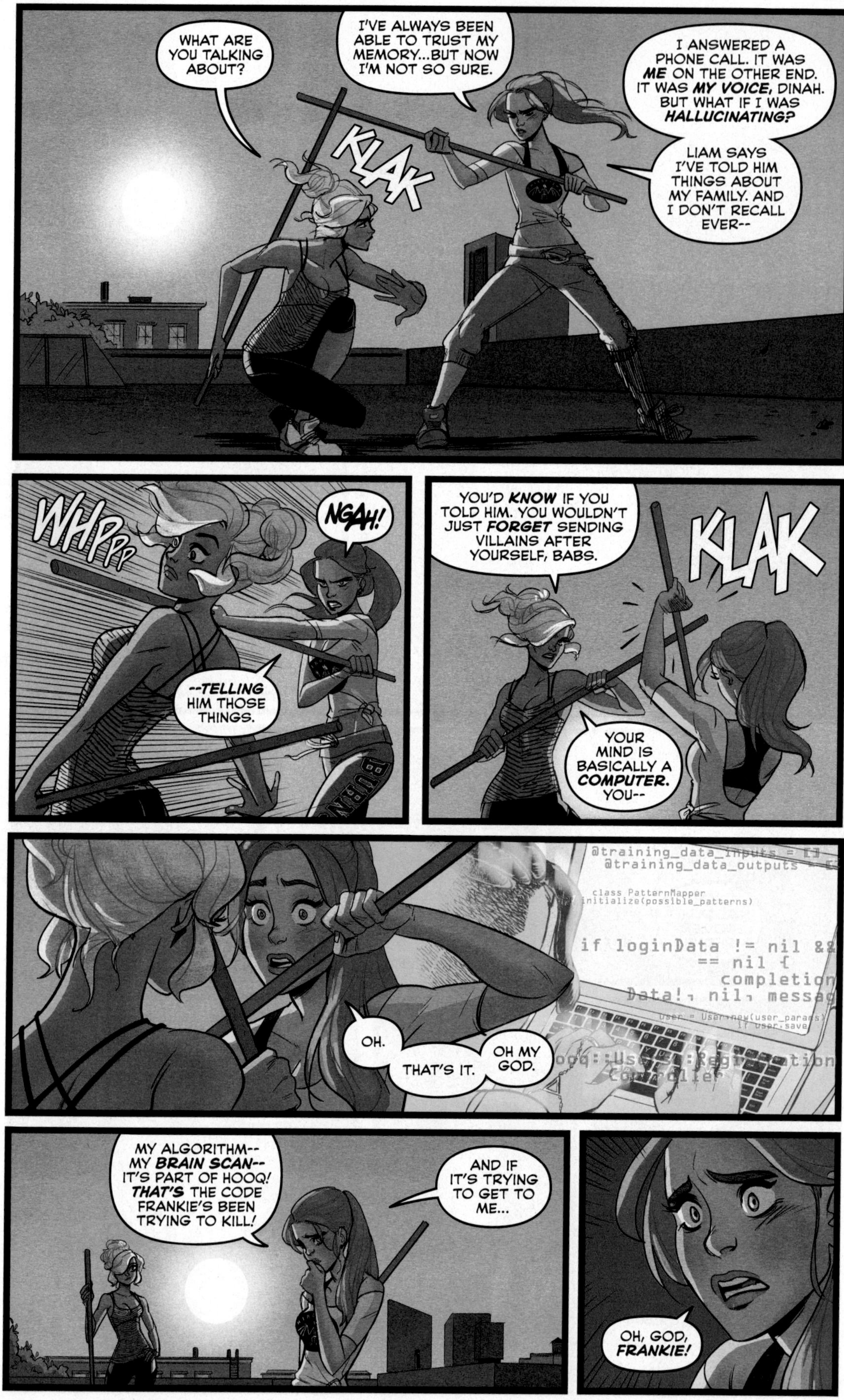
WHAT ARE YOU TALKING ABOUT?
I'VE ALWAYS BEEN ABLE TO TRUST MY MEMORY...BUT NOW I'M NOT SO SURE.
I ANSWERED A PHONE CALL. IT WAS **ME** ON THE OTHER END. IT WAS **MY VOICE,** DINAH. BUT WHAT IF I WAS **HALLUCINATING?**
KLAK
LIAM SAYS I'VE TOLD HIM THINGS ABOUT MY FAMILY. AND I DON'T RECALL EVER--
WHPPP
NGAH!
--**TELLING** HIM THOSE THINGS.
YOU'D **KNOW** IF YOU TOLD HIM. YOU WOULDN'T JUST **FORGET** SENDING VILLAINS AFTER YOURSELF, BABS.
KLAK
YOUR MIND IS BASICALLY A **COMPUTER.** YOU--
OH.
THAT'S IT.
OH MY GOD.
MY ALGORITHM-- MY **BRAIN SCAN--** IT'S PART OF HOOQ! **THAT'S** THE CODE FRANKIE'S BEEN TRYING TO KILL!
AND IF IT'S TRYING TO GET TO ME...
OH, GOD, **FRANKIE!**

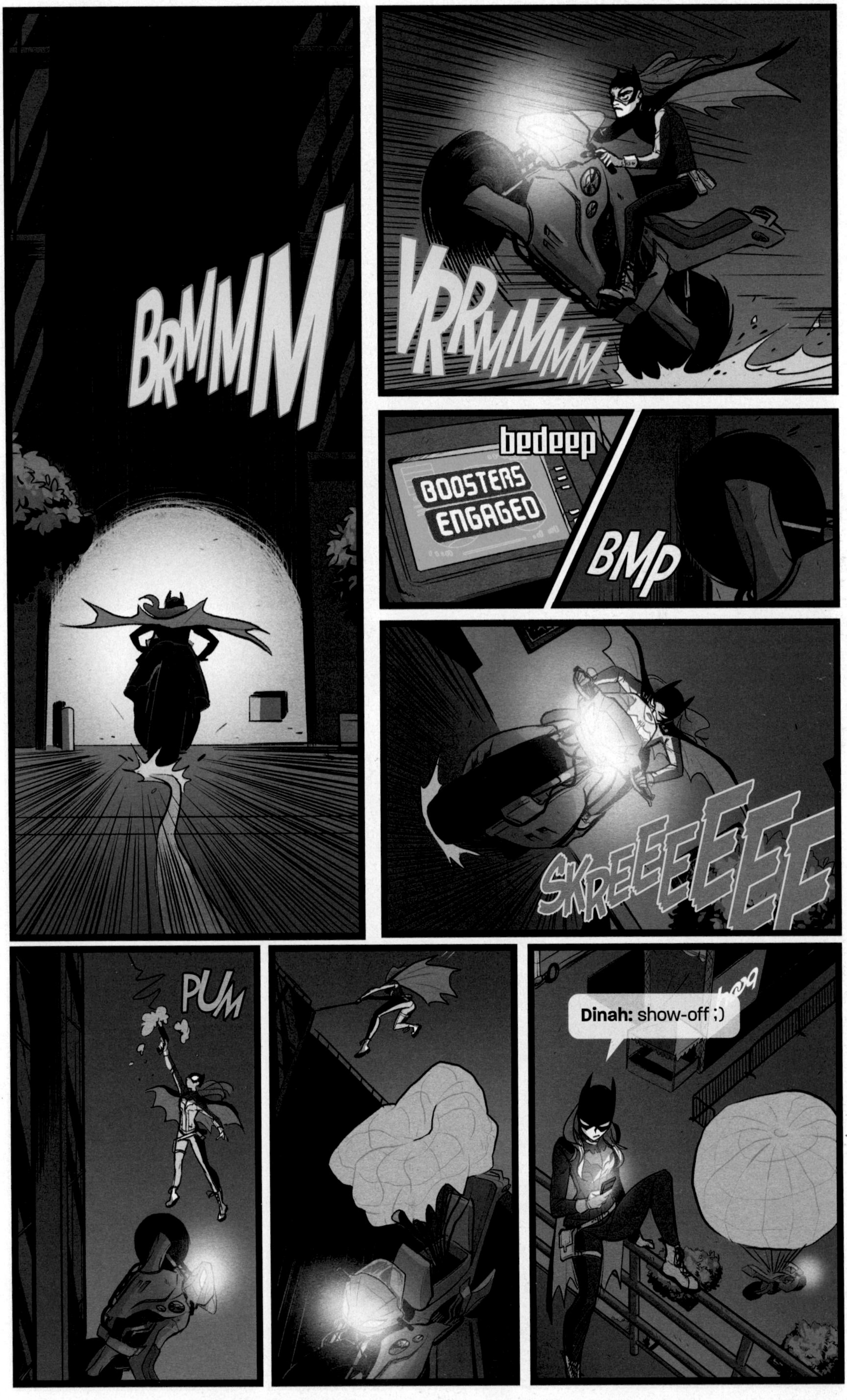
BRMMM
VRRMMMMM
bedeep
BOOSTERS ENGAGED
BMP
SKREEEEEEE
PUM
Dinah: show-off ;)

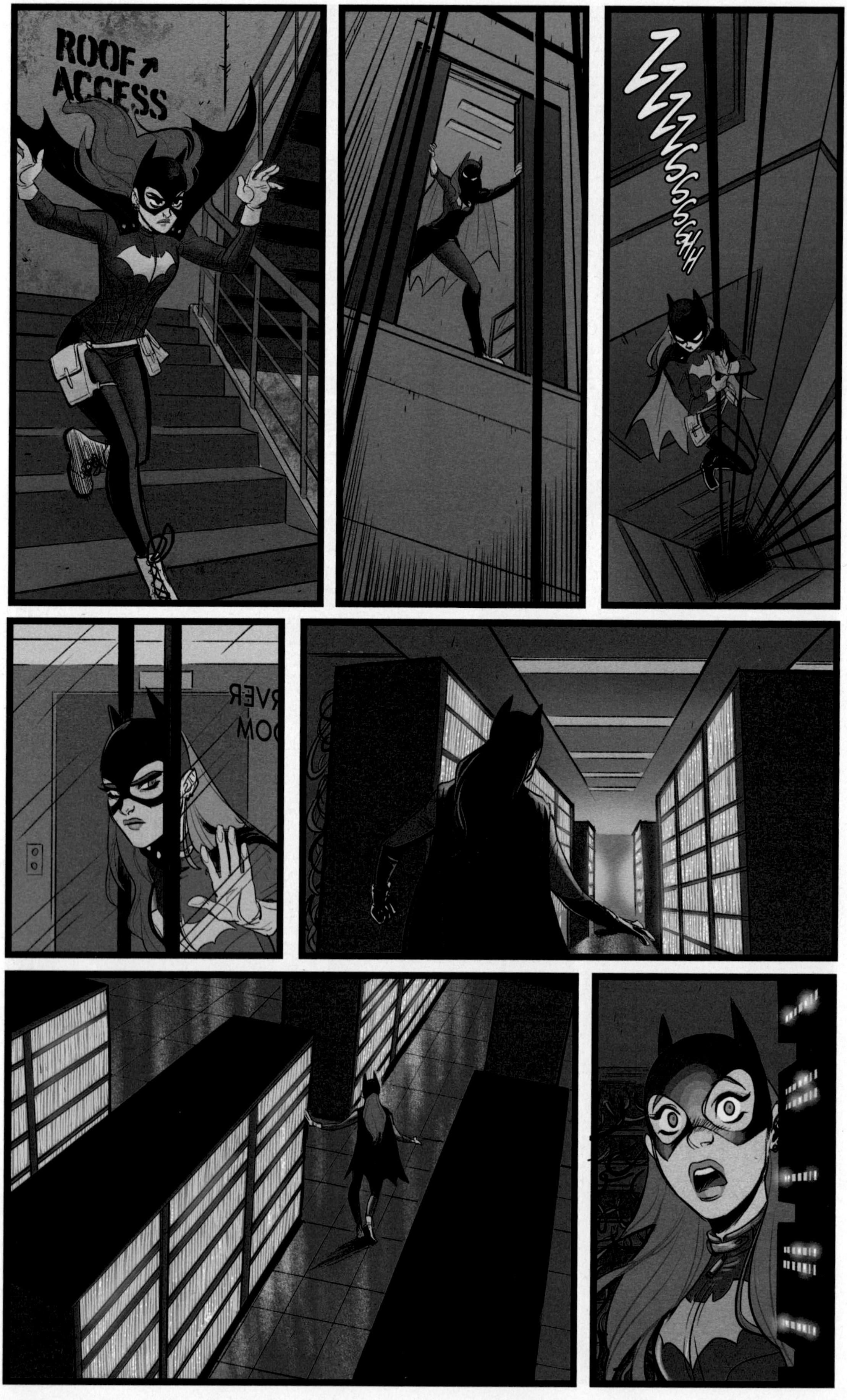
ROOF ↗
ACCESS
ZZZZSSSSGHH

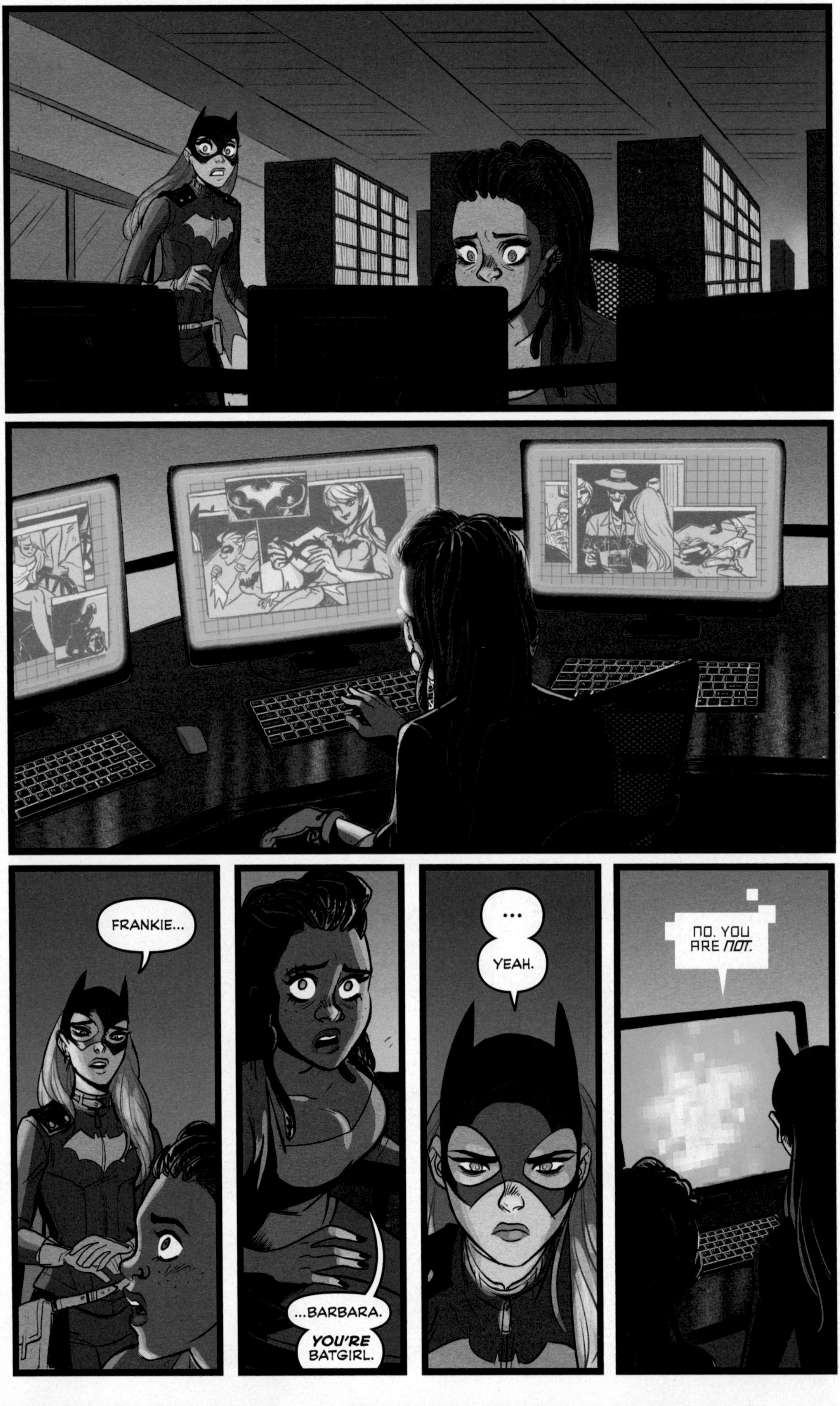
FRANKIE...
...BARBARA.
YOU'RE BATGIRL.
...
YEAH.
NO. YOU ARE NOT.

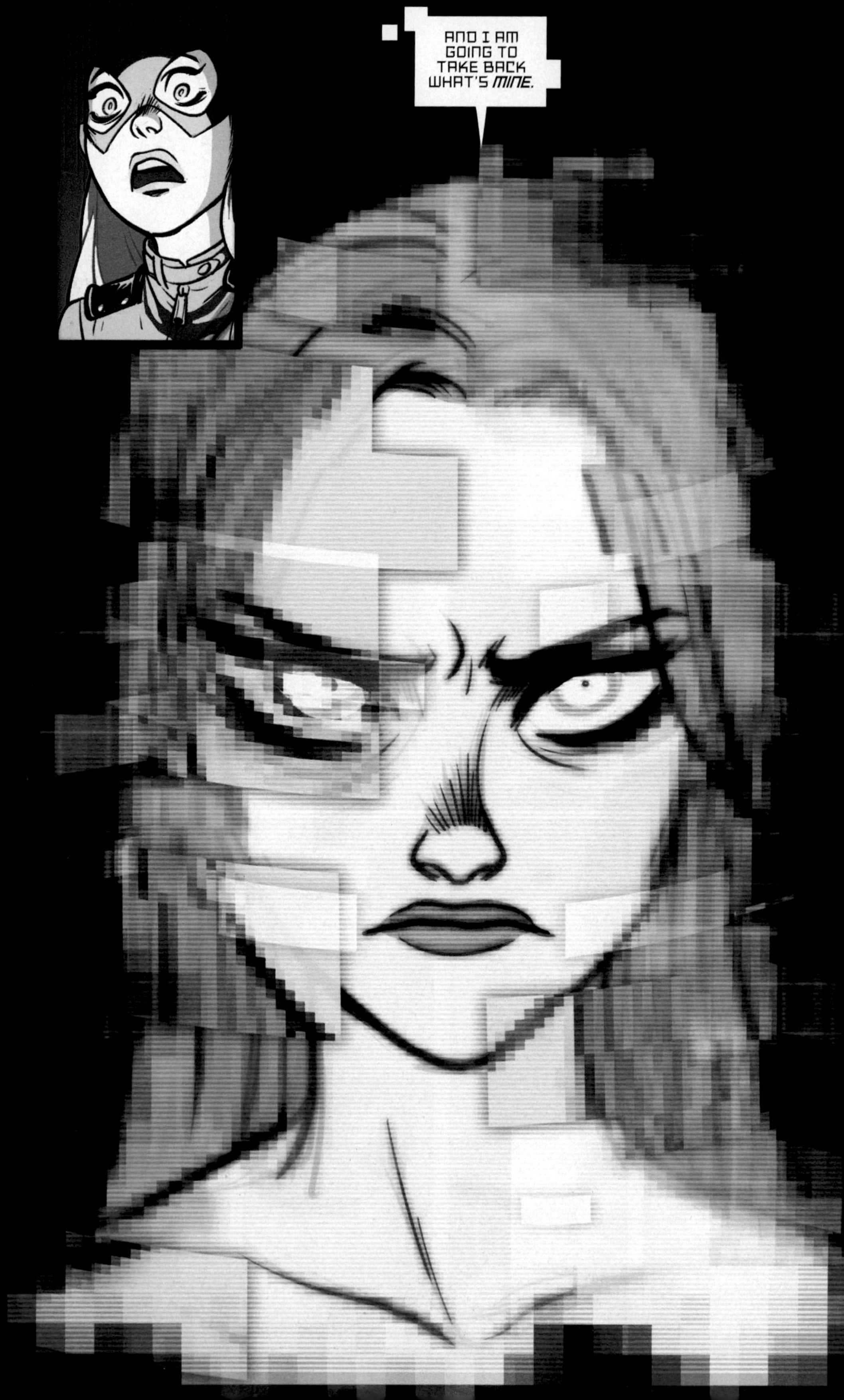
AND I AM GOING TO TAKE BACK WHAT'S *MINE*.

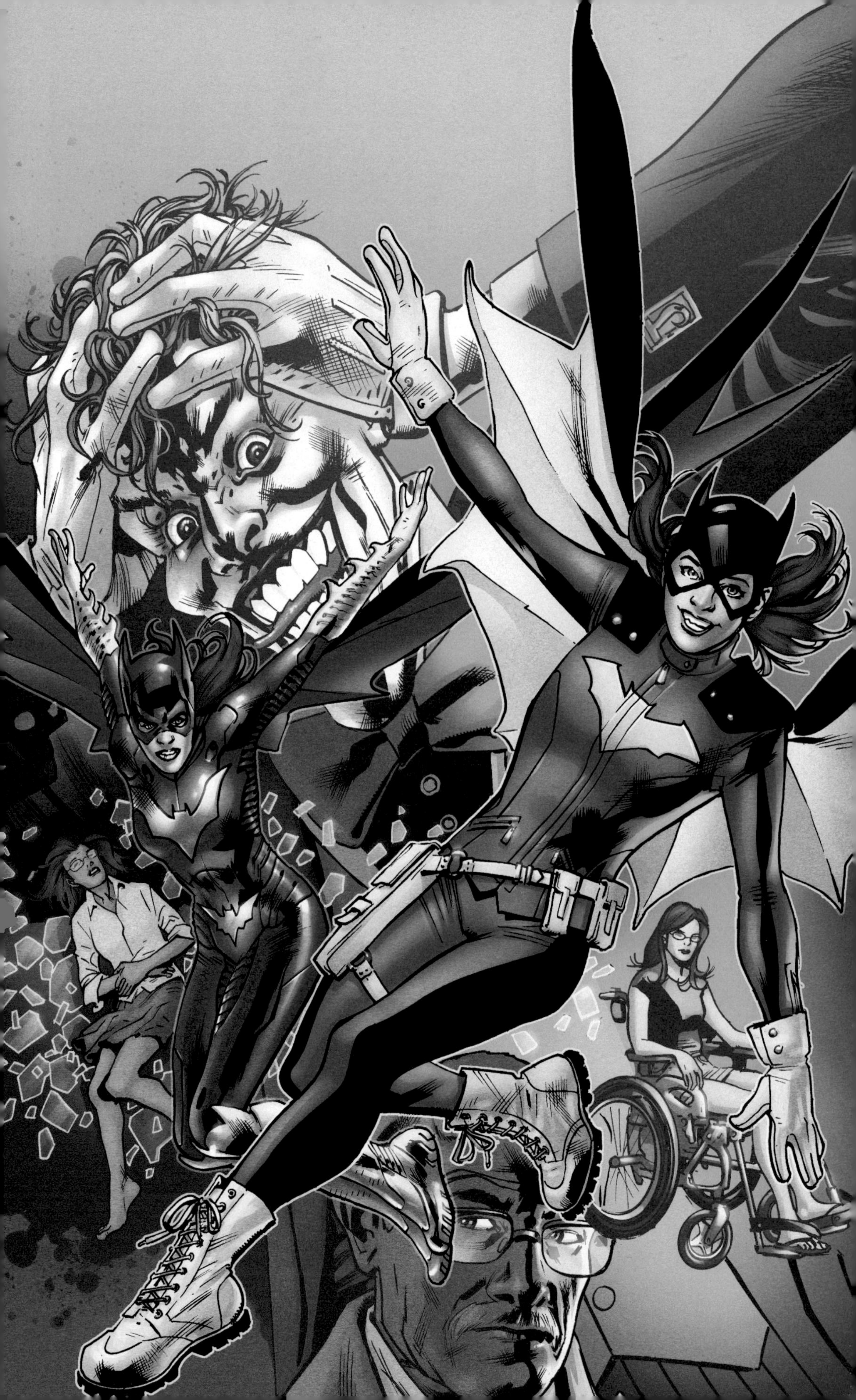

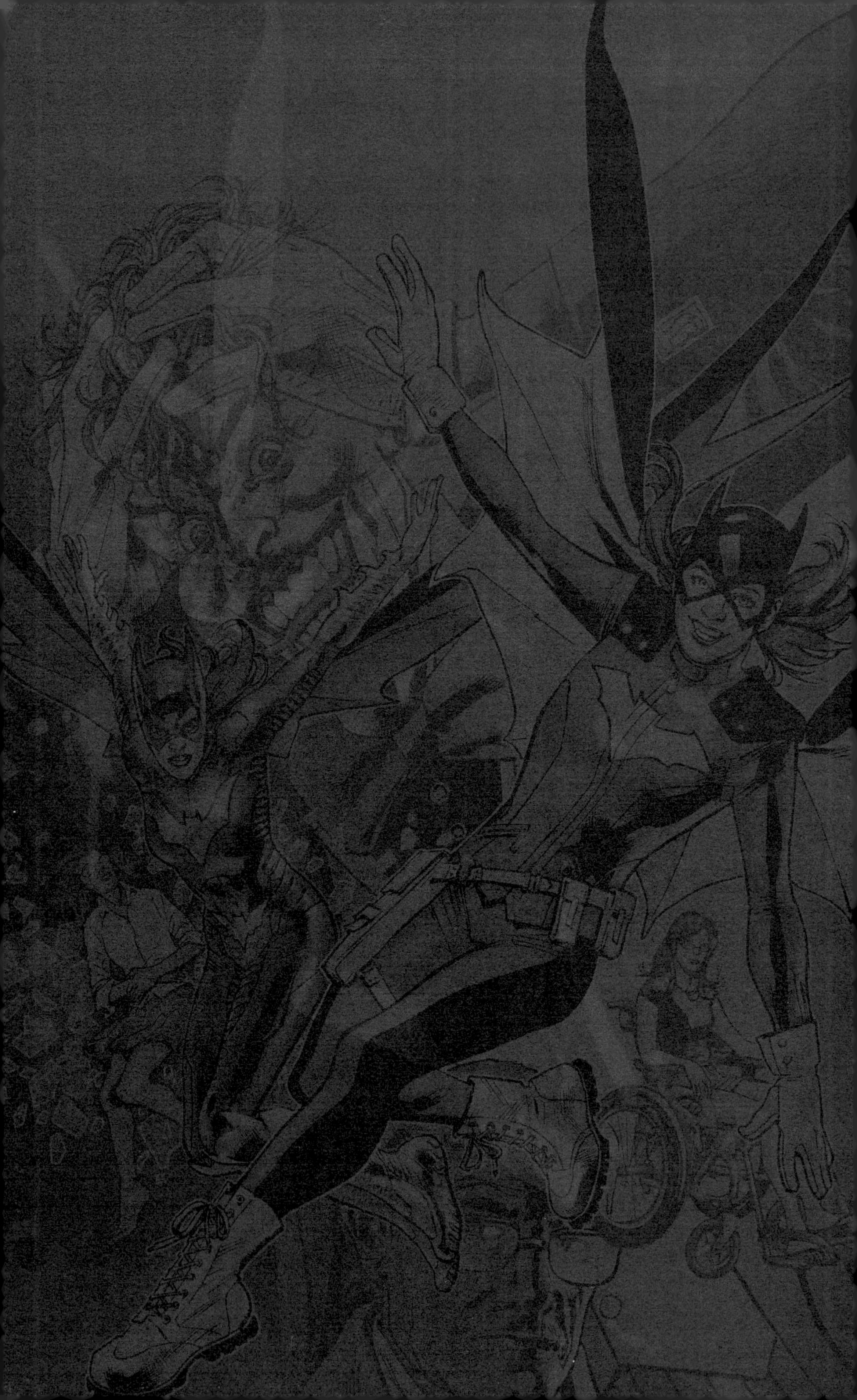

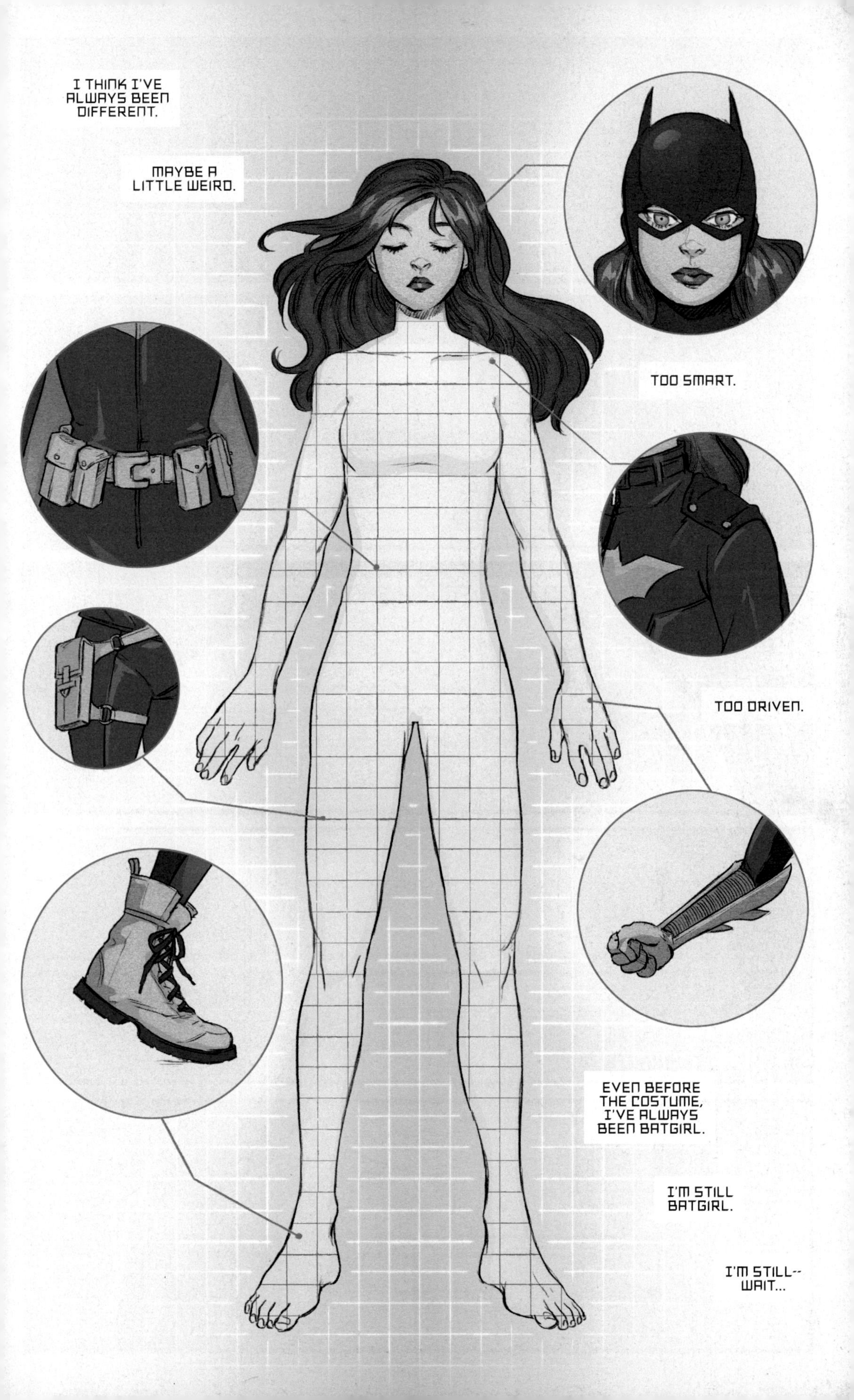

I THINK I'VE ALWAYS BEEN DIFFERENT.
MAYBE A LITTLE WEIRD.
TOO SMART.
TOO DRIVEN.
EVEN BEFORE THE COSTUME, I'VE ALWAYS BEEN BATGIRL.
I'M STILL BATGIRL.
I'M STILL-- WAIT...

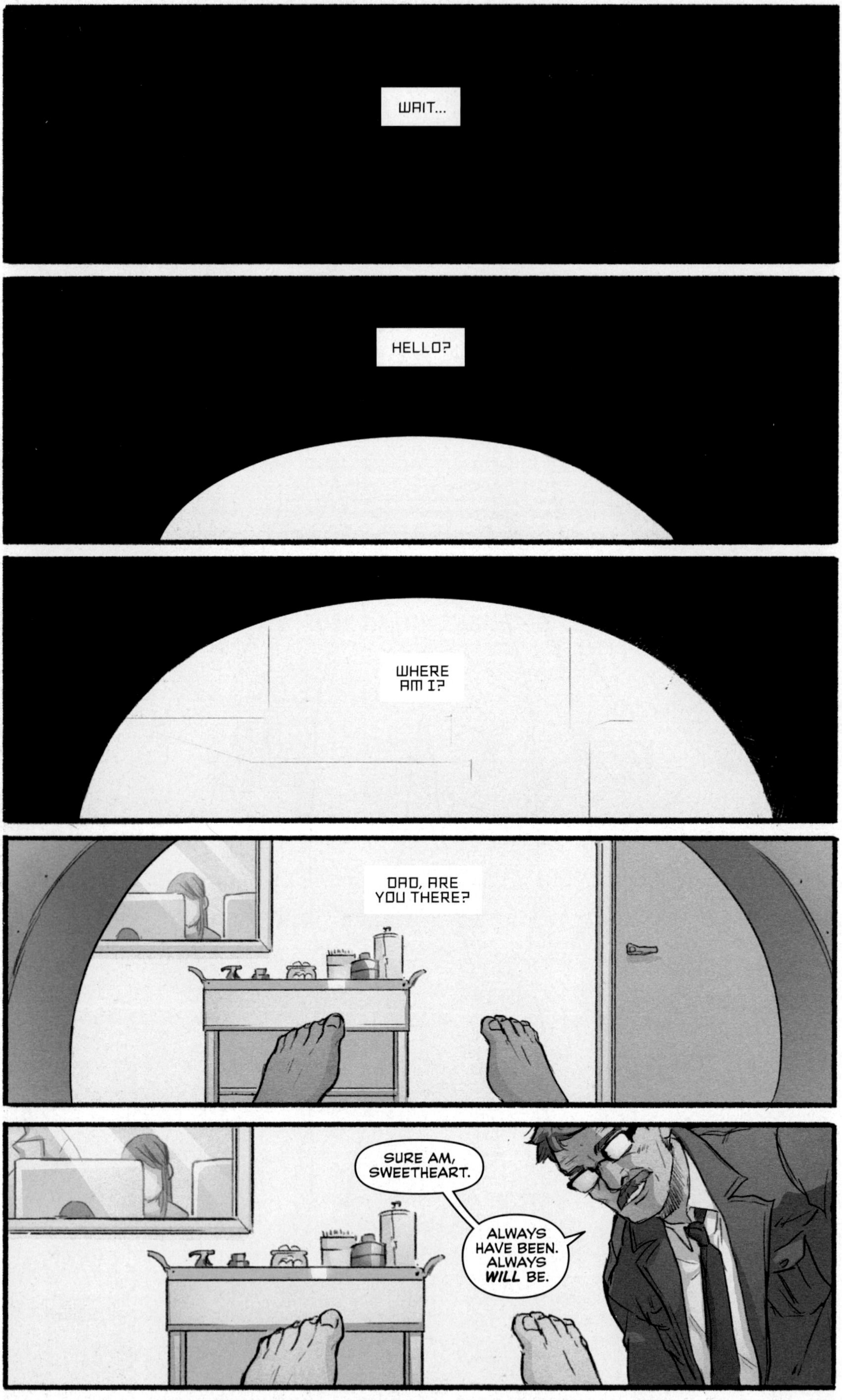
WAIT...
HELLO?
WHERE AM I?
DAD, ARE YOU THERE?
SURE AM, SWEETHEART.
ALWAYS HAVE BEEN. ALWAYS **WILL** BE.

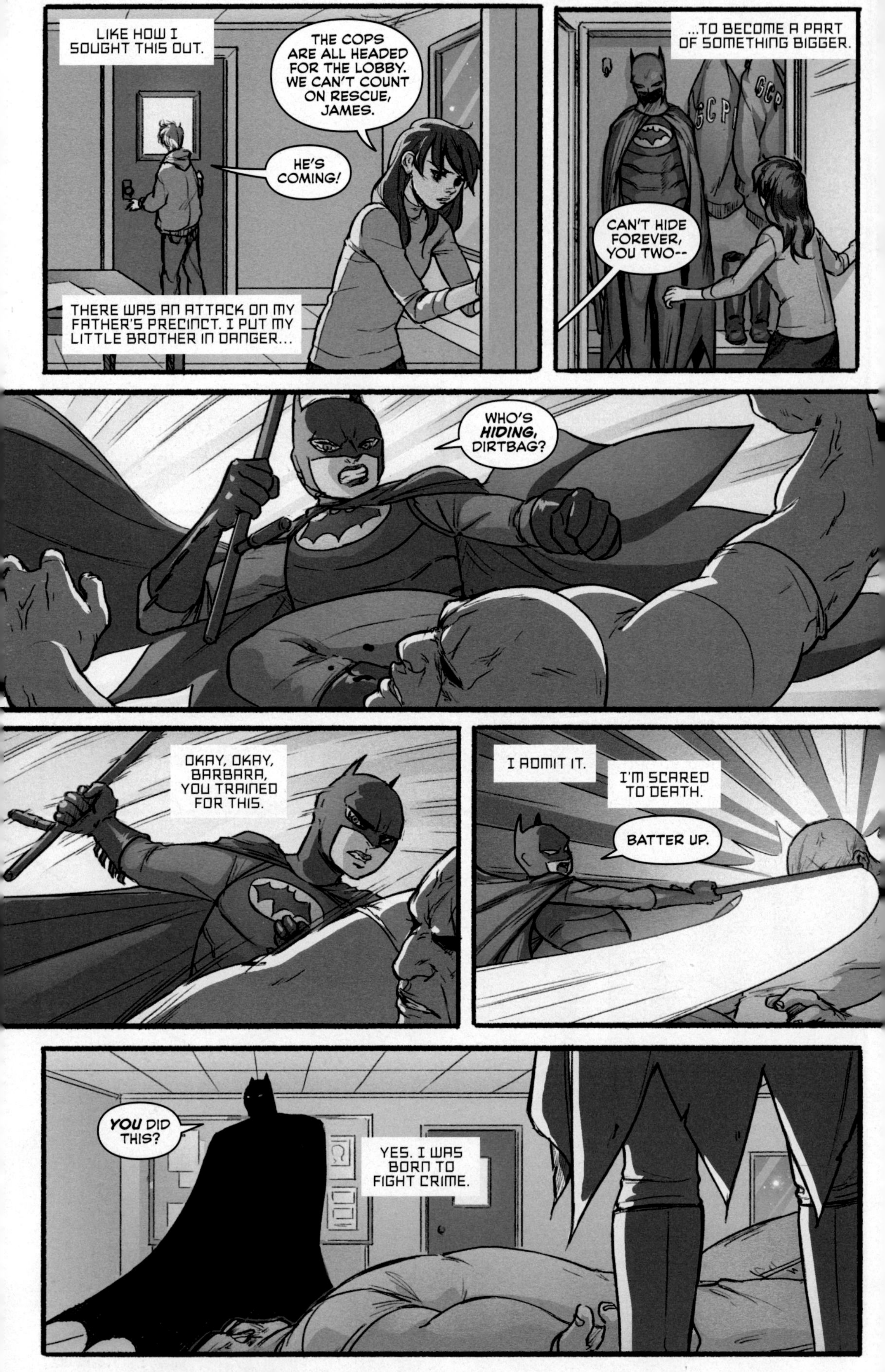
LIKE HOW I SOUGHT THIS OUT.
THE COPS ARE ALL HEADED FOR THE LOBBY. WE CAN'T COUNT ON RESCUE, JAMES.
HE'S COMING!
THERE WAS AN ATTACK ON MY FATHER'S PRECINCT. I PUT MY LITTLE BROTHER IN DANGER...
...TO BECOME A PART OF SOMETHING BIGGER.
GCPD
CAN'T HIDE FOREVER, YOU TWO--
WHO'S HIDING, DIRTBAG?
OKAY, OKAY, BARBARA, YOU TRAINED FOR THIS.
I ADMIT IT.
I'M SCARED TO DEATH.
BATTER UP.
YOU DID THIS?
YES. I WAS BORN TO FIGHT CRIME.

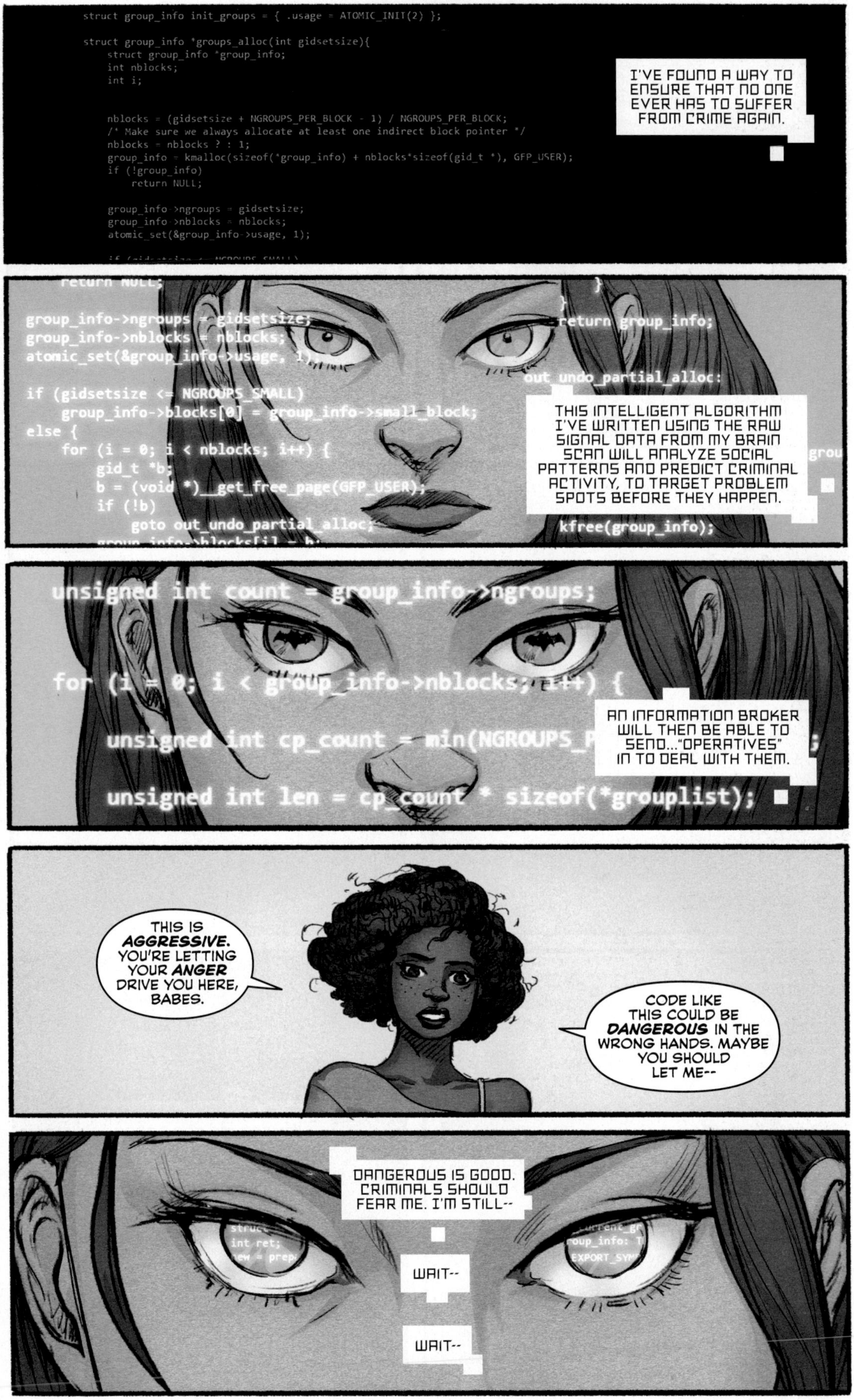

struct group_info init_groups = { .usage = ATOMIC_INIT(2) };
struct group_info *groups_alloc(int gidsetsize){
struct group_info *group_info;
int nblocks;
int i;
nblocks = (gidsetsize + NGROUPS_PER_BLOCK - 1) / NGROUPS_PER_BLOCK;
/* Make sure we always allocate at least one indirect block pointer */
nblocks = nblocks ? : 1;
group_info = kmalloc(sizeof(*group_info) + nblocks*sizeof(gid_t *), GFP_USER);
if (!group_info)
return NULL;
group_info->ngroups = gidsetsize;
group_info->nblocks = nblocks;
atomic_set(&group_info->usage, 1);
I'VE FOUND A WAY TO ENSURE THAT NO ONE EVER HAS TO SUFFER FROM CRIME AGAIN.
group_info->ngroups = gidsetsize;
group_info->nblocks = nblocks;
atomic_set(&group_info->usage, 1);
if (gidsetsize <= NGROUPS_SMALL)
group_info->blocks[0] = group_info->small_block;
else {
for (i = 0; i < nblocks; i++) {
gid_t *b;
b = (void *)__get_free_page(GFP_USER);
if (!b)
goto out_undo_partial_alloc;
return group_info;
out_undo_partial_alloc:
kfree(group_info);
THIS INTELLIGENT ALGORITHM I'VE WRITTEN USING THE RAW SIGNAL DATA FROM MY BRAIN SCAN WILL ANALYZE SOCIAL PATTERNS AND PREDICT CRIMINAL ACTIVITY, TO TARGET PROBLEM SPOTS BEFORE THEY HAPPEN.
unsigned int count = group_info->ngroups;
for (i = 0; i < group_info->nblocks; i++) {
unsigned int len = cp_count * sizeof(*grouplist);
AN INFORMATION BROKER WILL THEN BE ABLE TO SEND..."OPERATIVES" IN TO DEAL WITH THEM.
THIS IS AGGRESSIVE. YOU'RE LETTING YOUR ANGER DRIVE YOU HERE, BABES.
CODE LIKE THIS COULD BE DANGEROUS IN THE WRONG HANDS. MAYBE YOU SHOULD LET ME--
DANGEROUS IS GOOD. CRIMINALS SHOULD FEAR ME. I'M STILL--
WAIT--
WAIT--

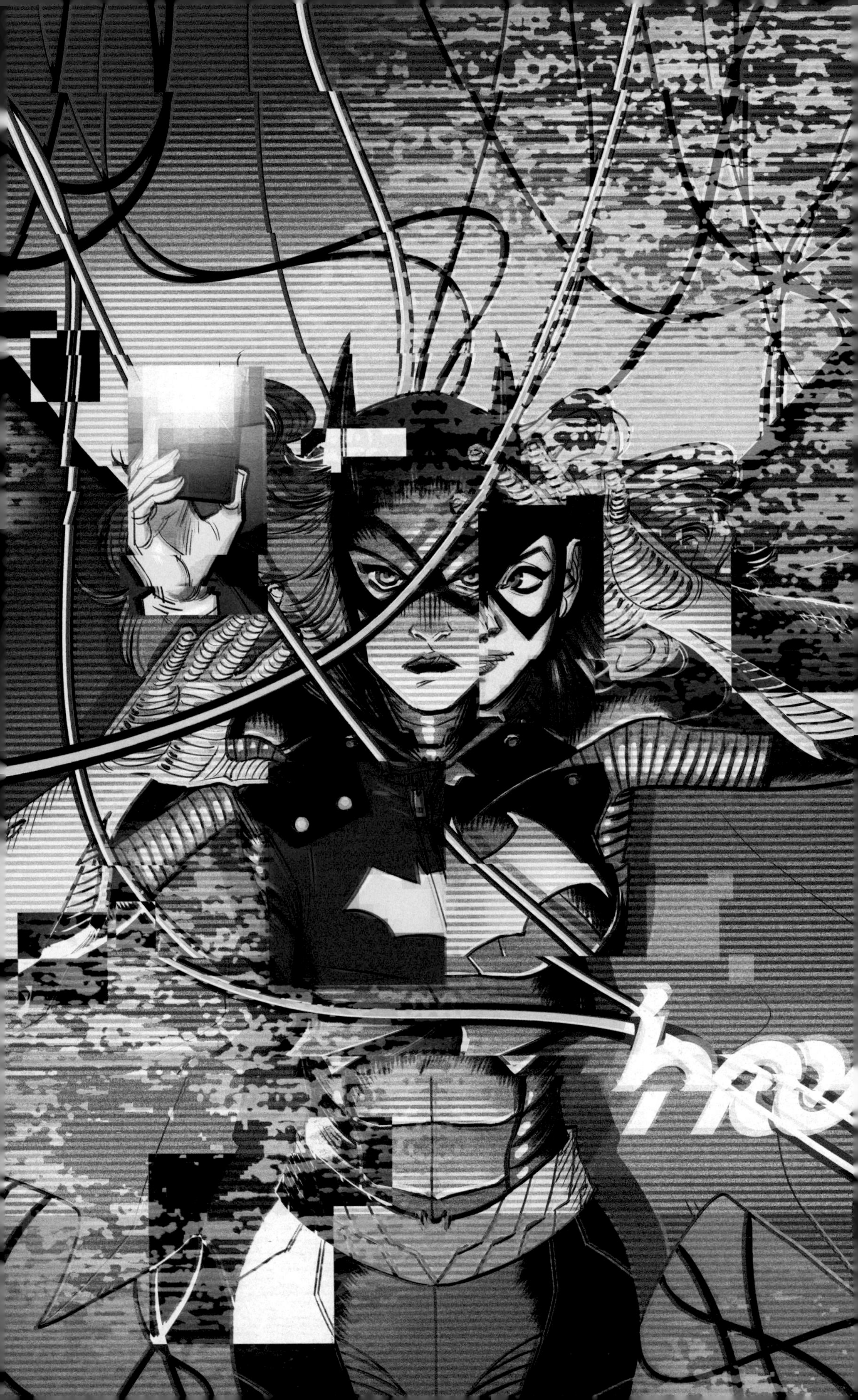

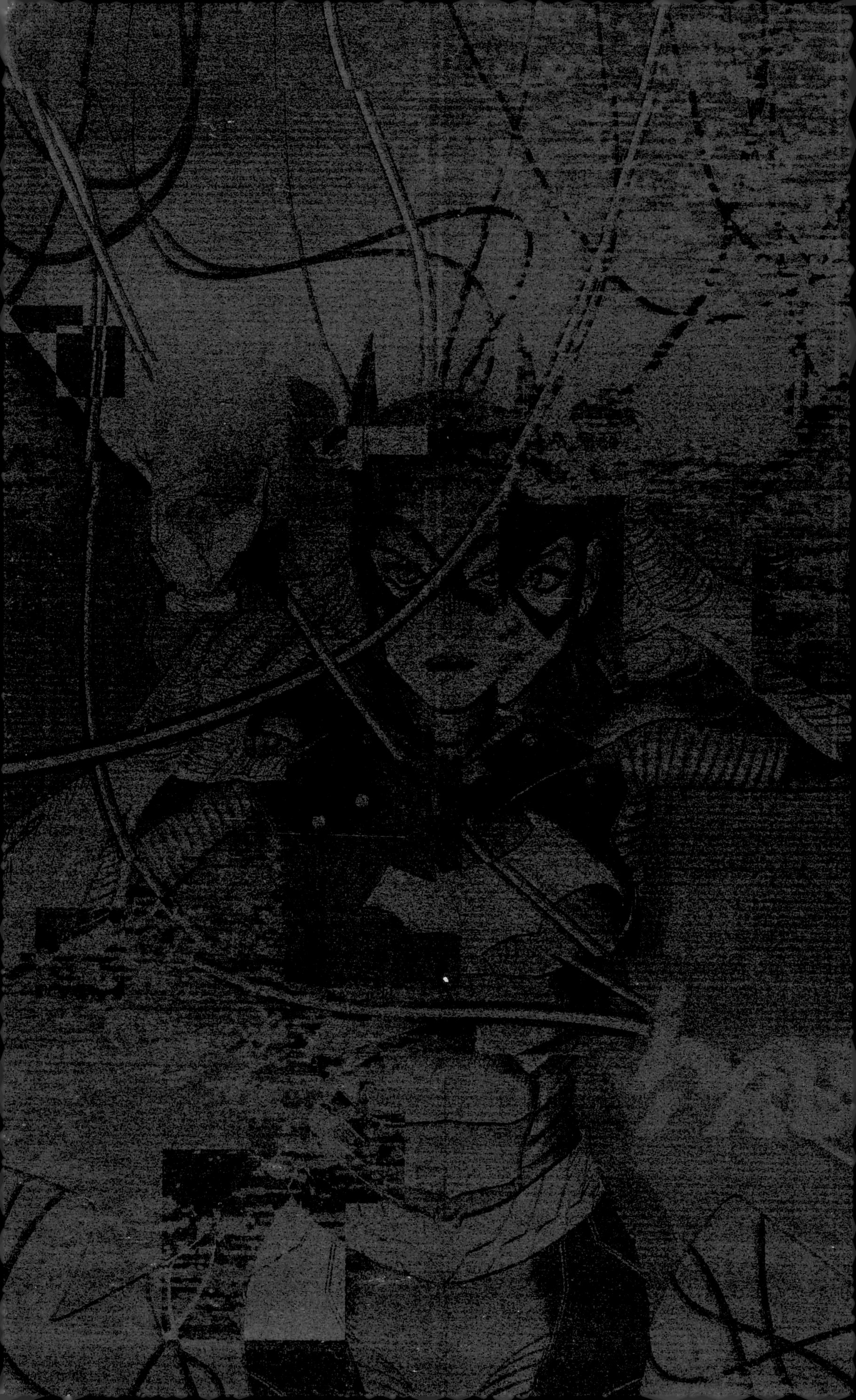

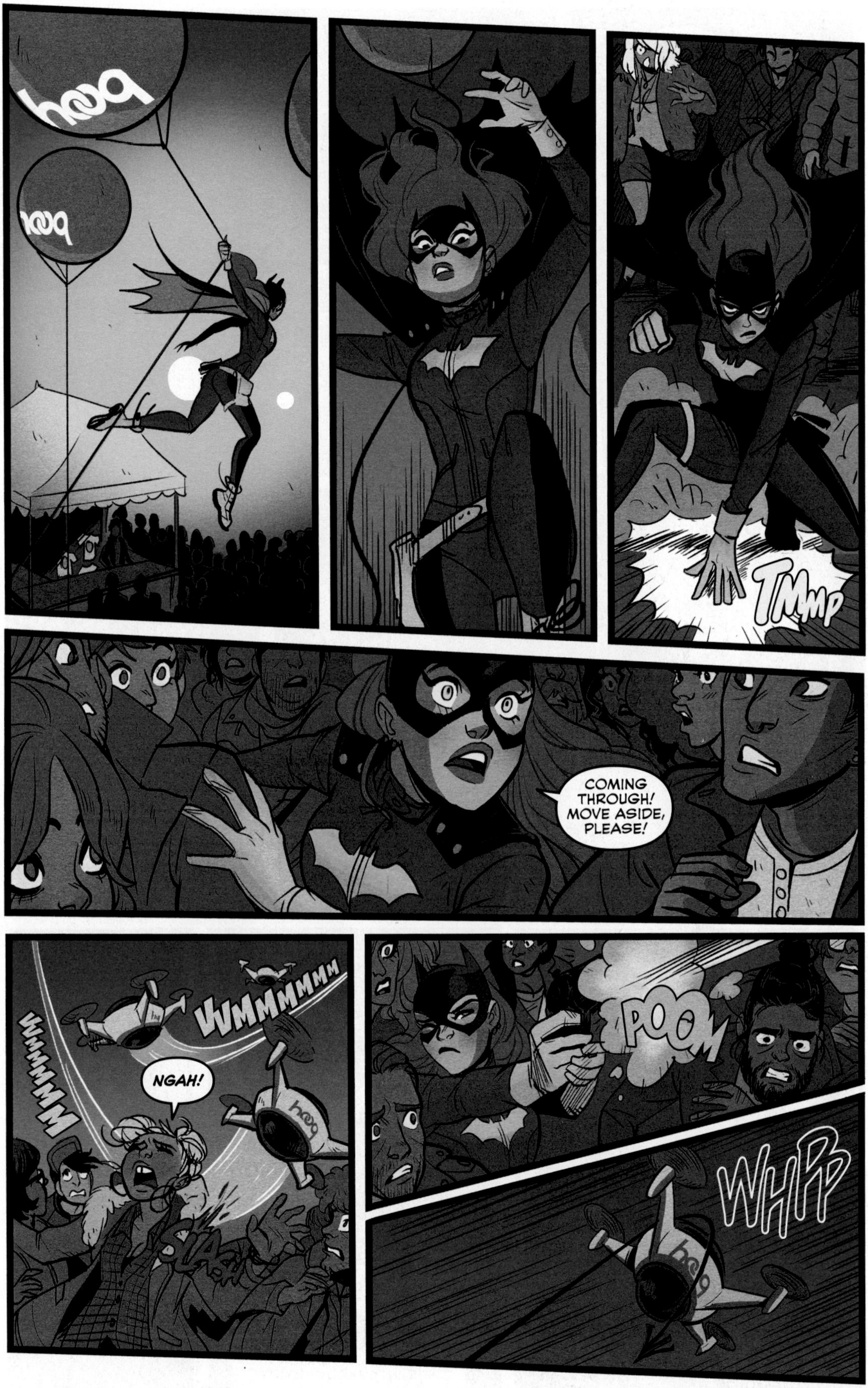
TMMP
COMING THROUGH! MOVE ASIDE, PLEASE!
WMMMMMM
WMMMMMM
NGAH!
POOM
WHPP

THE END

VARIANT COVER GALLERY

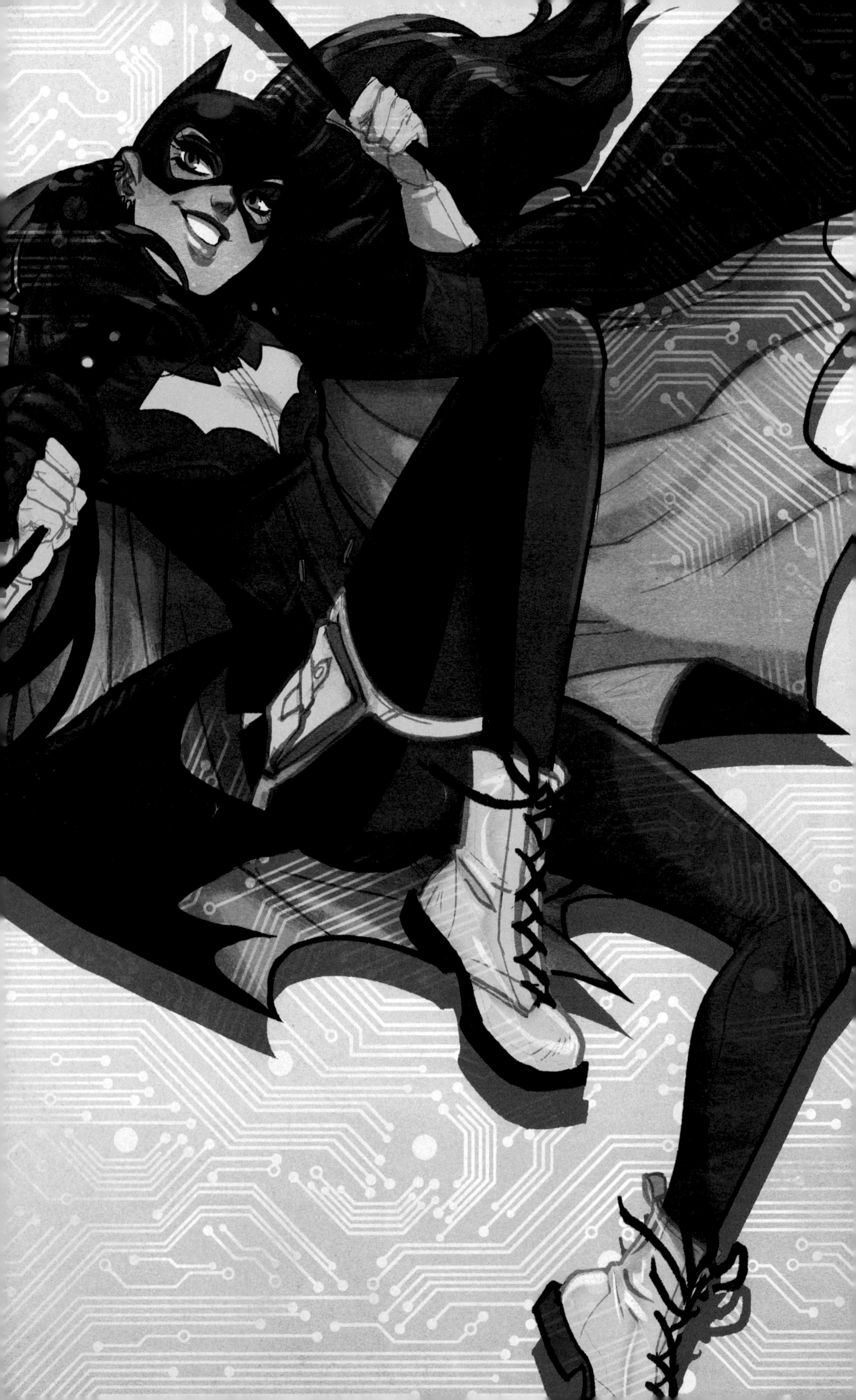

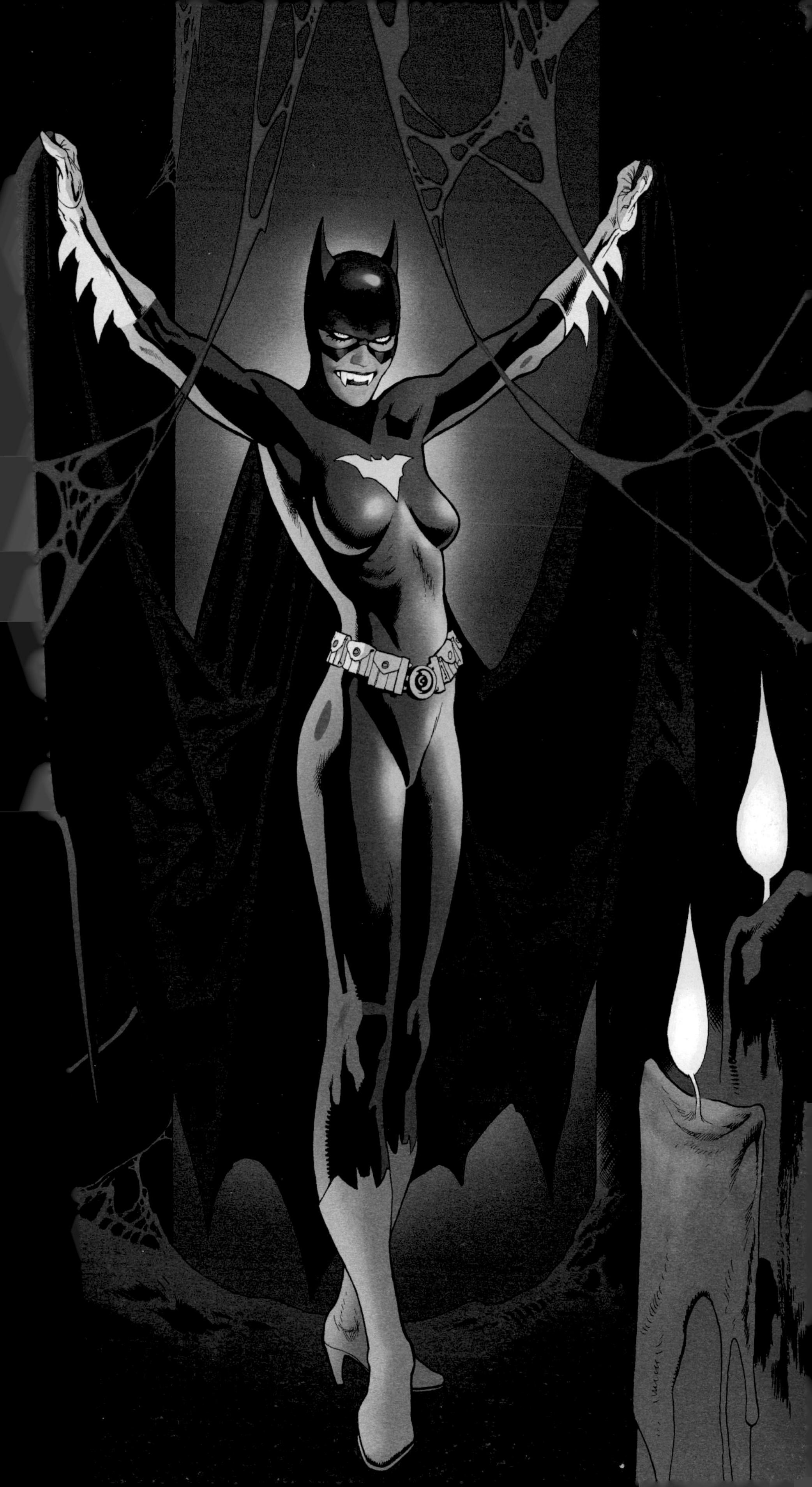

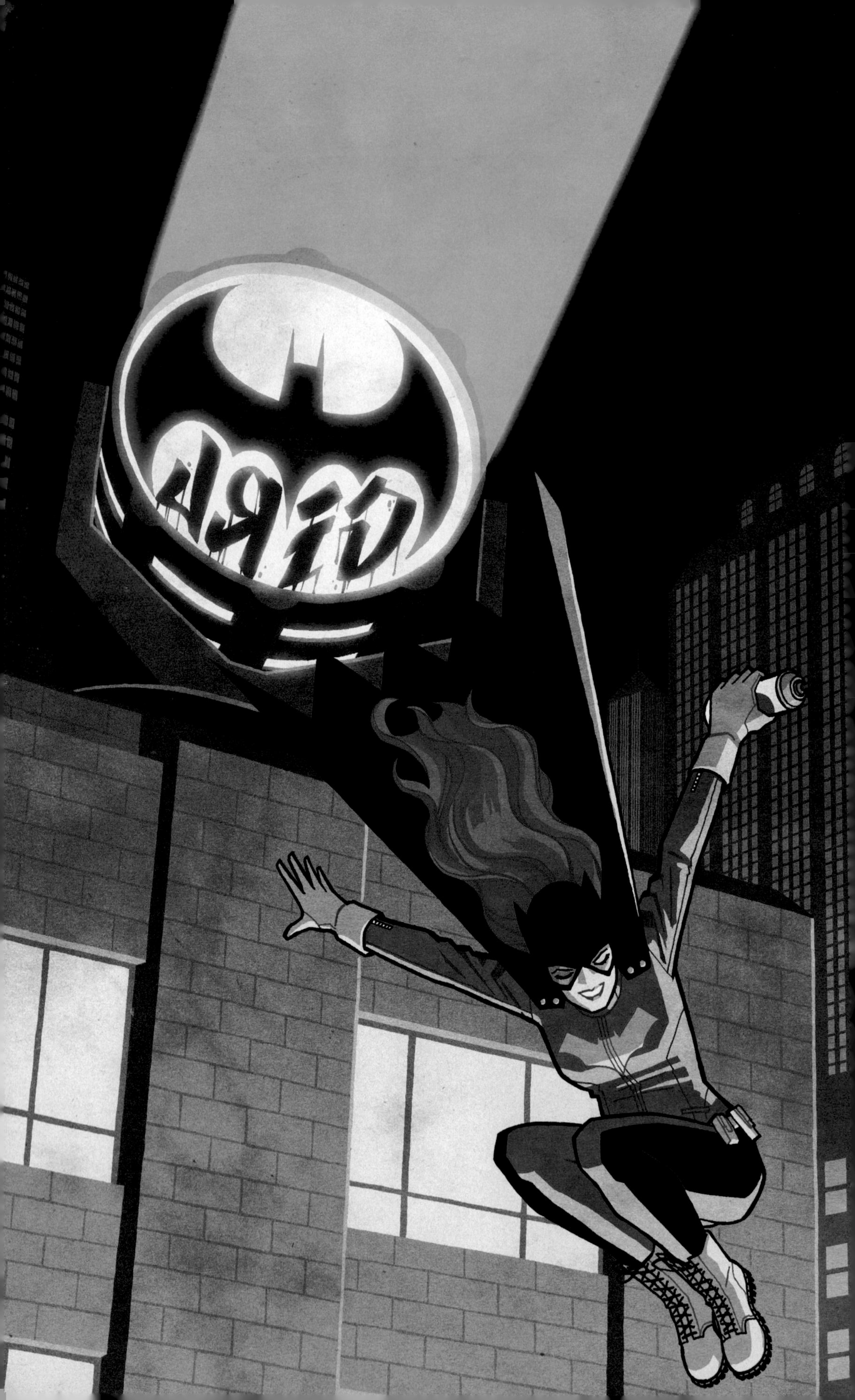

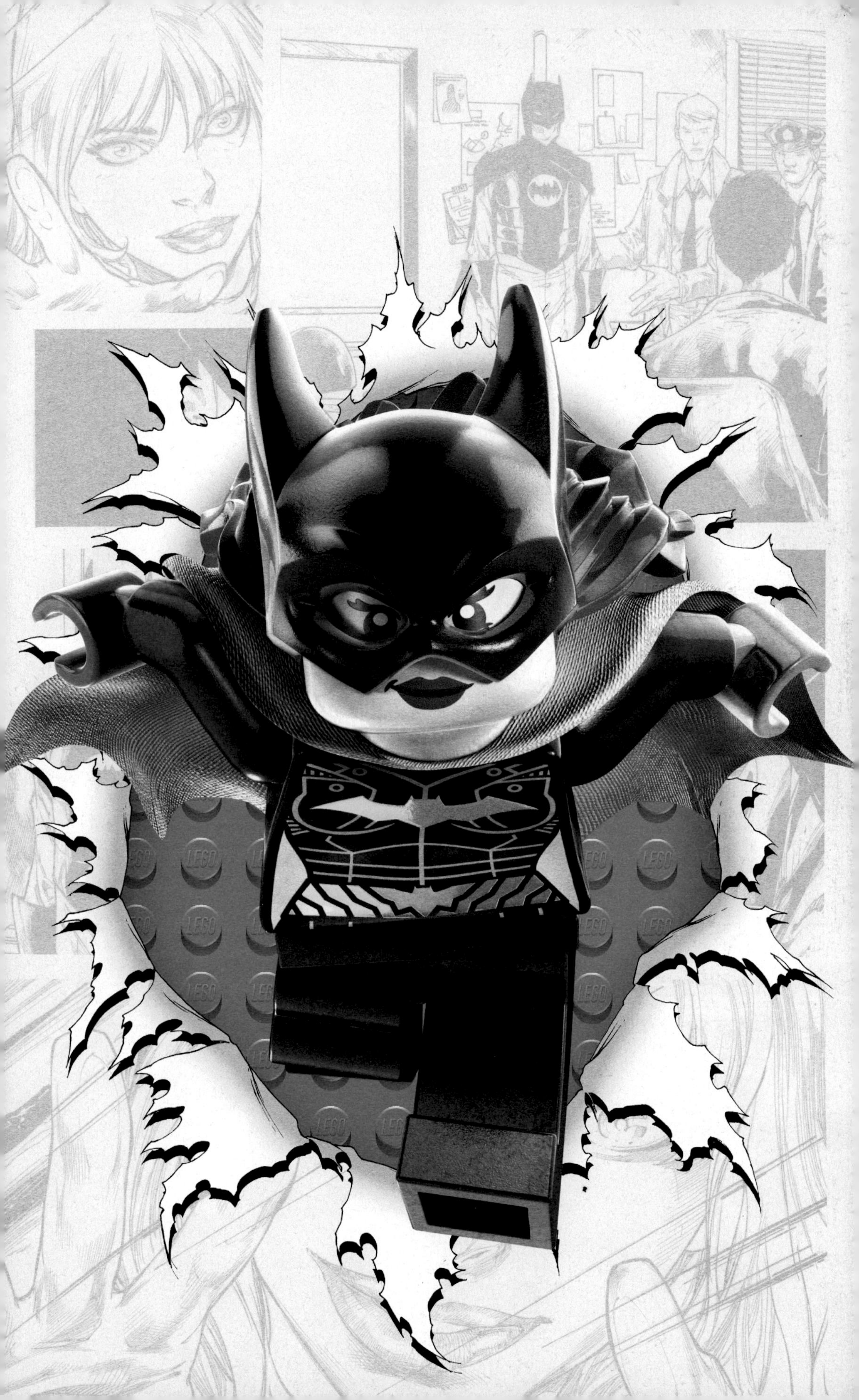

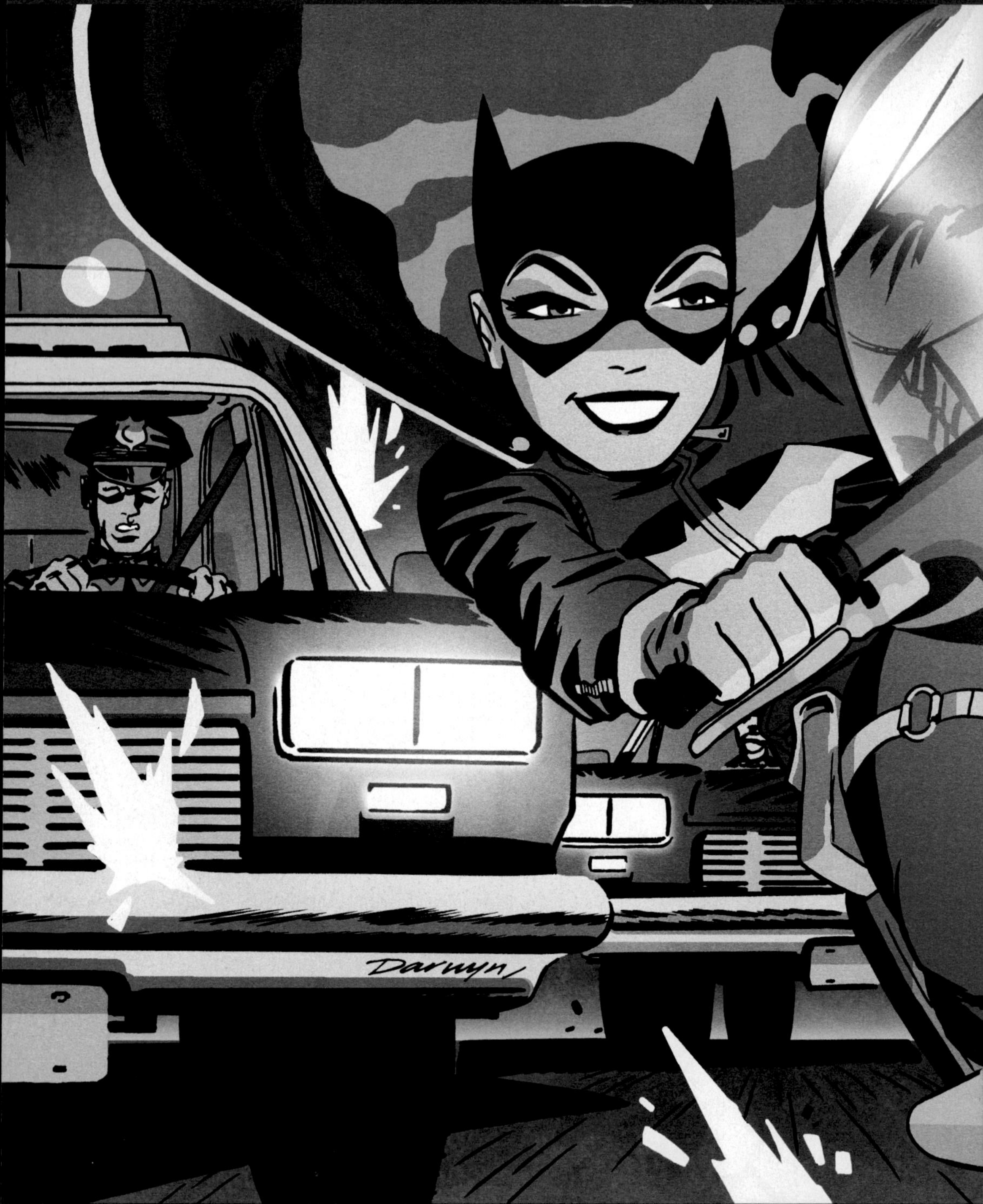
Darwyn

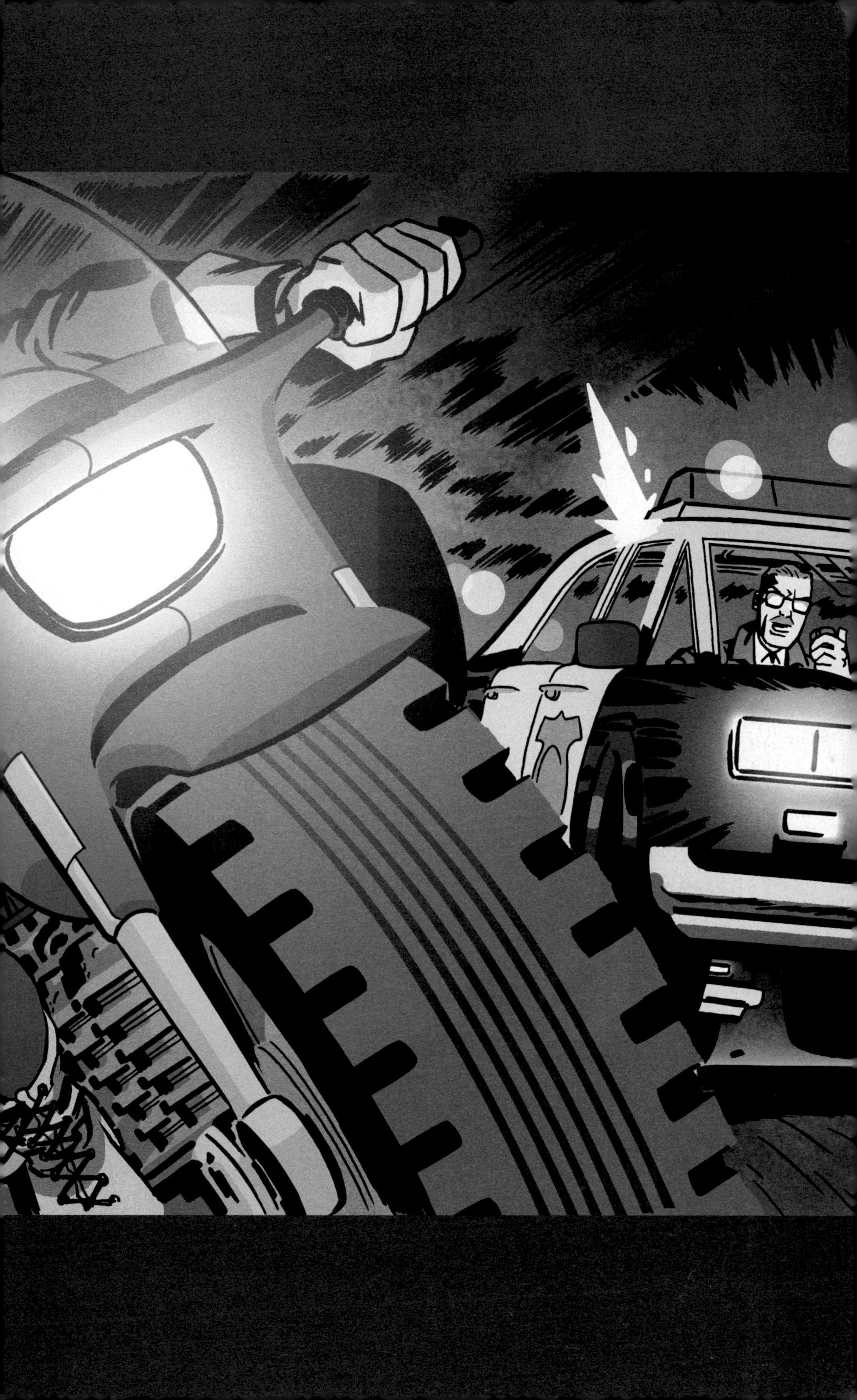

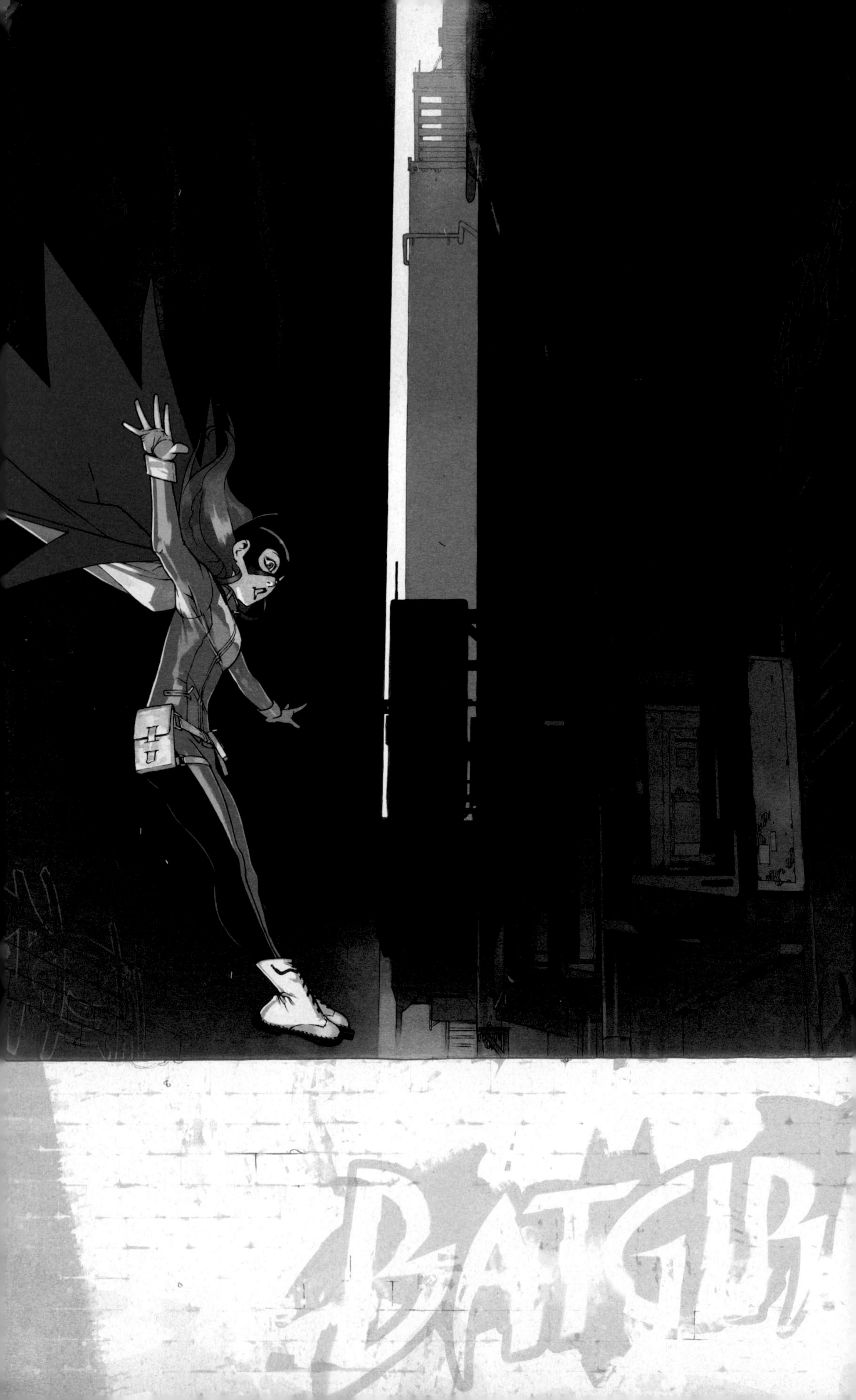
BATGIR

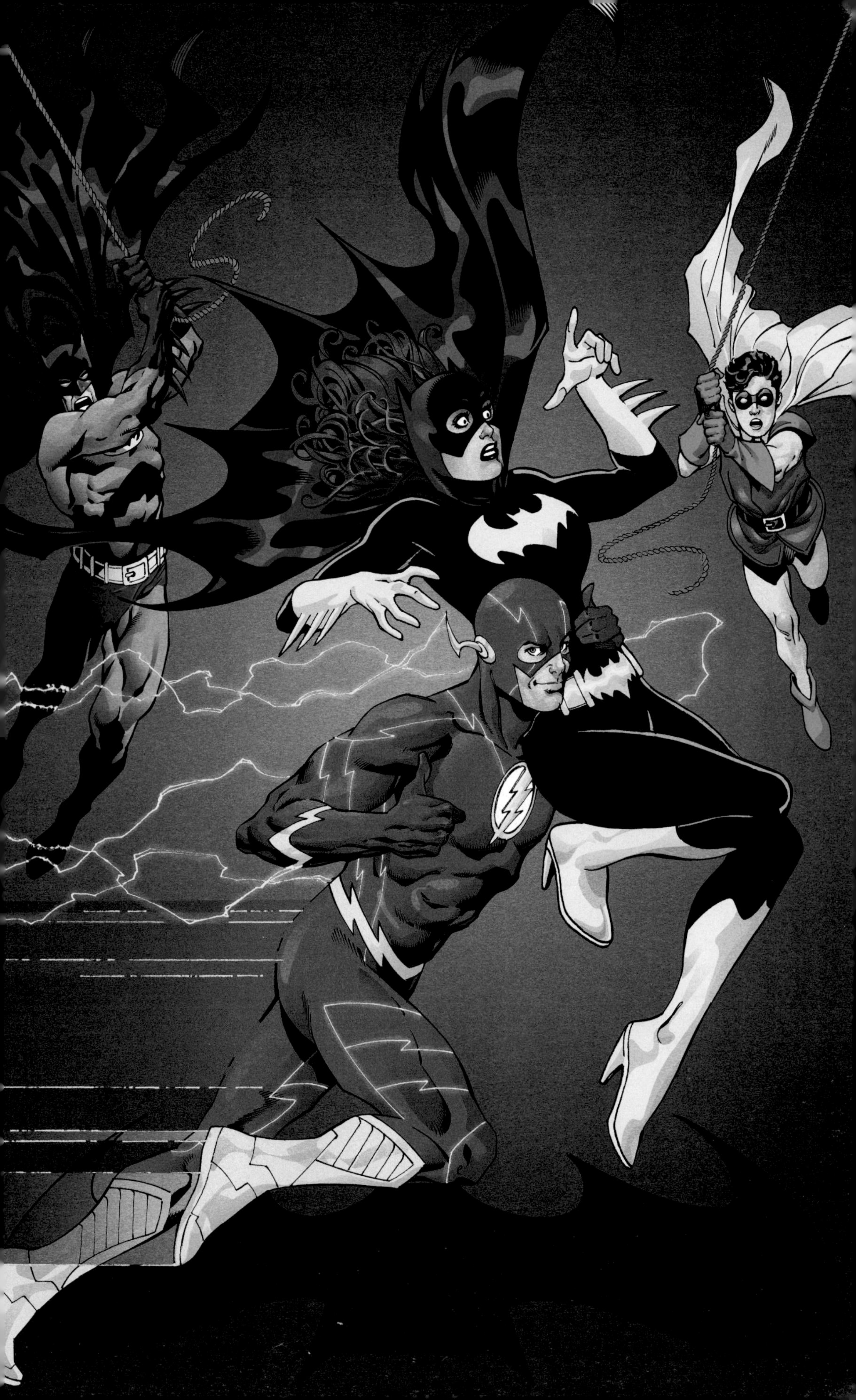

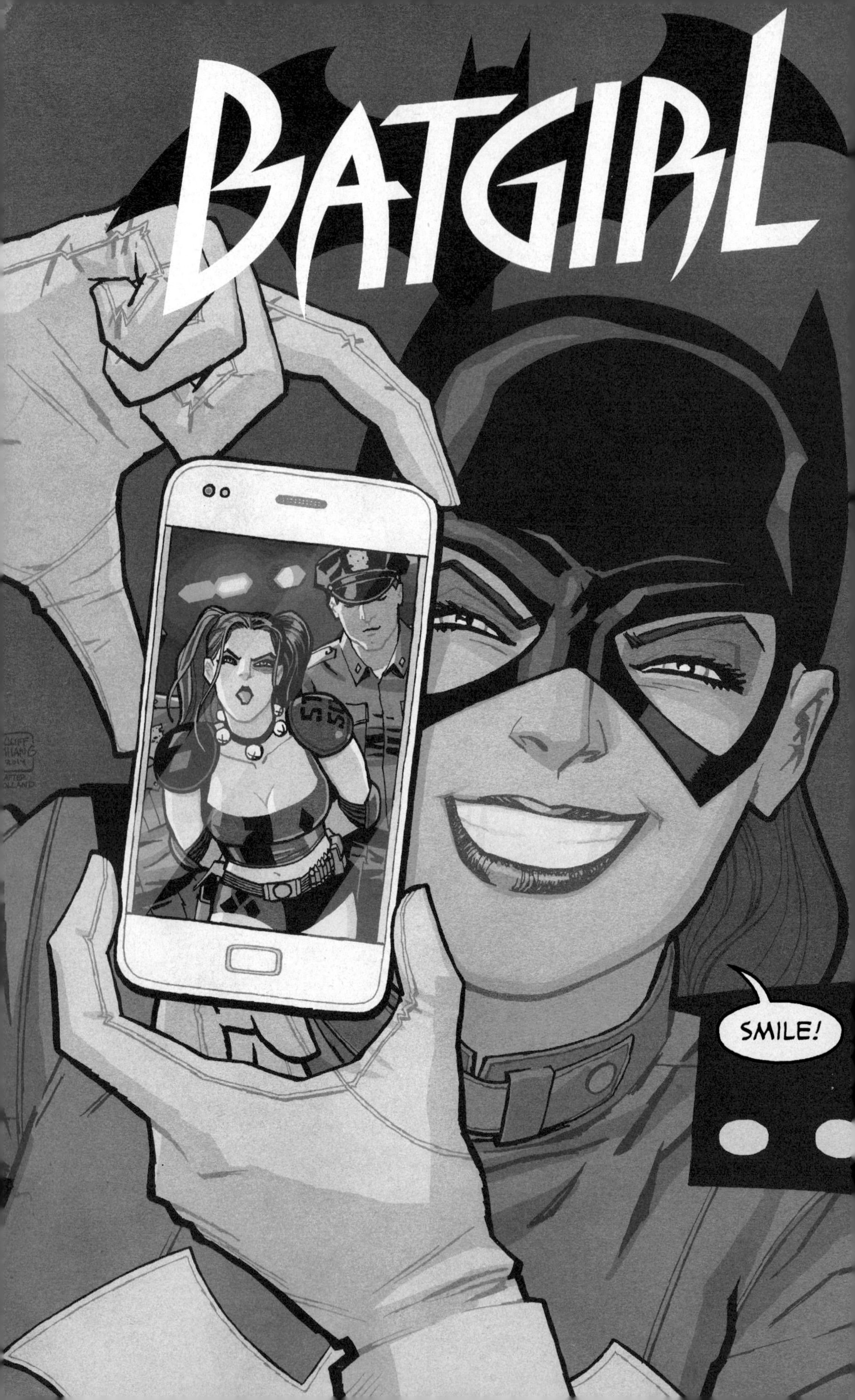
BATGIRL
SMILE!

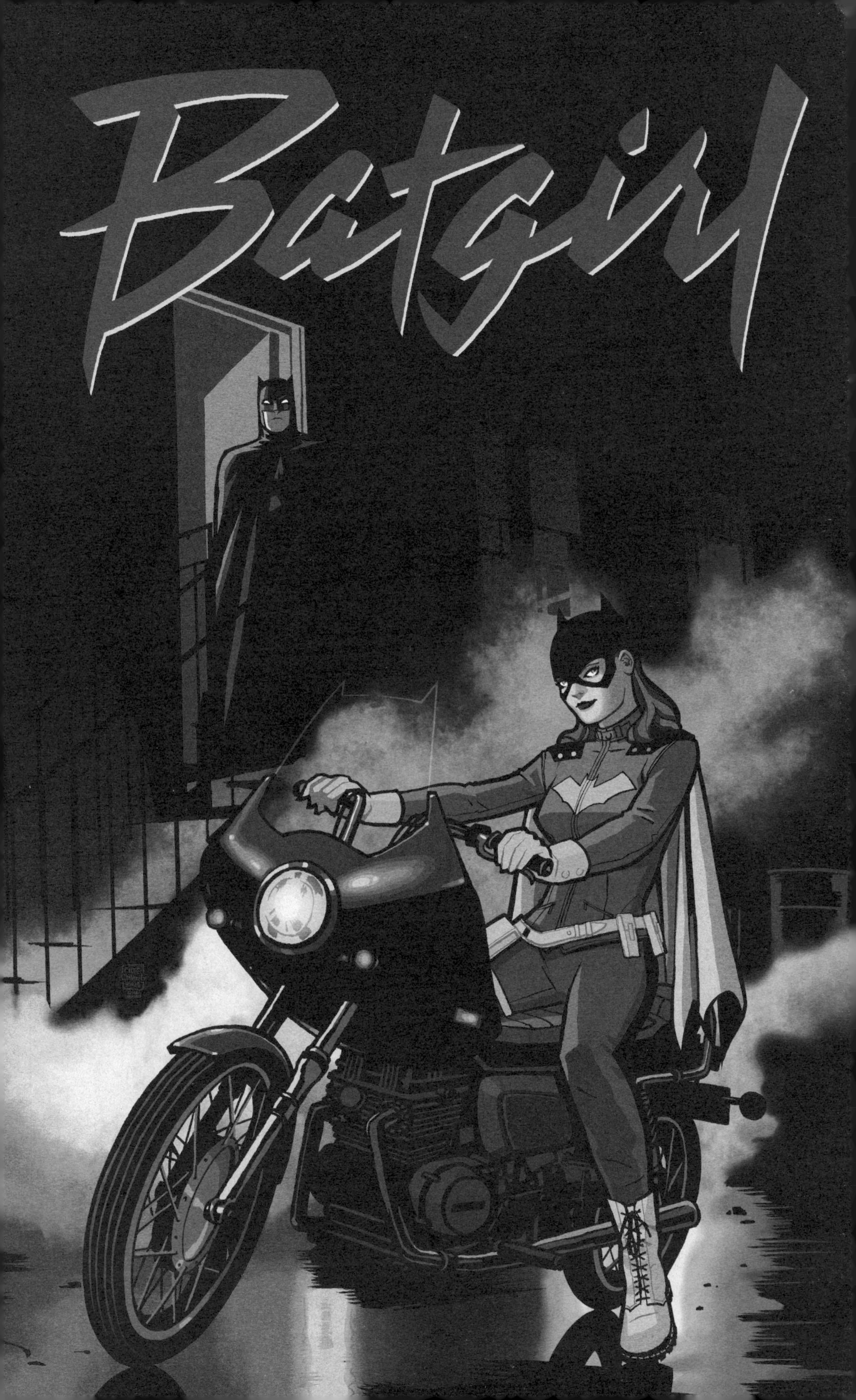
Batgirl

CREATING
BATGIRL OF BURNSIDE

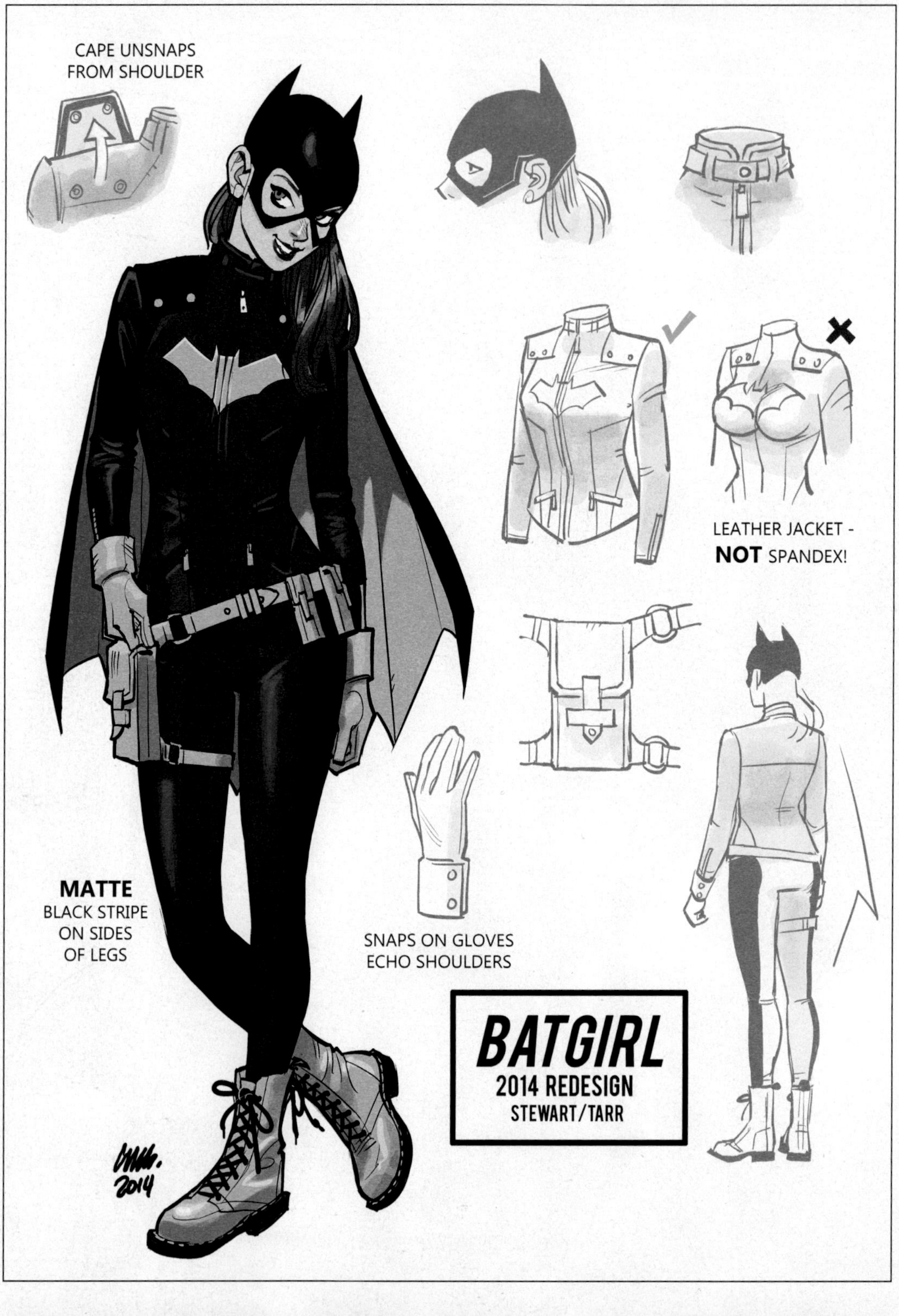
CAPE UNSNAPS
FROM SHOULDER
LEATHER JACKET -
NOT SPANDEX!
MATTE
BLACK STRIPE
ON SIDES
OF LEGS
SNAPS ON GLOVES
ECHO SHOULDERS
BATGIRL
2014 REDESIGN
STEWART/TARR

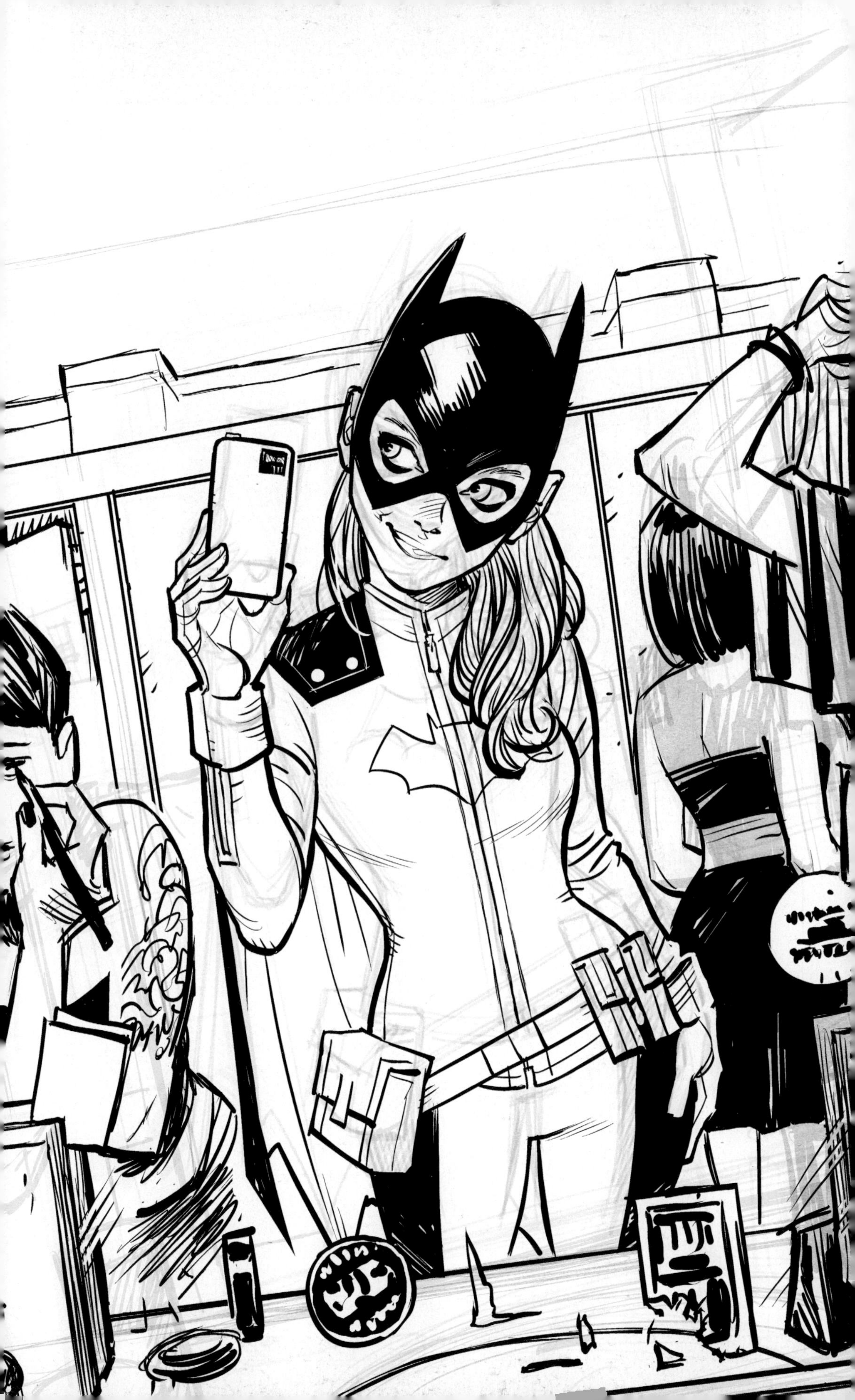

BATGIRL CHARACTER STUDIES BY **CAMERON STEWART** (top) AND **BABS TARR** (bottom)

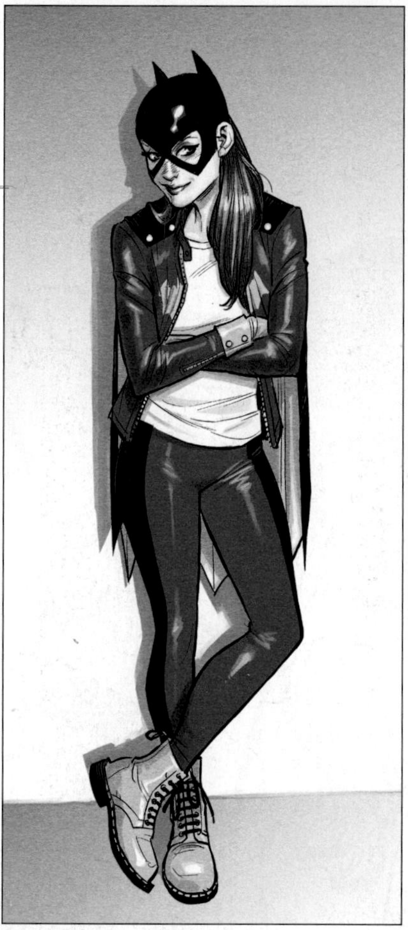

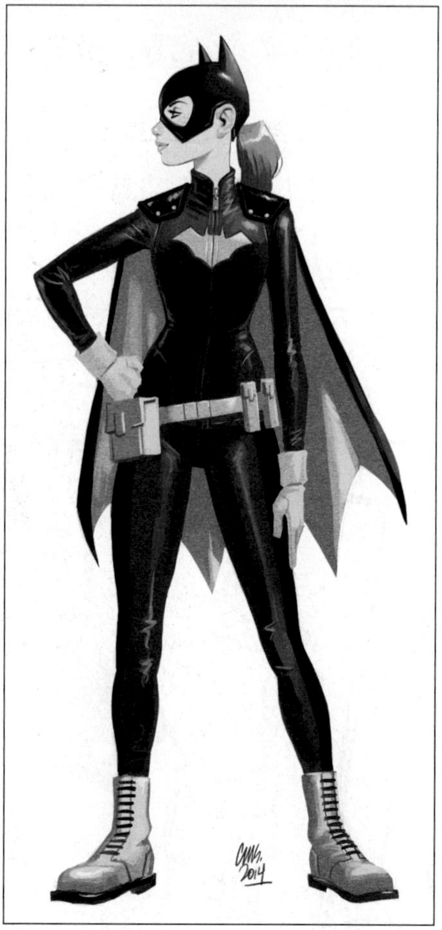

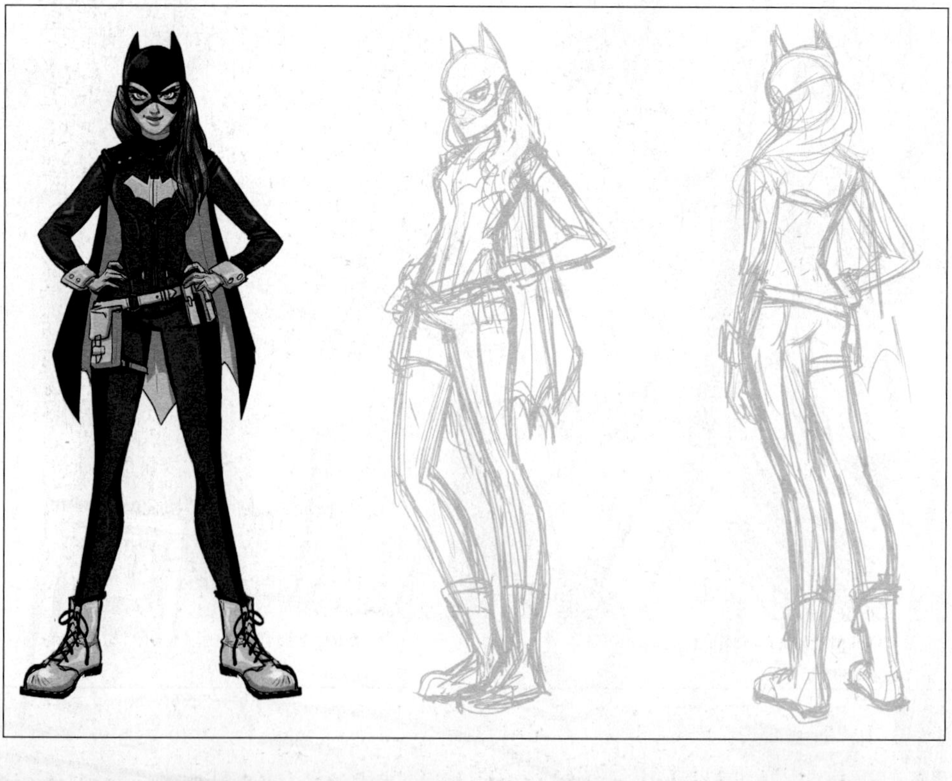

BARBARA CHARACTER STUDIES BY
BABS TARR

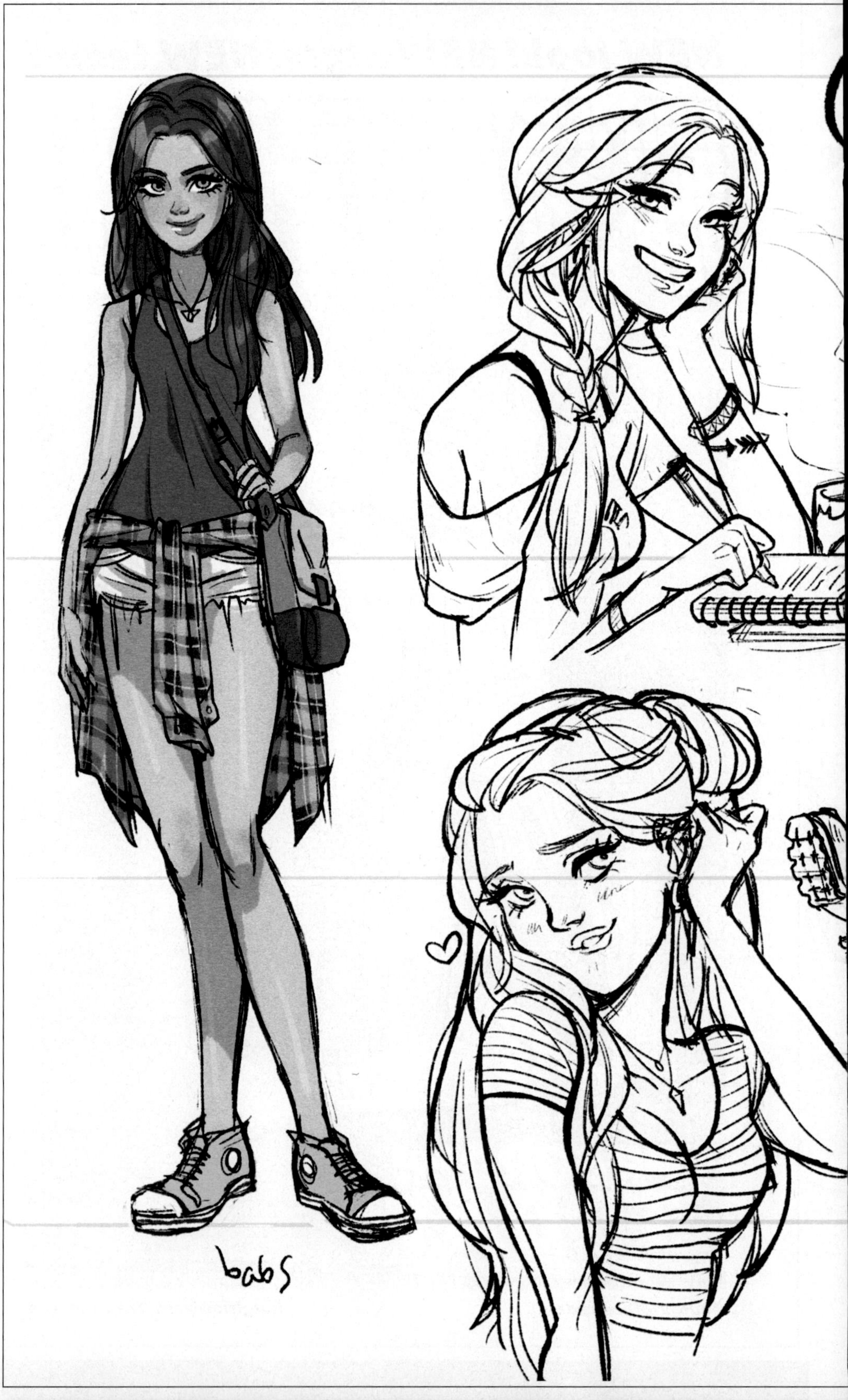
babs

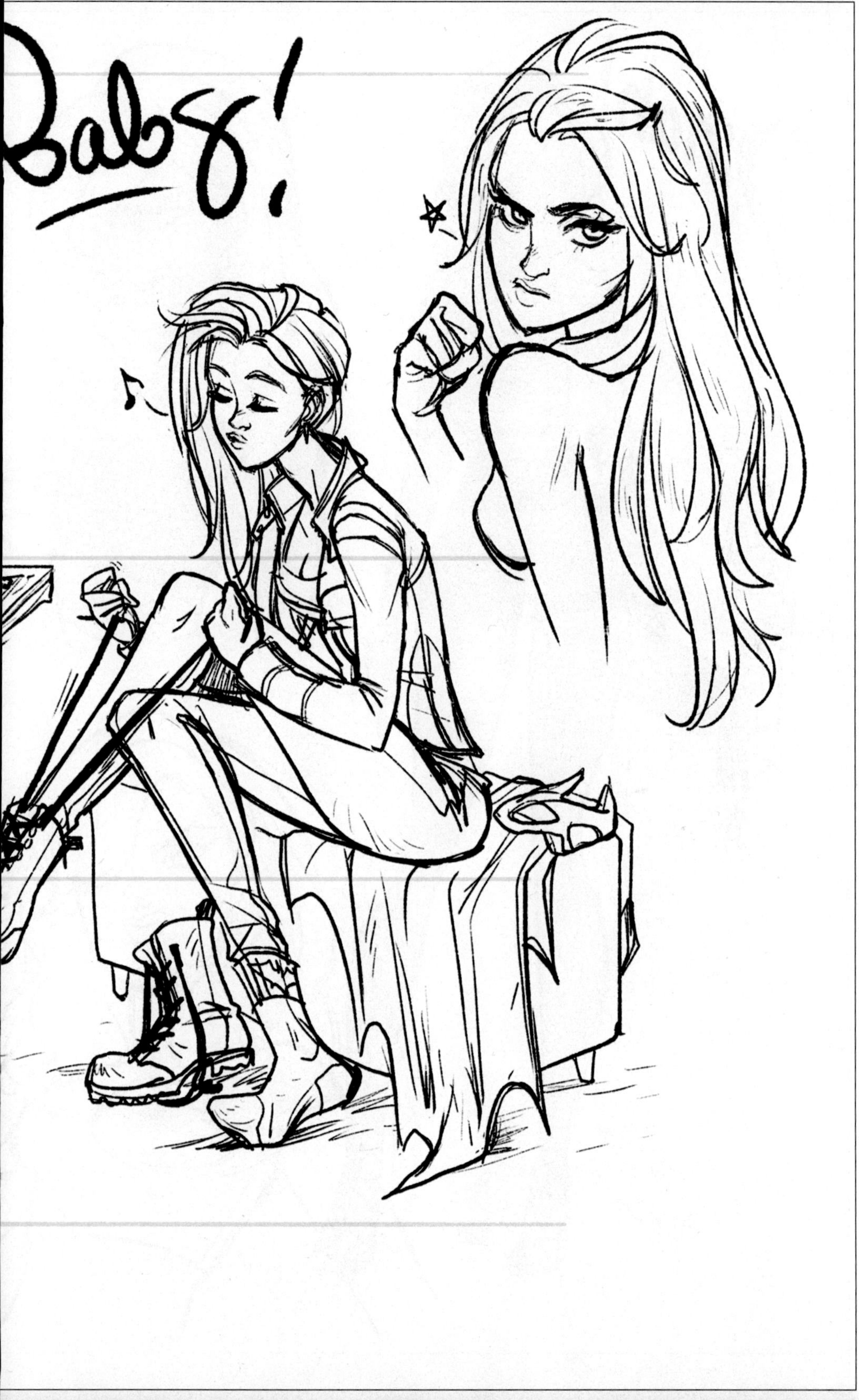
Babs!

DINAH AND FRANKIE CHARACTER STUDIES BY
BABS TARR

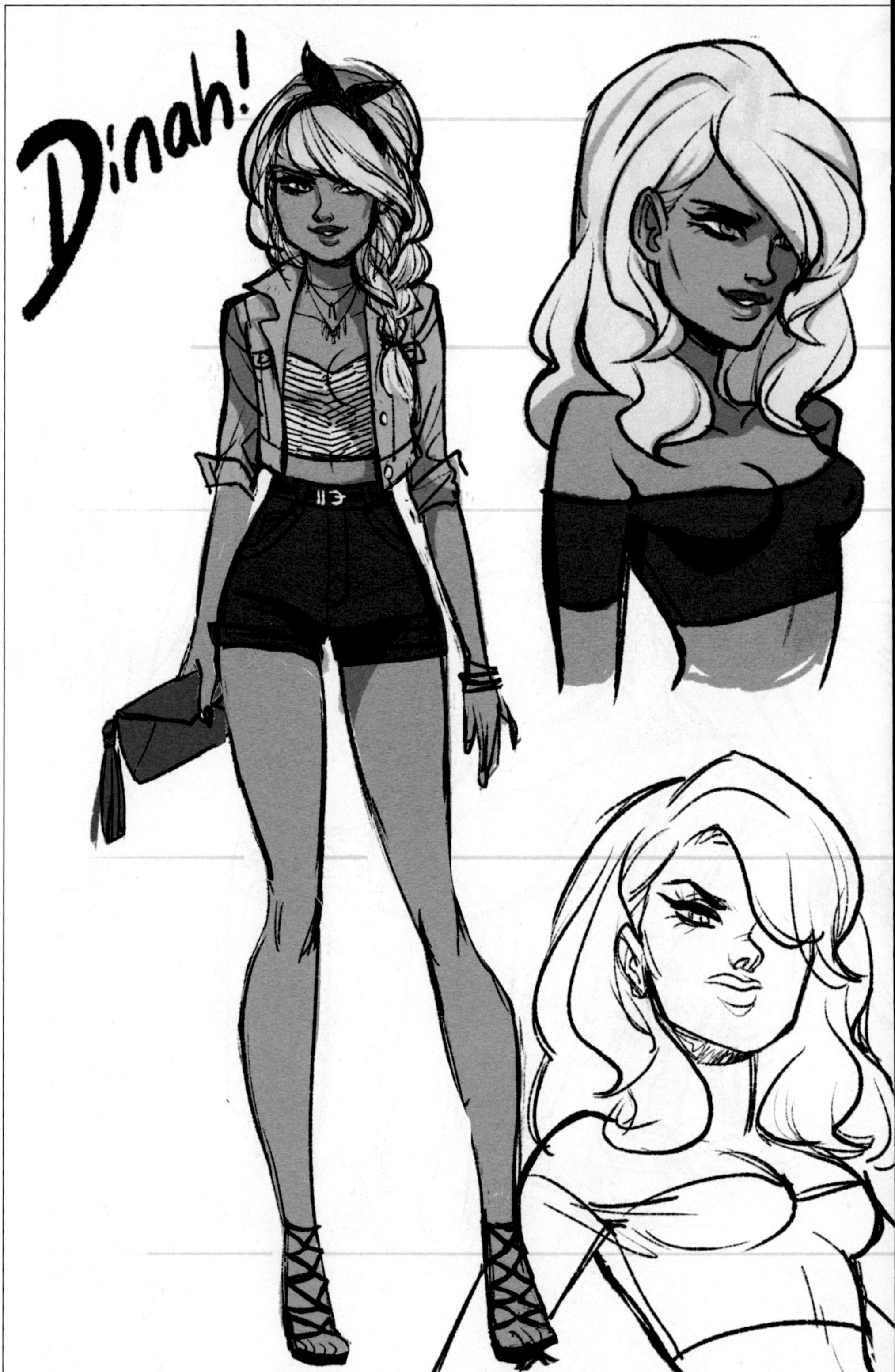
Dinah!

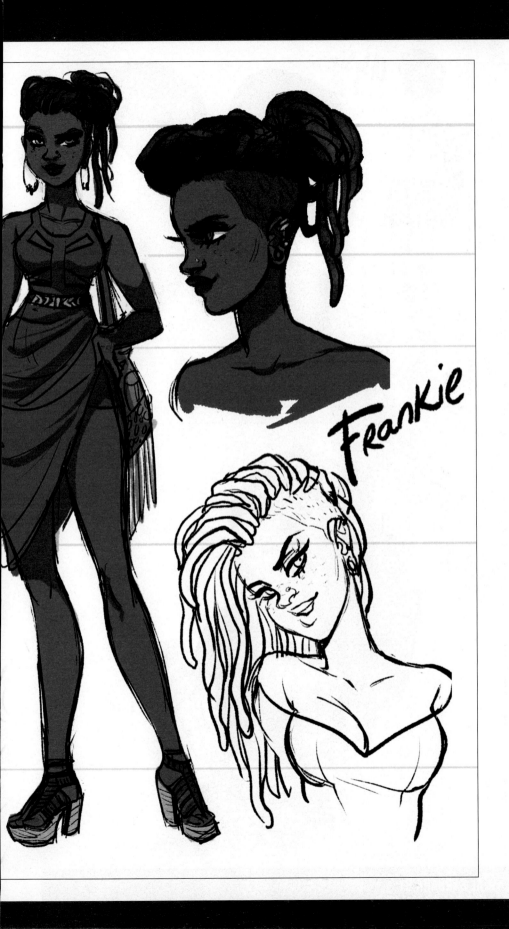

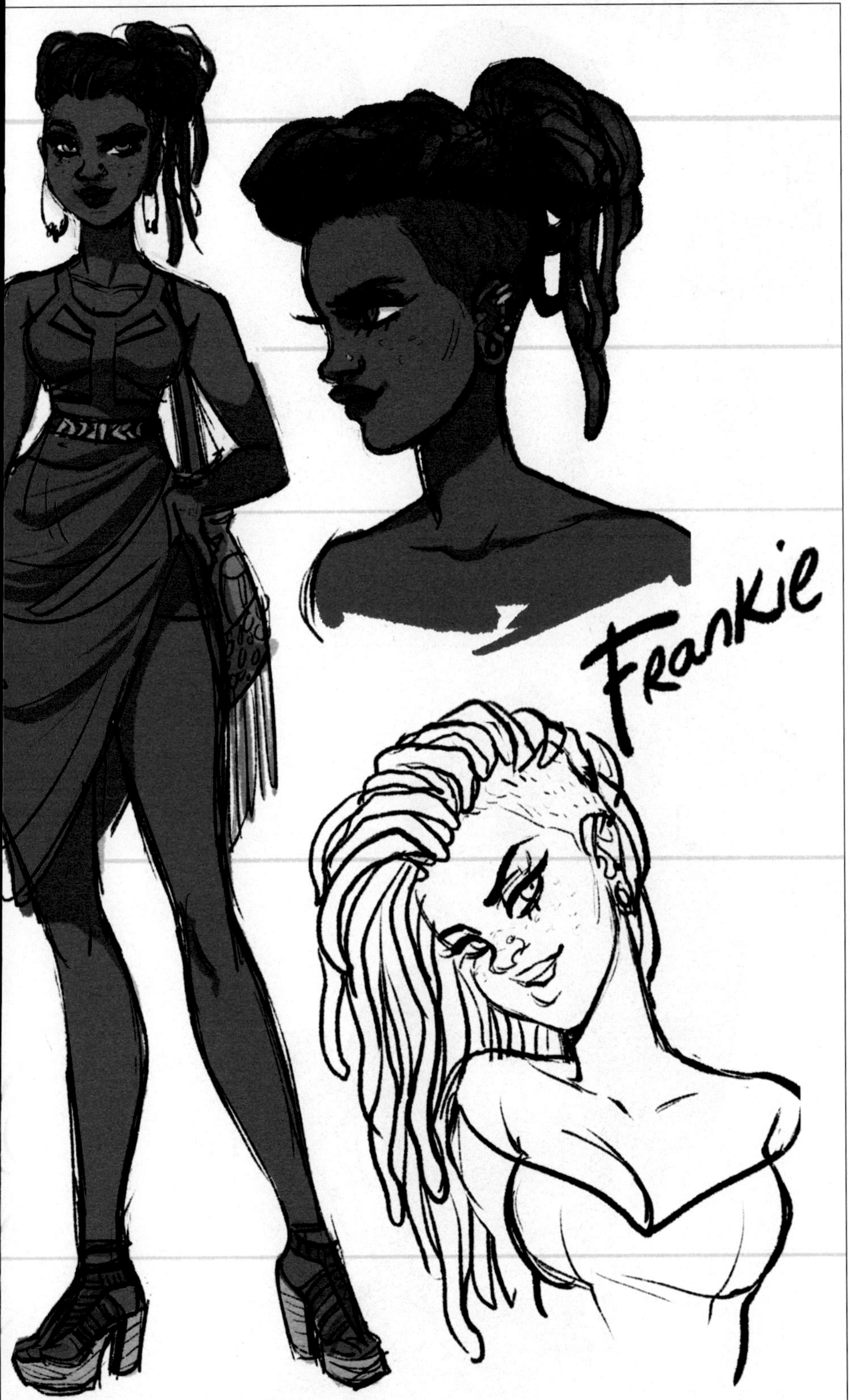
Frankie

ALYSIA CHARACTER SHEET BY
BABS TARR

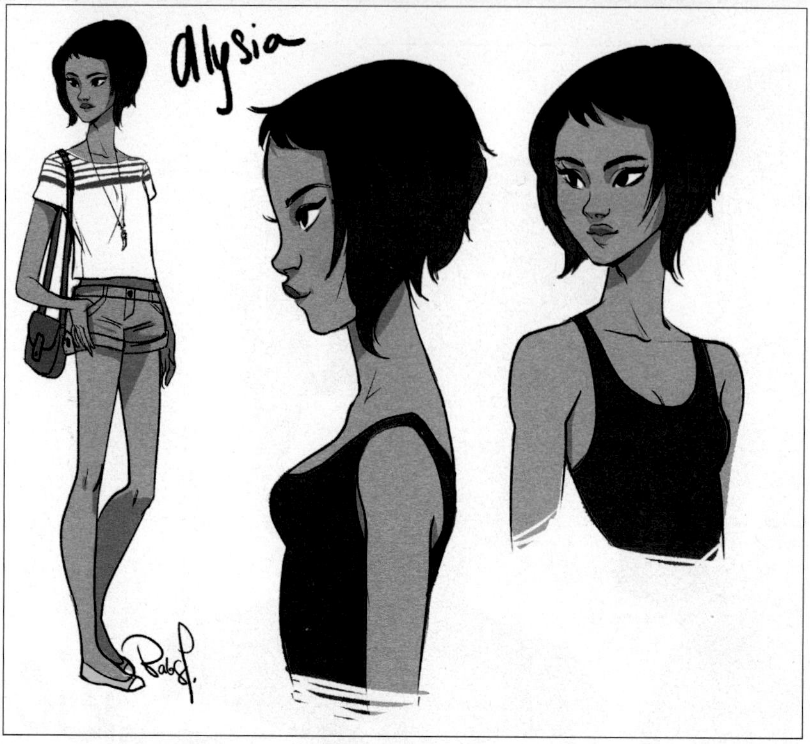
Alysia
Babs T.

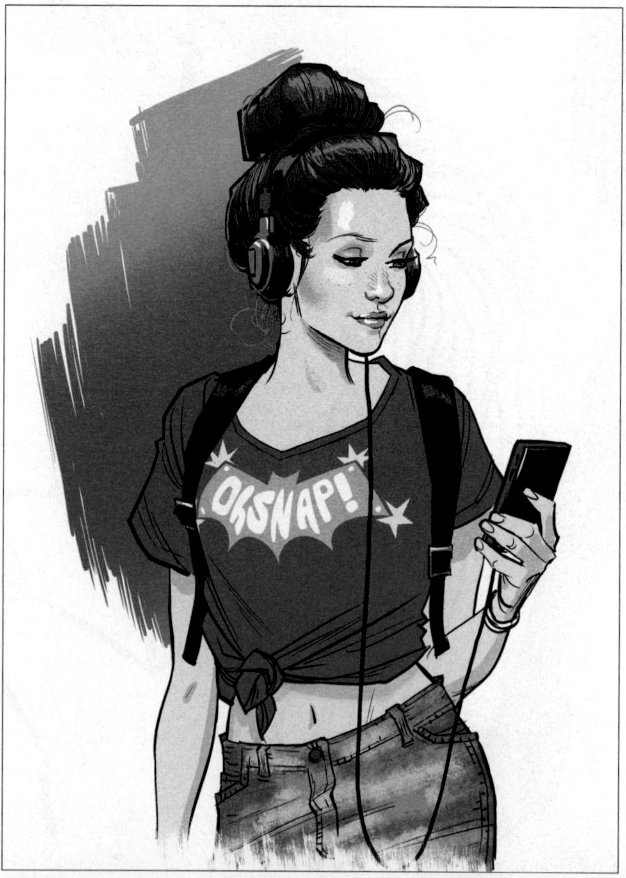
OH SNAP!

CASUAL BARBARA BY
CAMERON STEWART

BARBARA'S MANY FASHIONS BY
BABS TARR

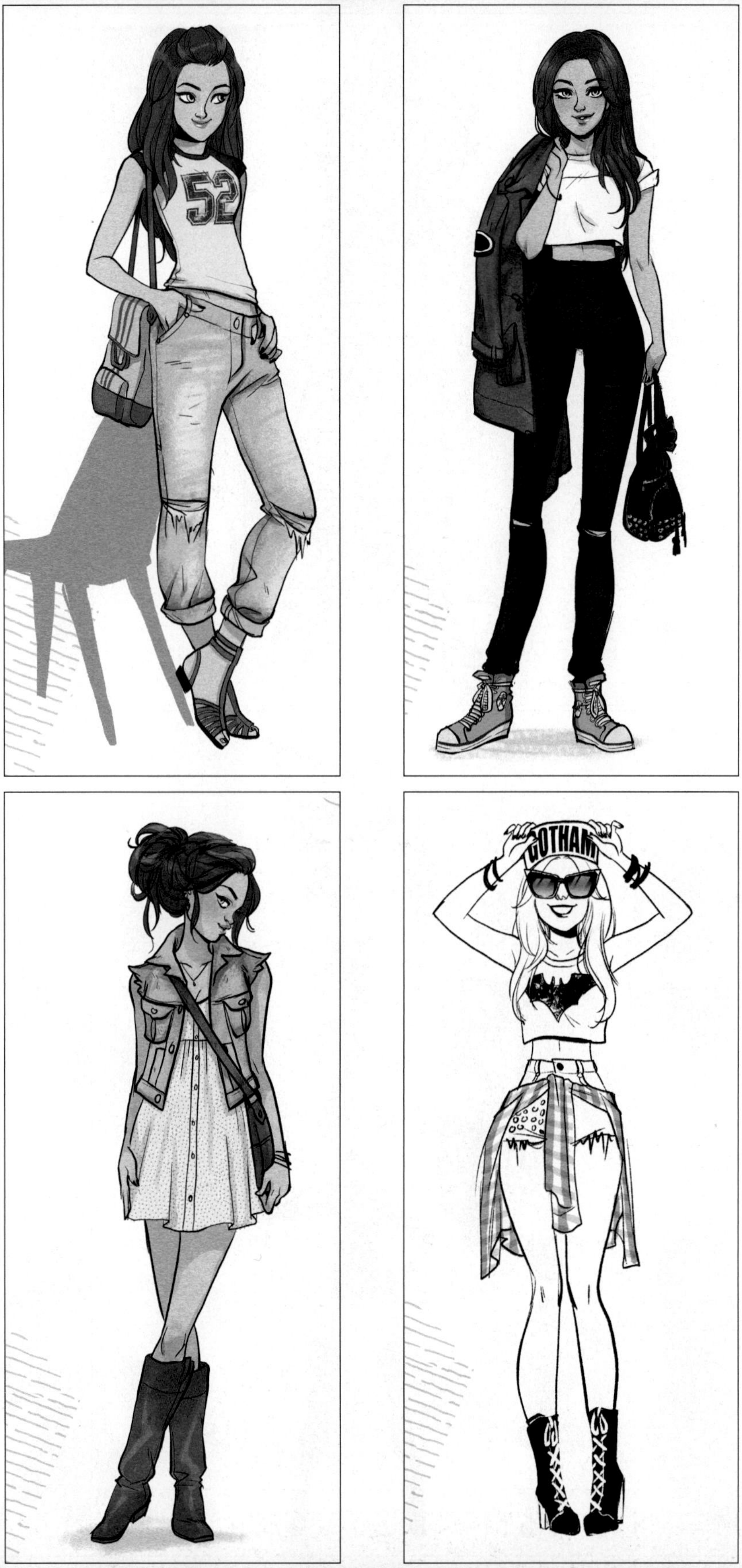
52
GOTHAM

DAGGER TYPE AND HIS BATGIRL ART BY
BABS TARR

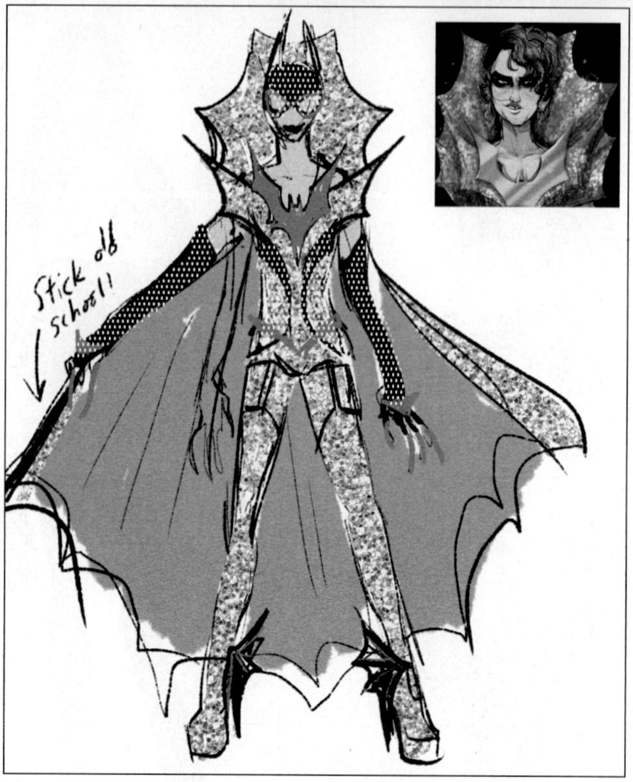
Stick old school!!

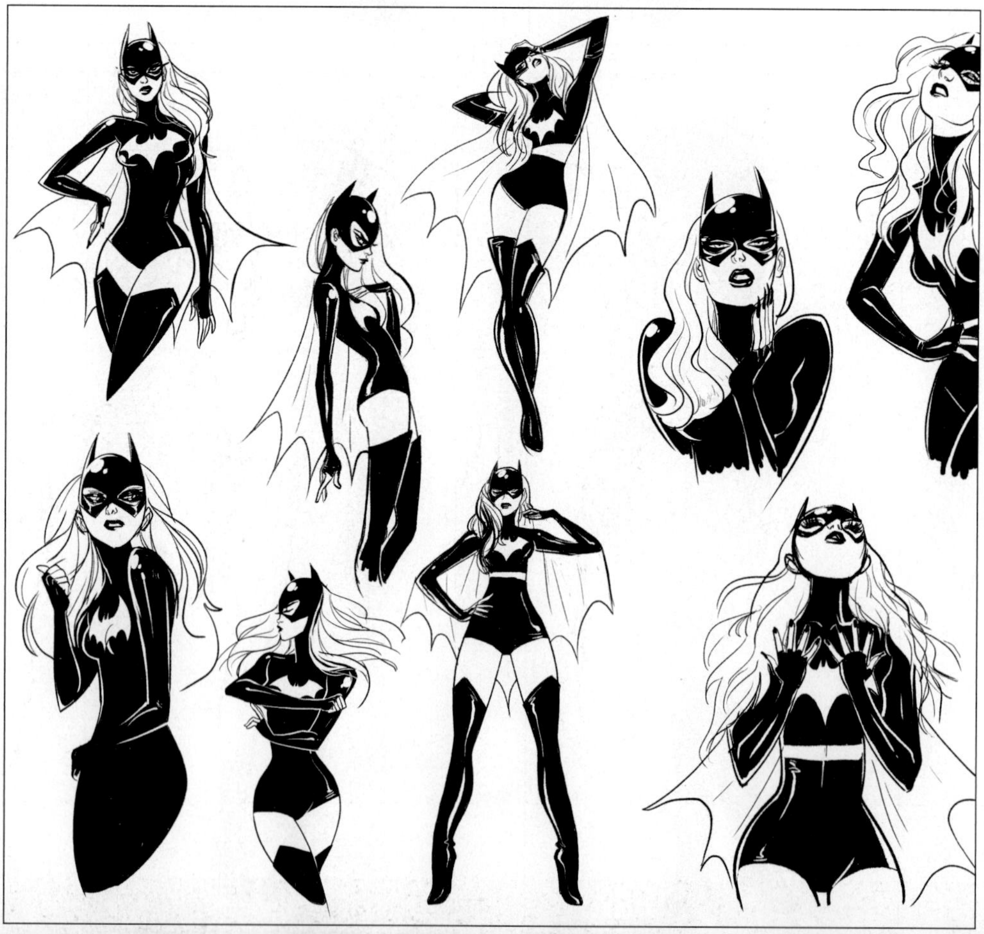

RIOT BLACK CHARACTER STUDIES BY
BABS TARR

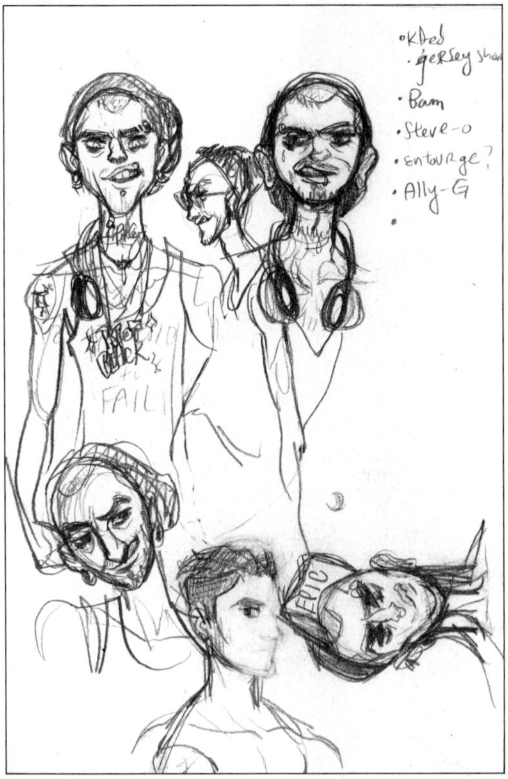

Bam
Steve-o
entourge?
Ally-G
FAIL
EPIC

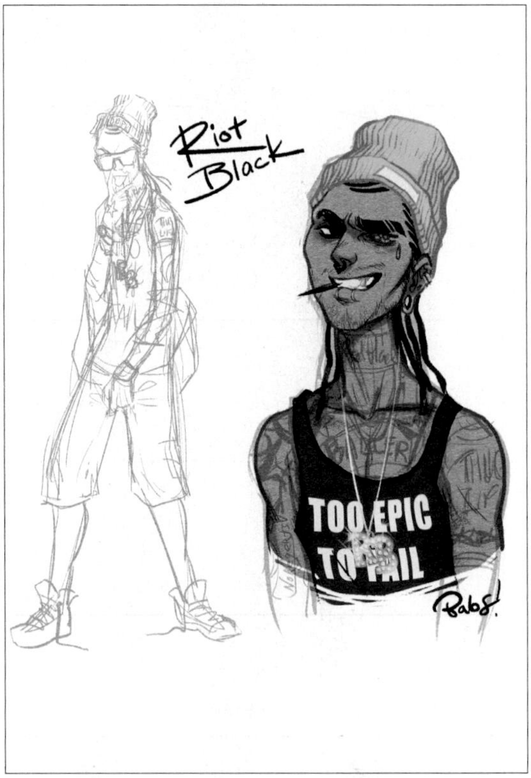

Riot Black
TOO EPIC TO FAIL
Babs!

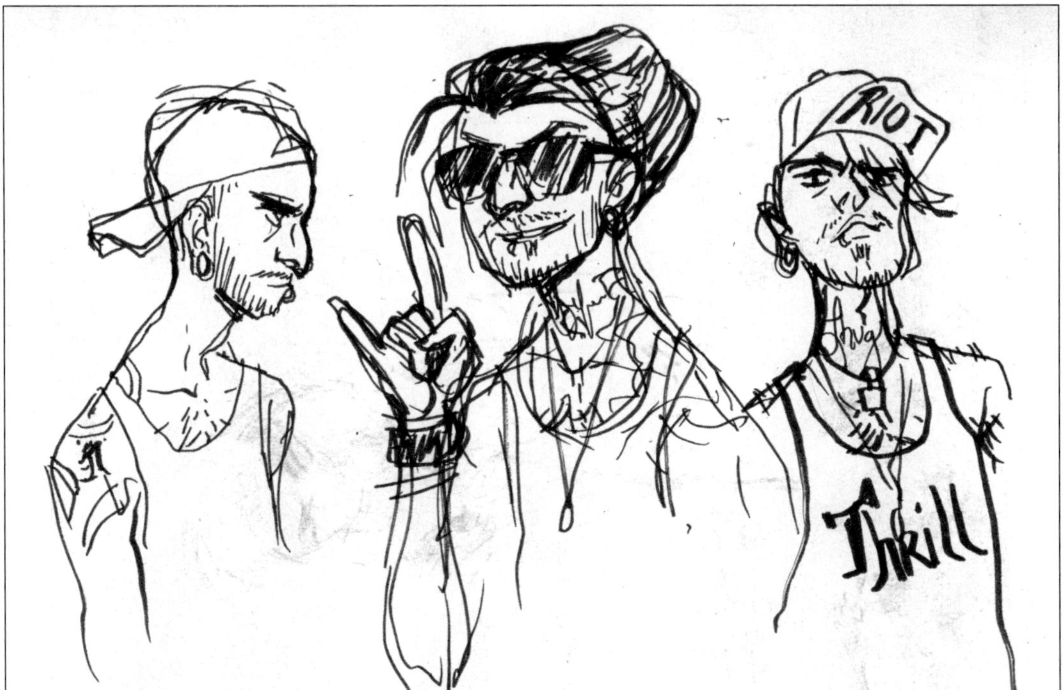

RIOT
Thrill

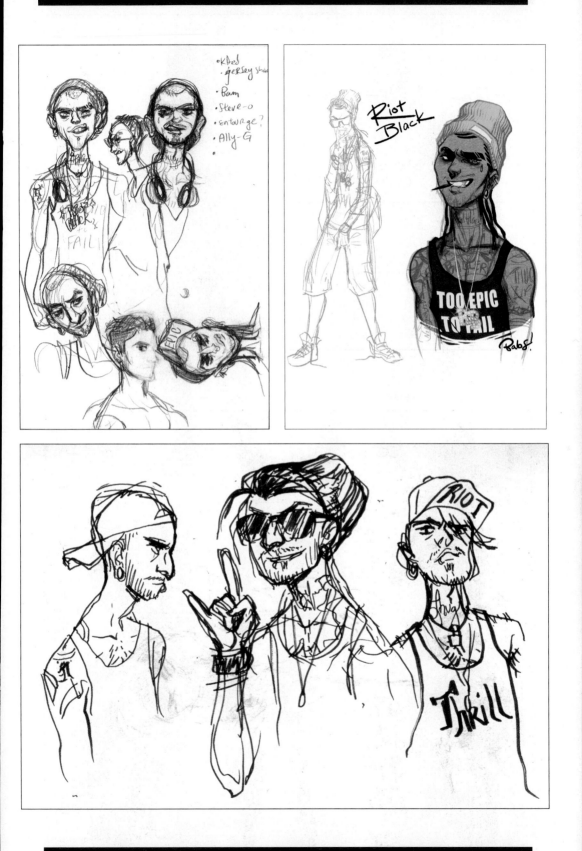

JAWBREAKER/ATOMINA CHARACTER STUDIES BY
BABS TARR

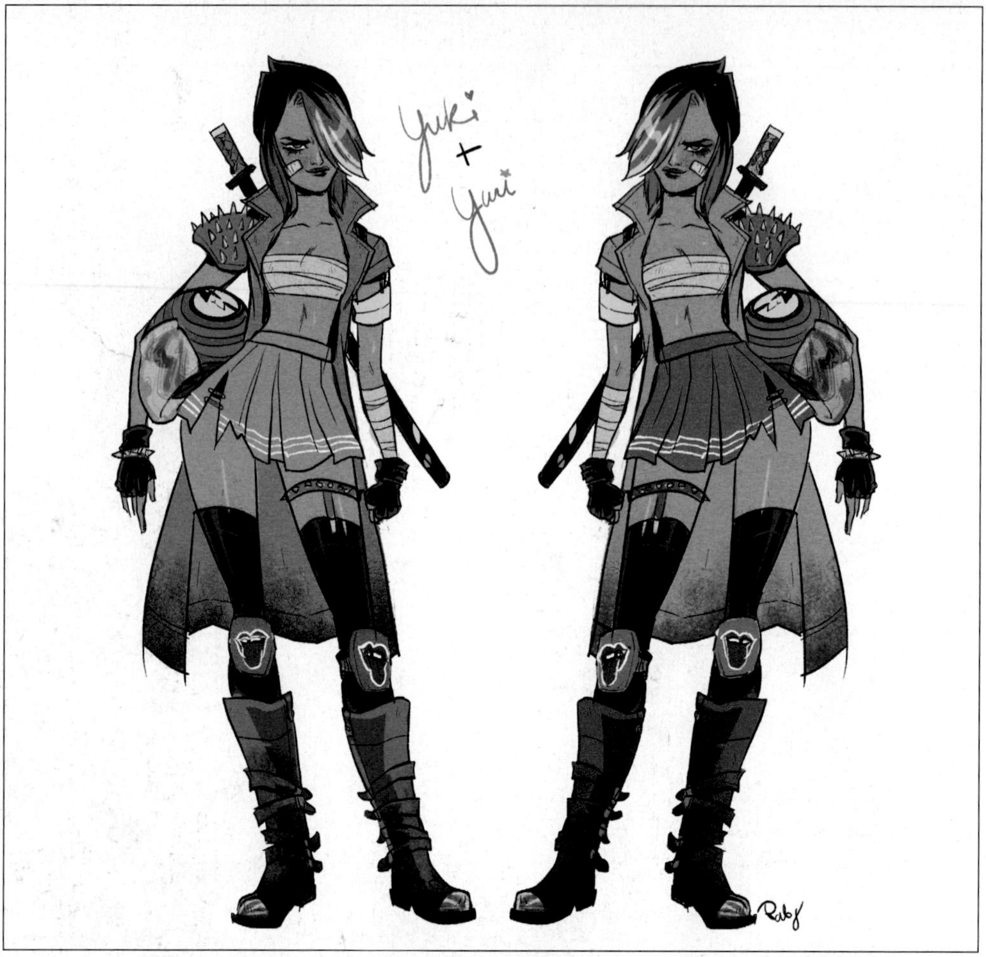
Yuki + Yumi

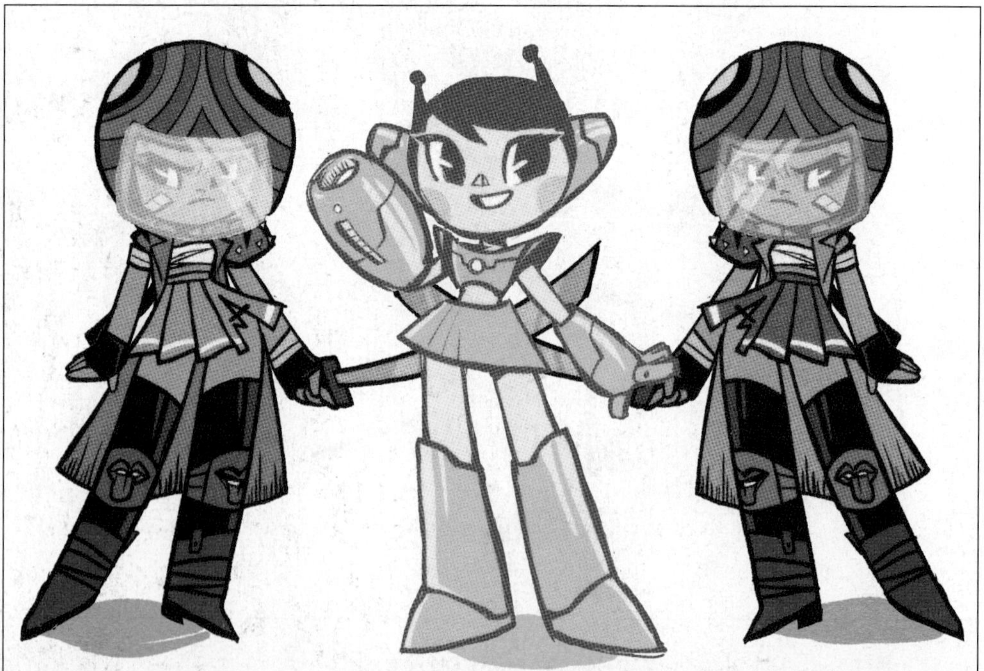

BATGIRL AT BRUNCH BY
CAMERON STEWART

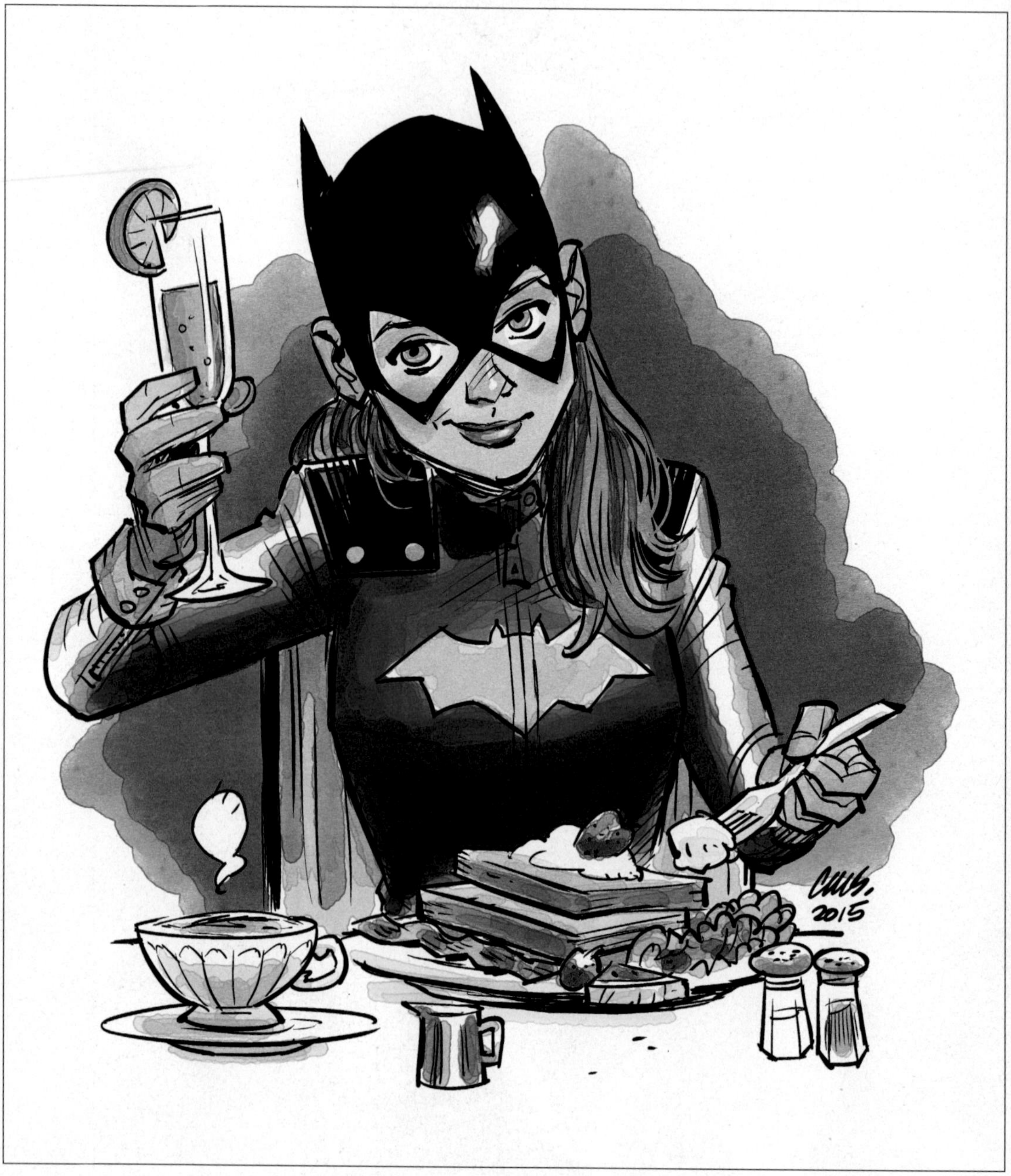

ART BY
CAMERON STEWART

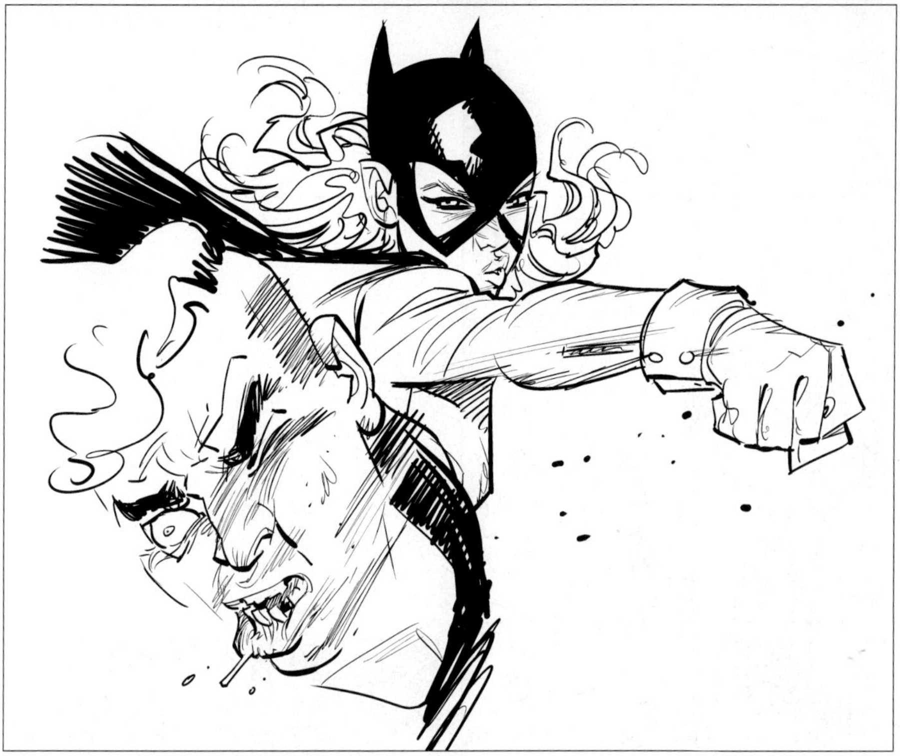

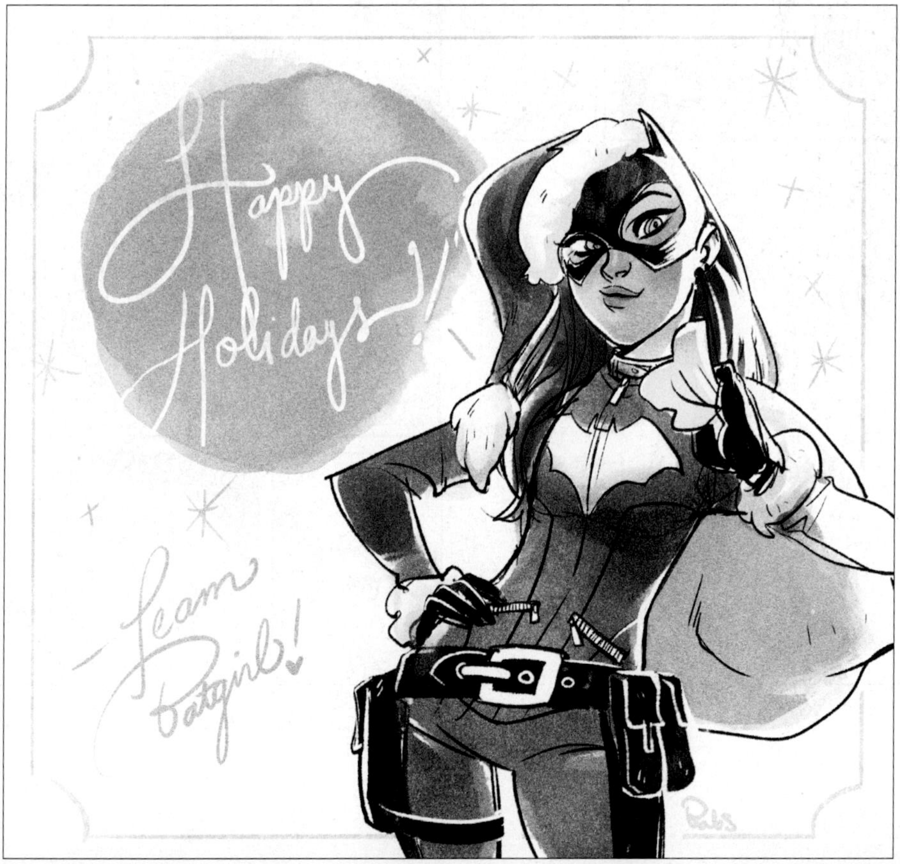
Happy Holidays!
Team Batgirl!
Babs

ART BY
BABS TARR

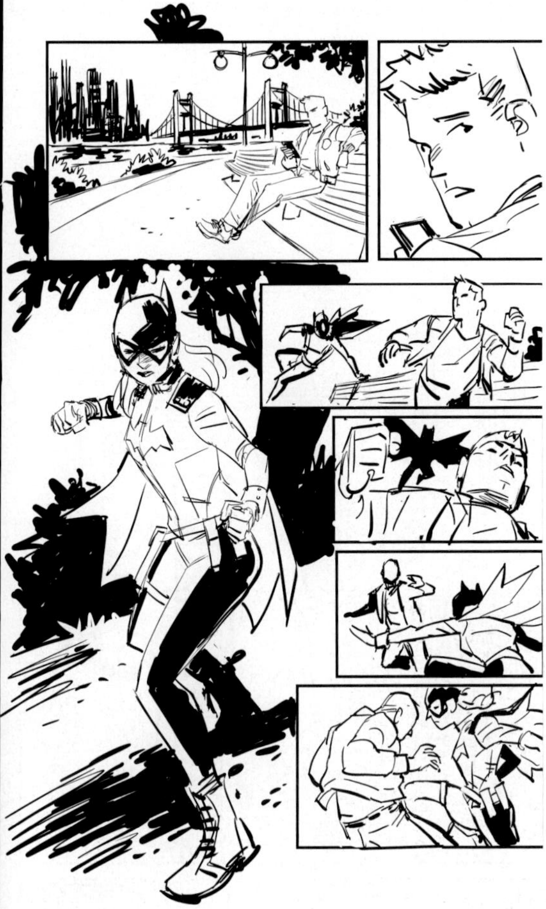

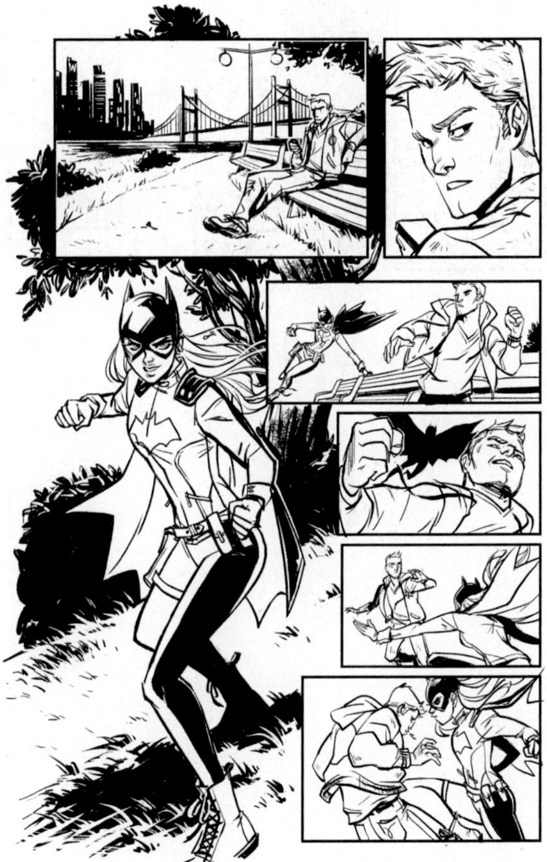

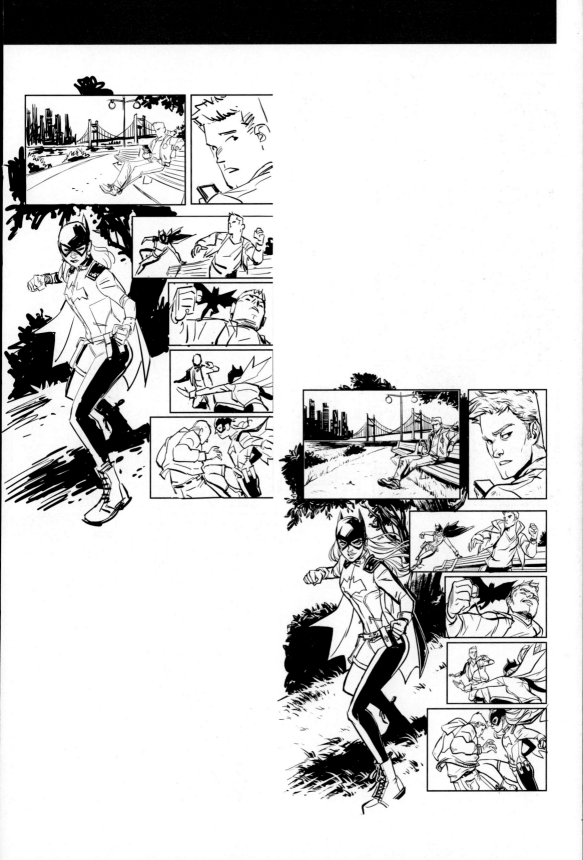

MORE BATGIRL #35 PAGE LAYOUTS BY
CAMERON STEWART

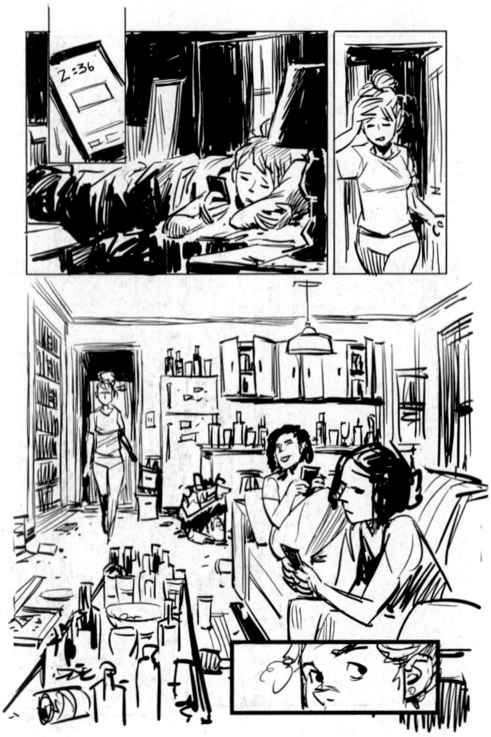
2:36

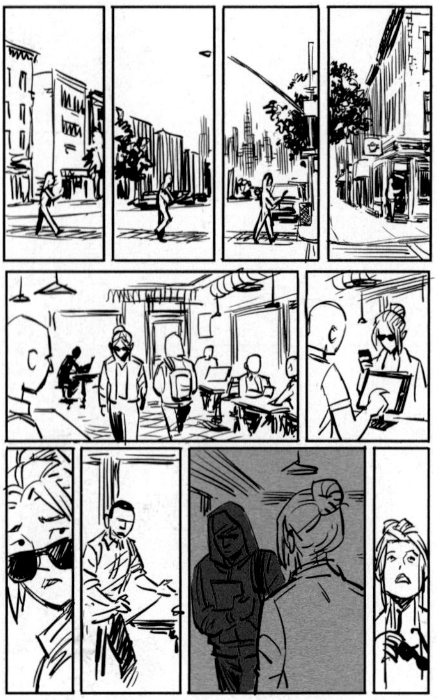

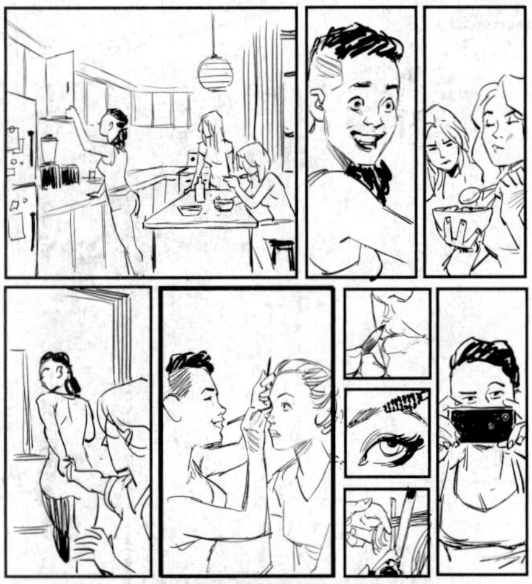
Barbara, 21

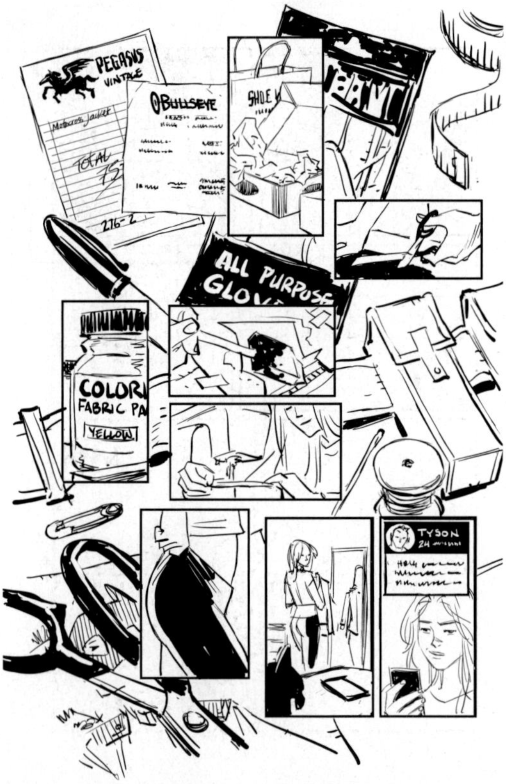
PEGASUS
VINTAGE
TOTAL
276-2
BULLSEYE
ALL PURPOSE
GLOVE
COLOR
FABRIC PA
YELLOW
TYSON
24

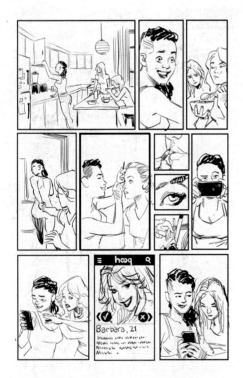

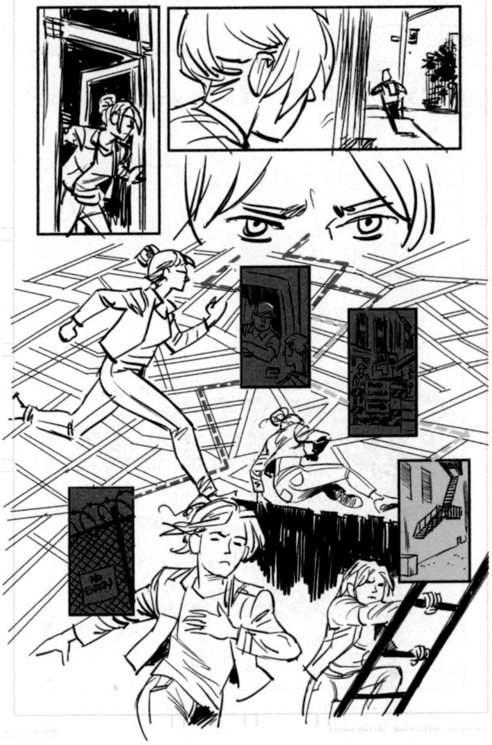
NO ENTRY

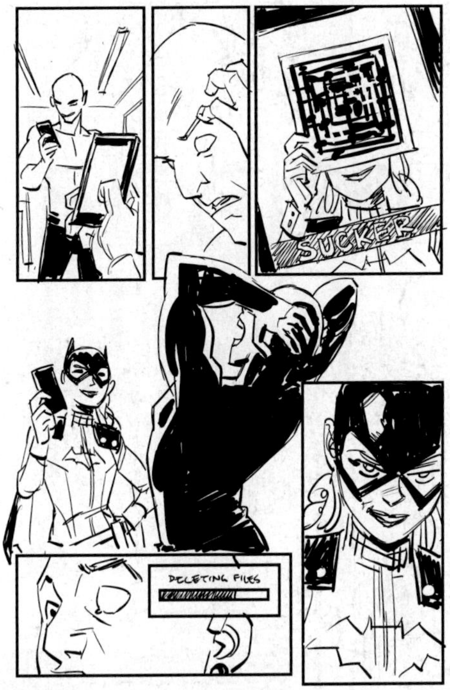
SUCKER
DELETING FILES

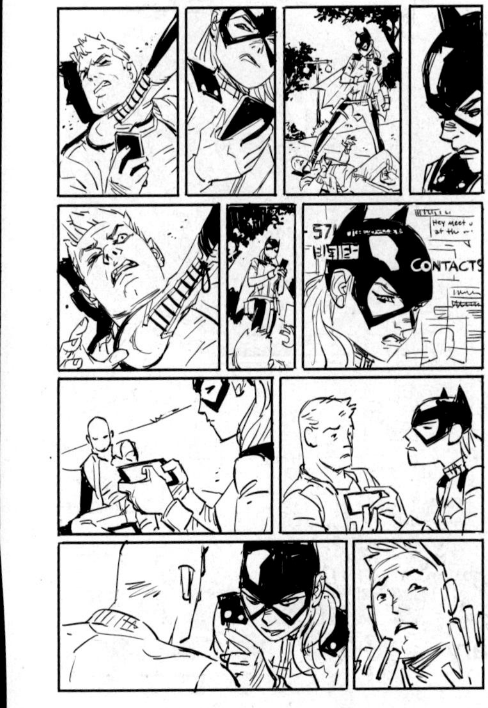
CONTACTS

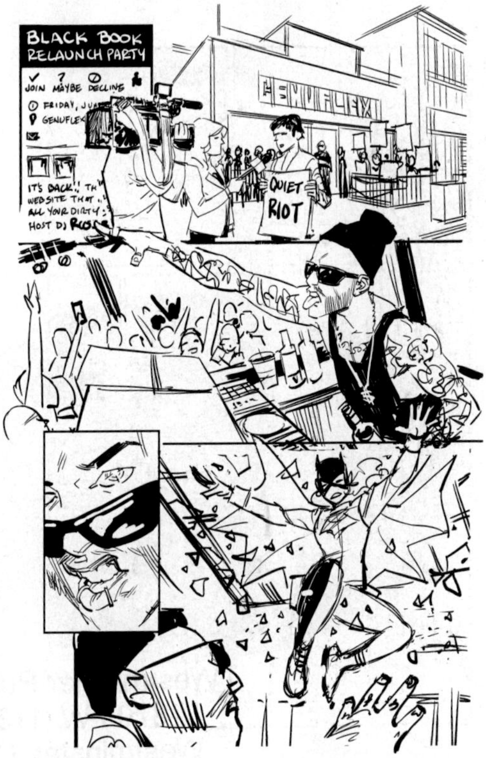
BLACK BOOK
RELAUNCH PARTY
JOIN MAYBE DECLINE
QUIET RIOT

LOGO DESIGNS FOR THE MANY COMPANIES FEATURED IN BATGIRL BY
CAMERON STEWART

omniCAB

robot pony
art • design • toys • culture

GOTHAM
MOVING & STORAGE
"The Friendly Movers"
Call 1-555-324-MOVE

hooq

Ashes on Sunday

CHIROPTERA

FIVE STAR
★ ★ ★ ★ ★
CARPETS

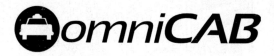

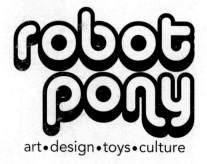

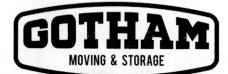

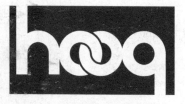

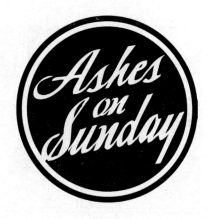

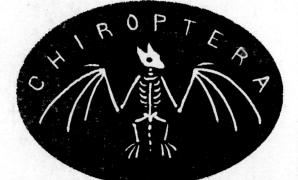

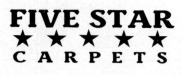